DISCARD

Work and Retirement

Work and Retirement

A Longitudinal Study of Men

Edited by Herbert S. Parnes

with contributions by

Gilbert Nestel

Thomas N. Chirikos

Thomas N. Daymont

Mary G. Gagen

R. Jean Haurin

Randall H. King

Frank L. Mott

and

Donald O. Parsons

The MIT Press
Cambridge, Massachusetts
London, England

This report was prepared under a contract with the Employment and
Training Administration, U.S. Department of Labor, under the authority
of the Comprehensive Employment and Training Act. Researchers
undertaking such projects under government sponsorship are encouraged to express their own judgments. Interpretations or viewpoints
contained in this document do not necessarily represent the official
position or policy of the Department of Labor.

This book was set in VIP Univers by Achorn Graphic Services Incorporated and printed and bound by Halliday Lithograph in the United States
of America.

Library of Congress Cataloging in Publication Data
Parnes, Herbert S., 1919–
  Work and retirement.

  Includes bibliographies and index.
  1. Age and employment—United States—Longitudinal studies.
2. Employment of men—United States—Longitudinal studies.
3. Afro-Americans—Employment—Longitudinal studies. 4. Aged—
Employment—United States—Longitudinal studies. 5. Retirement—
United States—Longitudinal studies.
I. Title
HD6280.P27   331.12′0973   81-1196
ISBN 0-262-16079-X   AACR2

BST
R

Contents

List of Figures

Foreword

Since 1965 the Center for Human Resource Research of The Ohio State University and the U.S. Bureau of the Census, under separate contracts with the Employment and Training Administration of the U.S. Department of Labor, have been engaged in the National Longitudinal Surveys (NLS) of labor market experience. Five subsets of the civilian population are being studied: men 45 to 59 years of age in 1966; women 30 to 44 years of age in 1967; young men between 14 and 24 in 1966; and young women 14 to 24 in 1968. In 1979 a new study of male and female youth 14 to 21 years of age was begun.

These groups were chosen because each is confronted with special labor market problems. The problems of youths revolve around occupational choice and include the preparation for work and the frequently difficult period of accommodation to the labor market when formal schooling has been completed. The problems of older women are associated with reentry into the labor force after children are in school or grown. The special problems of the middle-aged men stem in part from skill obsolescence, from the increasing incidence of health problems, and from employment discrimination, all of which are reflected in declining labor force participation rates and in spells of unemployment that are of longer than average duration.

For each of the four population groups originally covered by the NLS, a national probability sample of the noninstitutional population was drawn by the Census Bureau, and interviews have been conducted periodically by Census enumerators using schedules prepared by the Center for Human Resource Research. Originally planned to cover a five-year period, the surveys have been so successful and attrition so small that they have been continued beyond the originally planned expiration dates. The plan at the end of 1979 was to continue the surveys for a total of 15 years, with the final interviews in 1981 for the two groups of males, and in 1982 and 1983 respectively for the older and younger groups of women.

A substantial body of literature based on the NLS data has already appeared. Eighteen volumes of comprehensive reports have been published on surveys conducted through 1973: *The Pre-Retirement Years* (men, four volumes), *Career Thresholds* (young men, six volumes), *Dual Careers* (women, four volumes), and *Years for Decision* (young women, four volumes). In addition, about four hundred special reports on specific topics have been prepared by staff members of the Center for Human Resource Research and other researchers throughout the country who have acquired NLS public-use tapes.

This volume is based on the surveys of the older cohort of men through 1976. The change in title from the previous volumes in this series reflects the extension of the surveys beyond the originally planned five years. Under the original plan the oldest members of the sample would have been 64 years of age at the final survey, and under these circumstances *The Pre-Retirement Years* seemed a fitting title. By 1976, however, it was clearly inappropriate given that well over two-fifths of the sample had already retired.

Without attempting to escape ultimate responsibility for whatever limitations remain, the authors wish to acknowledge their debt to a large number of persons. Without their contributions neither the overall study nor the present volume would have been possible. Although personally unknown to us, the several thousand members of the sample who have generously agreed to repeated interviews over the years must be mentioned first, for they have provided the raw materials for our effort.

Officials of the Employment and Training Administration have been very helpful to us in providing suggestions for the design of the National Longitudinal Surveys and in reviewing preliminary drafts of our reports. We wish to acknowledge the continuous support and encouragement of Howard Rosen, director of the Office of Research and Development, and the valuable advice provided by Stuart Garfinkle, Frank Mott, Jacob Schiffman, Rose Weiner, and Ellen Sehgal, who have consecutively served as monitors of the project. This volume owes much to the conscientious assistance of Ms. Sehgal, who was generous with her own advice and recruited reviewers of a preliminary draft whose comments were very helpful.

The research staff of the Center for Human Resource Research has enjoyed the continuous expert and friendly collaboration of personnel of the Bureau of the Census, who have been responsible for developing the samples, conducting the interviews, coding and editing the data, and preparing the initial versions of the computer tapes. Those who have been involved in these activities over the years are too numerous to be mentioned individually, but we should like to acknowledge especially our debt to Marvin Thompson, chief of the Demographic Surveys Division, and to his predecessors, Earle Gerson, Daniel

Levine, and Robert Pearl; to George Gray, chief of the Longitudinal Surveys Branch; to Robert Mangold, his immediate predecessor; and to their colleagues Dorothy Koger and Tom Scopp. These are the individuals in the Census Bureau with whom we have had immediate contact in the recent past. In addition, we wish to express our appreciation to Robert C. Jung and Dwight Dean of the Field Division for directing the data collection; to David Lipscomb, Eleanor Brown, Mary Campbell, and their staff of the Systems Division for editing and coding the interview schedules; and to Lowell Wrucke, Kenneth Kaplan, and Emilye Williams for the preparation of the computer tapes.

The process of revising the computer tapes received from the Census Bureau and producing the tables and regressions was the responsibility of the Data Processing Unit of the Center for Human Resource Research under the able direction of Carol T. Sheets. To S. Rufus Milsted, production supervisor of the unit, and his staff, we express our thanks for serving so skillfully as intermediaries between us and the computer.

The authors profited from comments on earlier drafts of their work by their coauthors as well as by other members of the research staff of the Center, particularly Michael E. Borus, Ronald D'Amico, Russell Rumberger, and Steven Sandell. The authors of chapter 6 acknowledge also the helpful suggestions of Robert C. Atchley of Miami University and of Lola Irelan and the members of her staff in the Social Security Administration. The comments of three anonymous reviewers for the MIT Press were also valuable.

We thank Yvonne Holsinger and her staff at The Ohio State University Teaching Aids Laboratory for preparing the graphs in this volume. Finally, we are grateful to Ellen Mumma and Kezia Sproat for their editorial assistance and to Sherry McNamara for the exceptional skill and good humor with which she typed the several versions of the text and tables.

Herbert S. Parnes
March 1980

Work and Retirement

Most people would agree that individuals in their late forties or early fifties are middle-aged while those in their late sixties are old. In this volume we have the unique opportunity to follow a representative national sample of 45- to-59-year-old men as they aged by ten years between 1966 and 1976. Thus by any reasonable definition of the boundary substantial portions of the sample moved from their middle to their later years during the period covered by the study.

Important life cycle changes occur between 45 and 70. The physical, psychological, and social changes that generally characterize this period include the departure of children, the death of parents, increasing susceptibility to health problems, retirement, and reminders of mortality—including, for a not negligible minority, death.[1] From a labor market perspective these years also hold special significance. Because of the prevalence of age discrimination, the increasing likelihood of work-limiting health problems, and the possible obsolescence of skills, reaching age 40 or 45 has long been recognized as bringing special labor market disadvantage.[2] Among men in their early sixties, and especially at age 65, participation in the labor force drops sharply; fewer than three of ten men over 65 remain in the labor market.[3]

The studies in this volume examine the preretirement labor market behavior and the postretirement experience of men between 45 and 69. They are based on longitudinal data collected by periodic personal interviews with the same sample of men between 1966 and 1976. Since the data contain a comprehensive record of their labor market activity as well as periodic measures of their characteristics and attitudes, we can examine both the antecedents and the consequences of events and courses of action. We can see, for example, how individuals retiring under mandatory retirement plans had earlier assessed the prospect of forced retirement, and we can find out whether individuals who experienced labor market setbacks in their fifties or sixties were more likely than others to have suffered similar misfortunes at earlier ages.

The ten years 1966 to 1976 are an unusually interesting decade. There were substantial variations in economic conditions: a three-year span (1966 to 1969) in which the labor market was

The research assistance of Nan Maxwell and Mary Gagen is gratefully acknowledged.

relatively tight and improving, with unemployment rates ranging from 3.8 percent to 3.5 percent; a two-year period (1969 to 1971) in which conditions deteriorated, with unemployment rates moving to 4.9 percent and 5.9 percent; a two-year period of some improvement, with unemployment dropping again to 4.9 percent in 1973; and finally a three-year period in which unemployment reached its highest levels since the beginning of World War II—8.5 percent in 1975 and 7.7 percent in 1976.[4] These fluctuations permit analysis of the effects of changes in the economic environment on the labor market experience of the men under consideration. The decade covered by the data is fortuitous from yet another point of view: it should reflect whatever short-run impact the civil rights movement has had on the relative employment status of middle-aged and older black men.

Plan of the Volume

This volume is the fifth in a series of reports based on the same data base, the first to take advantage of information covering ten full years in the lives of the men in the sample. The remainder of this introduction describes the sample and the nature of the information collected in the surveys, briefly summarizes major findings of the earlier reports in this series, and presents an overview of the changes in the lives of the men in the sample between 1966 and 1976.

The remaining chapters do not purport to analyze in a single framework all aspects of the labor market experience of middle-aged and older men that the data base would permit. Each is a self-contained study of a problem or aspect of behavior that is of interest to its author(s) and has a significant bearing on the welfare of this group. There has been no attempt to force individual interests into a common mold or to induce any of the researchers to accept uncongenial conceptual frameworks or methods of analysis in the interest of some a priori notion of theoretical or methodological integrity. We hope that whatever may have been lost in the logic of organizational structure or methodological consistency will have been fully compensated by the resulting eclecticism.

Chapter 2 addresses the question whether there was any change in the employment security and earnings of black men relative to white men during the decade 1966 to 1976. More specifically, it attempts to ascertain the extent to which such changes were attributable to the civil rights movement and to variations in economic conditions.

Chapter 3 examines a problem that poses special difficulties for middle-aged and older workers—the involuntary loss of job. The study identifies more than one-hundred sample members who suffered involuntary separations from the jobs they had held for at least five years when first interviewed in 1966. The authors first inquire whether the incidence of such involuntary separations varies among men with different demographic and economic characteristics. Then, by comparing the status of this group in 1976 with that of otherwise comparable men who suffered no involuntary loss of job, the study probes the impact of displacement on long-service workers.

The extent and character of physical and mental impairments among this cohort of men and the labor market consequences of health problems are the subject of chapter 4. The authors exploit detailed information on functional limitations that was collected in 1976 and analyze the effects of degrees of impairment on work activity and earnings.

Chapter 5 examines white-black differences in the labor market participation of middle-aged and older men and seeks an explanation for the increasing differential over the past two decades. Between 1966 and 1976 this gap widened from 2.1 to 9.1 percentage points for men 45 to 54 and from 5.0 to 9.7 points for men 55 to 64. The author develops an economic model of the labor force participation decision to test the hypothesis that the increasing liberality of disability benefits has caused larger proportions of black men than of white men to withdraw from economic activity.

Chapter 6 deals with members of the sample who reported having retired during the decade 1966 to 1976. On the basis of criteria provided by their ten-year records, these individuals are classified according to their route into retirement: (1) involuntarily as the result of mandatory retirement provisions; (2) by virtue of health problems; and (3) purely voluntarily, either (a) before the conventional retirement age or (b) at age 65 or later. The postretirement experiences and attitudes of these groups are then examined.

Chapter 7 is concerned with the more than eight hundred members of the sample who died between 1966 and 1976 and explores socioeconomic patterns discernible in the years immediately preceding death. For example, attention is directed to changes in family income levels, the man's attachment to the labor force, including shifts in occupational affiliation, and the wife's attachment to the labor force. The last chapter summarizes and synthesizes the findings of the previous chapters and draws implications for public policy.

The Sample and the Data

The NLS Sample

The studies in this volume are based on data from the National Longitudinal Surveys (NLS).[5] The members of the sample who provided the information were selected to be representative of the approximately 15 million men in the U.S. civilian non-institutionalized population who in 1966 were between 45 and 59.[6] However, to provide sufficient observations for reliable racial comparisons, the sampling ratio for black men was three to four times as high as for whites. Of the 5,020 men originally interviewed in 1966, 3,518 were white, 1,420 were black, and 82 were of other races. Because this last group is small, it has been eliminated from all the analyses in this volume. The tables in the report show numbers of sample cases rather than blown-up population estimates. However, in most of the chapters all calculations (percentage distributions, means, regression coefficients) are based on weighted observations.[7]

Of the 5,020 men interviewed in 1966, 3,487 remained in the sample as of 1976. In some of the chapters the analysis is restricted to the records of individuals interviewed in 1976. Since sampling weights have been adjusted to reflect the effects of attrition, the samples used in these chapters represent men in the civilian population who were between 55 and 69 in 1976.[8]

Nature of the Data Base

The data were collected in a series of eight surveys. Extended face-to-face interviews with members of the sample were conducted in 1966, 1967, 1969, 1971, and 1976. In 1968 a brief mailed questionnaire was used, and in 1973 and 1975 short telephone interviews were conducted.[9] It is neither necessary nor possible to describe in detail the rich body of information collected. It includes an abbreviated lifetime work history of each respondent up to the time of the first survey, a detailed work history during the period covered by the remaining surveys, and information about social, psychological, and economic characteristics of the respondents that are hypothesized to influence labor market behavior.[10]

The NLS data provide unique research opportunities because

of their rich content, and more particularly because of their longitudinal or panel character—because observations of the same individuals have been taken at several points over a ten-year period. This makes it possible to measure the extent and character of change in important aspects of the labor market status of the men, thus providing relatively uncommon information. More important, however, is the ability to relate an individual's characteristics at one time to his characteristics or status at a later point or to examine changes in one set of characteristics in the light of changes in another set. These kinds of analysis permit insights into developmental processes and into the direction of causation between correlated variables that can be gained in no other way.

All the chapters exploit the longitudinal nature of the data. Chapter 2, for instance, uses data on earnings and unemployment reported at different survey dates to investigate trends in black-white differentials. The study of mortality in chapter 7 and the study of black-white differentials in labor force participation in chapter 5 take advantage of information collected before the deaths of sample members known to have died by 1976. The study of retirement experience (chapter 6) uses the periodic reports of the respondents prior to retirement, rather than retrospective explanations, to categorize the circumstances of the retirement decision. The study of the incidence and impact of job loss (chapter 3) relates attitudinal and other characteristics of the individuals before their displacement to the likelihood of job loss and to its consequences. The analysis of health limitations (chapter 4) compares the extent of physical and mental impairments of the same subsample of men in 1971 and 1976. These types of analysis would not have been possible on the basis of conventional cross-sectional (moment-of-time) data.

Earlier Findings

These studies supplement substantial earlier research based on waves of interviews conducted between 1966 and 1971 with the same sample of men. While the number of studies is too large for a comprehensive review, it is instructive to mention the highlights of these earlier investigations.[11]

While middle-aged and older men have been singled out for study because of their potentially serious labor market problems, our research to date shows that facile generalizations about the labor market problems of men in their forties and fifties are dangerous. A substantial majority of men in this age range have

no special labor market problems. When they were first interviewed in 1966 at ages 45 to 59, their labor force participation
was very high: 19 of 20 were in the labor force at the time of
the survey, and over 16 of 20 were continuously in the market
for 52 weeks in the preceding calendar year. Unemployment
was quite low, less than 1.5 percent in the survey week. The
employed men were, by and large, in better jobs than the average of all males. Almost 9 of 10 were in occupations different
from those in which they had started their work careers, and
over one-half had moved up the occupational ladder. Two-thirds
regarded their current occupational assignment as the best of
their career. The employment relationship appeared to be stable
and satisfactory for large majorities of the men. Three-fifths had
served their current employers (or had been self-employed) for
ten years or more; two-fifths professed an unwillingness to
consider another job at any conceivable wage rate; more than 9
of 10 claimed that they liked their jobs.[12]

Even after five years, when the oldest members of the sample were 64, conditions remained good for a substantial majority
of the men in 1971. Almost one-half reported that they had
made progress in their work during the preceding five years, and
less than one-tenth believed they had become worse off. A
substantial majority of the men remained full-year, full-time
workers, experienced no unemployment, served in jobs with
which they expressed satisfaction, and continued to experience
gains in real income even as the burden of dependency
diminished.[13]

On the other hand, the fortunate position of the majority made
no more tolerable the misfortunes of those who suffered substantial unemployment, held degrading jobs, and earned low
incomes. Even at the time of the initial survey in 1966 a nonneg-
ligible proportion of the men were at the very bottom of the occupational hierarchy either because they started and remained
there or because they had slipped during their working lives.
One in 12 was an unskilled laborer; 1 in 10 earned less than
$1.50 per hour; almost 1 in 6 was in an occupation of lower so-
cioeconomic status than that of his first job. Moreover, not all
displayed the stable work attachments that characterized the
majority. About one-fifth claimed that they would not work except for financial necessity; a tenth had served less than one
year with their current employer; as many as one in eight re-

ported that they would accept another job at the same or lower wage rate.[14]

Factors in Labor Market Success

Race   All our studies have shown dramatic differences between whites and blacks in virtually every aspect of labor market success. The substantial disparity between the two races in earnings, occupational status, and unemployment experience hardly comes as a surprise, for these differences would be expected on the basis of racial differentials in educational attainment alone. However, there is evidence that the differentials in rewards between blacks and whites are greater than can be accounted for by racial differentials in human capital. Although none of our earlier studies has been aimed specifically at measuring or identifying racial discrimination in the labor market, several have adduced evidence of it. For example, the relation between educational attainment and earnings is less systematic for middle-aged blacks than for their white counterparts. Similarly, there is evidence that black men in this age group do not reap the same returns to initiative as do whites. Finally, for given qualifications, black men are less likely than whites to have moved up the occupational ladder within firms over the five-year period from 1966 to 1971.[15]

Nevertheless, our analyses have also provided some grounds for limited optimism on this score, for they suggest that at least some of the gross differentials between whites and blacks narrowed between 1966 and 1971. For instance, among men who were employed at the survey dates in both years, hourly earnings rose more in percentage terms for blacks than for whites, thus reducing the relative differential. This trend was even more pronounced in the case of annual earnings.[16]

The labor market behaviors of black and white men are also similar in some respects. There is no evidence, for instance, that black men differ from whites in the strength of their attachments to their current employers. Moreover, the factors that influence the strength of these attachments appear to be largely the same and to operate in similar ways for blacks and whites. Nor are the probabilities of voluntary interfirm job changes different for blacks and whites. Other things equal, black and white men are equally likely to make such changes and tend to respond to opportunities in substantially the same way.[17]

Health   There is abundant evidence that health has an important effect on the labor market position of middle-aged men. A
substantial minority of the sample—27 percent—reported
health conditions that limited either the amount or the kind of
work they could do in the initial survey when they were between 45 and 59.[18] Among those who were in their early sixties
in 1971 the proportion was as high as two-fifths. Poor health is
important in explaining withdrawal from the labor force before
the conventional age of retirement. It also accounts for a major
portion of the differential in labor force participation between
white and black men. Among men with no health problems the
labor force participation of blacks is actually slightly higher than
that of whites. Finally, even among men who remain in the labor
force health has a powerful influence on earnings and employment experience. When other human capital variables such as
education and training are controlled, men who report health
limitations have lower hourly and annual earnings than those
with no such limitations, and they suffer more unemployment.[19]

Education and training   Other types of investment in human
capital also have a salutary effect on the labor market status and
experience of middle-aged men. For instance, other things being
equal, number of years of school completed is strongly related
to hourly and annual earnings. Over the five-year period between 1966 and 1971 better-educated men were more likely
than men with less education to have moved up the occupational hierarchy and less likely to have moved down.[20] These
findings suggest that some of the labor market disadvantage of
middle age will be reduced as the educational attainment of
men in this age category increases.

  Certain types of training outside the formal educational system also appear to have a favorable influence on the earning
power of middle-aged men. The association is much clearer for
training obtained earlier in life than for that obtained during middle age. However, even in the latter case there appear to be
payoffs at least for some categories of men, notably black men
with some previous training experience.[21]

Labor Mobility

Even though older men are known to be less mobile than
younger men, there is evidence of a considerable amount of job
changing among middle-aged men. Over one-eighth of the

sample made at least one voluntary change of employer between 1966 and 1971, and an additional one-twelfth had moved involuntarily. About a third of the group changed occupations during the period—one-fourth across the boundaries of major occupation groups.[22]

Most of the job changes made by men in this age group appear advantageous. More men moved up the occupational ladder between 1966 and 1971 than moved down. The voluntary interfirm movement that occurred led, on average, to higher levels of job satisfaction and to economic gains.[23]

Retirement

The trend toward earlier retirement is amply documented by analyses of the retirement expectations of the sample. A dramatic example is that among men aged 50 to 60 who were employed in 1971, 38.5 percent intended to retire before age 65. Five years earlier the corresponding proportion of the identical group of men had been ten percentage points lower. The intention to retire early is especially prevalent among those who expect liberal retirement benefits, those with relatively unfavorable attitudes toward their jobs or toward work in general, and those without dependents.[24]

On the other hand, a substantial number of early retirements are not planned or intended but are instead attributable to traumatic illness or injury or to a gradual deterioration in health. In many of these cases the retirees have woefully inadequate incomes and meager assets.[25]

Economic Conditions

Much of our earlier work demonstrated the profound influence of general economic conditions on the labor market experience of the sample. To illustrate, most of the increase in the differential between the labor force participation rates of blacks and whites that occurred between 1966 and 1971 developed between 1969 and 1971, suggesting that the loosening of the labor market in that two-year period had a differentially adverse effect on blacks. The trend of unemployment rates for whites and blacks over the period tells pretty much the same story.[26] As another illustration, virtually the entire gain in real annual earnings between 1965 and 1970 occurred during the first three years of the period.[27] Finally, there is evidence that both the propensity of men to change jobs and the rate of actual voluntary movement are sensitive to the level of economic activity; the likelihood that voluntary movement will produce a relative wage advantage is greater in a buoyant than in a depressed economy.[28] These findings, all consistent with what is known about the operation of the labor market in general, underscore the importance of policies directed at achieving high levels of employment, particularly for middle-aged men who tend to suffer labor market disadvantage.

The Ten-Year Period 1966–1976

The remaining chapters explore the ten-year records of the sample for specific analytical purposes. However, none systematically describes the changes in the life and work experience of the men under consideration; the rest of this chapter is designed to do that. It constitutes a backdrop for the more detailed and more analytical presentations of later chapters. The data are also interesting in their own right, for they are the first data based on a representative national sample that permit a description of the patterns of change over a decade in the work lives of middle-aged men.

Of course, one must not claim too much for the data, for they are linked to a specific time period. The experiences over the decade 1966 to 1976 are colored by the configurations of the social and economic environment of that decade. In addition, the subjects of our examination belong to a cohort whose entire lives have been shaped by circumstances and events that are unique. Thus the influences that have operated on this 15-year age group are different from those affecting the same age group at any other point in history.

Even though the cohort is unique, we can examine the patterns of change over the previous decade in a number of important aspects of their lives. By dividing the entire cohort into three five-year age groups and by measuring their characteristics at three points in time—1966, 1971, and 1976—we can undertake several types of analysis simultaneously. First, we can examine the pattern of age differentials in a characteristic at any point in time and note any changes in that pattern over the ten-year period. Second, by following the total cohort or any of the three age subgroups over time, we can observe the combined effects of aging and environmental change. In particular, we can discern the differences between the two five-year

periods 1966 to 1971 and 1971 to 1976, which were characterized by quite different labor market conditions. Third, we can
also compare three cross sections of individuals of the same
age (55 to 59) at three points—1966, 1971, and 1976—in
order to discern the effects of different economic environments
on behavior and experience. Finally, in all cases we can compare
the experiences of black and white men.[29]

Attrition

The appendix to this chapter (table 1A.1) describes the extent
and character of attrition from the sample over the ten-year
period. Of the 5,020 men who were interviewed in 1966, 3,487
participated in the 1976 survey. Over half of the 1,533 men who
disappeared from the sample (17 percent of the original sample)
died.[30] This left 4,179 members of the original sample who were
alive in 1976 and who were therefore representative of the 1976
male population between the ages of 55 and 69. Of these, more
than 83 percent were interviewed in 1976.[31]

Variations in mortality   Although variations in the mortality
rate among members of the original sample do not bias the
1976 sample, the issue is nevertheless of interest. The difference between the mortality rates of whites and blacks is pronounced. Overall the mortality rate of black men was almost half
again as high as that of white (22 percent versus 15 percent). A
differential is discernible within almost every age, occupation,
education, and income category shown in table 1A.1, although
its magnitude varies considerably. Especially interesting is that
the black-white difference in death rate is much larger within
educational categories than within occupational categories. For
instance, among men with 9 to 11 years of education the mortality rate of blacks is one-third higher than that of whites, and
among men with 12 years of education the differential is even
higher. On the other hand, among all men in white-collar positions there is a difference of only two percentage points in the
mortality rate of whites and blacks. Indeed, the only occupational categories in which the mortality rate differential exceeds
three percentage points are professional workers, operatives,
service workers, and farm workers. It appears, then, that the
large racial differential within educational categories at least

partly reflects the channeling of black men of this generation into less desirable occupations than white men with ostensibly comparable educational backgrounds.

The differences in mortality rates by indicators of socioeconomic status are also dramatic. For example, for both whites and blacks the rates are almost twice as high among farm laborers as among white-collar workers. For both racial groups they are well over twice as high among those whose total family income in 1966 was less than $3,000 as among those whose income was $10,000 to $15,000.

Representativeness of 1976 sample Attrition from the original sample for reasons other than death, if not distributed randomly, can cause the sample of men interviewed in 1976 to be unrepresentative of the total age group at that time. It is therefore worthwhile to inquire to what extent the noninterview rate among those original sample members still alive in 1976 varied according to important characteristics of the respondents. These 1976 noninterview rates are shown in table 1A.1 by selected 1966 characteristics of the respondents. The attrition rate, which was 17 percent for the total sample of respondents, was consistently higher for whites than for blacks, and there are also fairly systematic differences by socioeconomic status indicators. For example, the attrition rate was 19 percent among white-collar workers versus 16 percent among blue-collar workers. It was 20 percent among those with annual incomes between $15,000 and $19,999 and 12 percent among those with incomes less than $3,000.

These variations are probably not large enough to bias seriously the representativeness of the sample. In over two-thirds of the 132 cells shown in table 1A.1 the difference between the noninterview rate and the overall average noninterview rate is smaller than four percentage points, and in two-fifths of the cases it is smaller than two percentage points. It seems fair to conclude that attrition has not departed sufficiently from a random pattern to constitute a serious problem, especially since the principal objectives of the research are to explore relationships rather than to produce population estimates of individuals with differing characteristics. Moreover, sample cases have been reweighted to compensate for differential attrition by race, education, and geographic mobility (see appendix B).

Demographic Characteristics

Family structure The decreasing burden of dependency with the increasing age of married couples is dramatically indicated in figure 1.1. For the cohort as a whole the proportion of men who were married and had dependents other than their wives declined by more than half over the ten years covered by the surveys. Increasing age has a less substantial effect in reducing the dependency burden among blacks than among whites, reflecting the historically higher level of fertility among that generation of black men and women. At the beginning of the decade approximately 60 percent of both racial groups had dependents other than their wives, but ten years later this proportion was 22 percent for the whites and 31 percent for the blacks.

Health While the economic circumstances of middle-aged men improve with time because of the reduction in dependency, there is a clear deterioration in health (figure 1.2).[32] Over the decade the proportion of individuals with work-limiting health problems grew substantially for the cohort as a whole and in each of the five-year age groups. The trend is more pronounced for blacks than for whites; by 1976 two-fifths of the white men and almost half of the black men reported problems that affected the amount or kind of work they could do.

Labor Market Activity

The aging of the sample over the decade 1966 to 1976 is best reflected in the exodus from the labor force as measured by survey week labor force participation rates (figure 1.3). Only 4 percent of the white men and 6 percent of the blacks were neither working nor looking for work when surveyed in 1966; by 1976 these percentages were 37 and 38 percent, respectively. Among those who were 65 to 69 in 1976 slightly over two-thirds of each racial group were out of the labor force.

These changes result not only from the aging of the sample but also from the trend toward reduced labor force participation over the decade for men of given ages. One can compare the cross-sectional relationships in 1966 with the longitudinal data for the ten-year period. When the survey began, cross-sectional relationships implied that white men who were then 45 to 49 would decrease their labor market participation over the ten-year period by only 4 percentage points. By the end of the decade

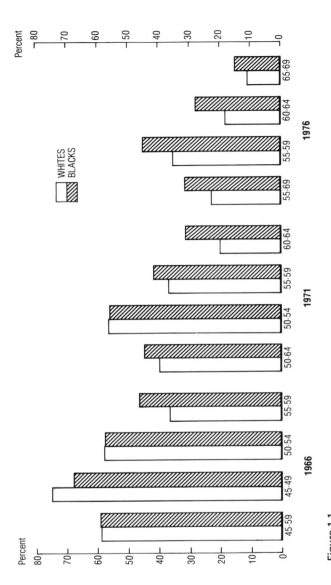

Figure 1.1
Percent Married with Dependents other than Wife, by Age and Race, 1966, 1971, 1976

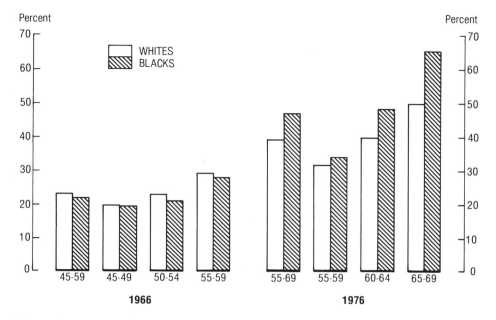

Figure 1.2
Percent with Work-Limiting Health Problems, by Age and Race, 1966, 1976

this cohort of men had actually registered a decline in labor force participation of 12 percentage points. The same phenomenon is evident in the data for men who were 55 to 59 in each of the three survey years shown.

These trends suggest the increasing prevalence of early retirement. More direct evidence on this issue is provided by figure 1.4, which shows the proportion of respondents not yet 65 by the 1976 survey who reported that they either intended to retire early (before 65) or had already retired. This proportion is shown for each of the three survey years 1966, 1971, and 1976; the figures relate to precisely the same group of respondents in each of the three years.

The increasing trend toward early retirement discernible in our data for 1971 continued at least until 1976.[33] Among white men aged 45 to 49 in 1966, 28 percent either had already retired or intended to do so before 65. In 1971, when these men were 50 to 54, the corresponding proportion was 39 percent, 11 percentage points higher than in 1966. By 1976, when the group had reached 55 to 59, the overall proportion had risen an additional 12 percentage points; 14 percent had already retired, and an ad-

15

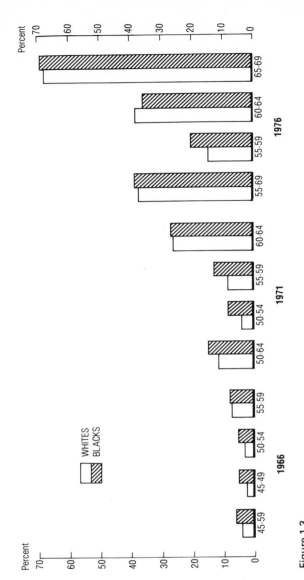

Figure 1.3
Percent Out of Labor Force in Survey Week, by Age and Race, 1966, 1971, 1976

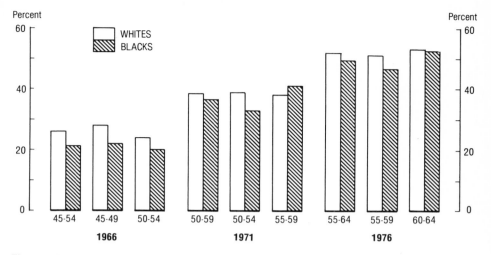

Figure 1.4
Percent of Men under 65 Who Plan to Retire Early or Have Already Retired, by Age and Race,
1966, 1971, 1976

ditional 36 percent intended to do so before 65. These same
trends are evident for those between 60 and 64 in 1976, and for
blacks as well as whites. Indeed, the increasing trend for blacks
between 1966 and 1971 was steeper than that for whites, so
that the proportion of blacks opting for early retirement in 1971
was nearly identical to that of whites.

The same general conclusions may be drawn from the cross-
sectional relationships. For instance, comparing white men 50 to
54 in 1966 with men of the same age in 1971 shows that the
proportion of actual or prospective early retirees grew from 24
percent to 39 percent. Some observers have asserted that the
trend toward early retirement would probably reverse itself as
the result of inflation and other factors.[34] While continued high
rates of inflation may ultimately produce this result, it was not
evident by 1976.

Changes in Job Status

We have been examining changes in the characteristics of the
entire group of respondents. Now we turn to the subset who
were employed at all three survey dates in order to depict the
changes in employment status as men move from middle into
older age.[35]

Occupational distribution   Among those employed in the survey weeks of 1966, 1971, and 1976, the proportion who were involved in professional and managerial activity was remarkably stable, ranging between 30 percent and 33 percent for white men and 8 percent and 10 percent for black men (figure 1.5).

Hours of work   The cohort of men under consideration took increased leisure over the decade not only in the form of decreased labor force participation rates but also through the reduction in hours of work among those who remained employed (figure 1.6). For the age group as a whole, average weekly hours dropped by 5 for whites and by 3 for blacks between 1966 and 1976, with most of the decrease occurring in the second half of the decade. As might be expected, the decrease was closely related to age, being most pronounced among those 65 to 69 in 1976. This, of course, reflected the increased relative importance of part-time work in postretirement jobs.[36] Nevertheless, perceptible decreases in weekly hours of work occurred over both five-year periods and, for whites, in every age group. The cross-sectional data for men 55 to 59 years in each year also depict a declining trend. For example, white men in this age group worked an average of 49 hours a week in 1966, but only 46 and 44 hours in 1971 and 1976, respectively. The decrease in weekly hours for all production or nonsupervisory employees in the economy as a whole was much smaller over the decade 1966 to 1976—from 38.6 in 1966 to 36.2 in 1976.[37]

Earnings   Figure 1.7 shows median hourly earnings expressed in terms of 1976 dollars for 1966, 1971, and 1976. The inverse relationship between hourly earnings and age clearly discernible in the cross section does not prevail longitudinally, at least until postretirement jobs become a significant factor. For instance, in 1966 white men 45 to 49 enjoyed a differential of 45 cents per hour over the group who were five years older and an even larger advantage over those who were ten years older. Nonetheless, as that youngest age group aged by five years, their real earnings in 1971 were higher than in 1966 by approximately 50 cents per hour, and by 1976 they had increased by about another 20 cents. Even among the oldest of the three five-year age categories there was no deterioration in the median real hourly earnings of white men between 1966 and 1971. By 1976 there was a decline of over one dollar per hour, reflecting the movement into postretirement jobs by large num-

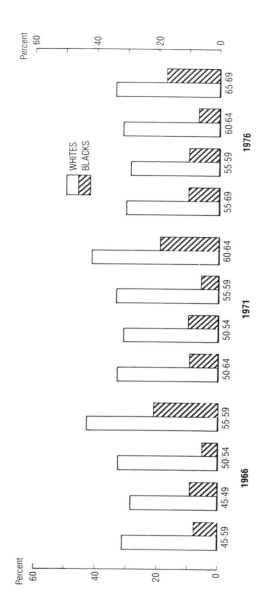

Figure 1.5
Percent Employed as Professionals or Managers, by Age and Race, 1966, 1971, 1976 (respondents employed in all three years)

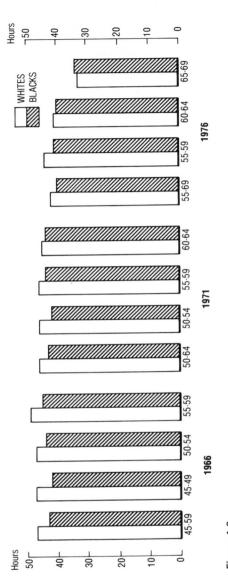

Figure 1.6
Mean Number of Hours Usually Worked in Survey Week Job, by Age and Race, 1966, 1971, 1976 (respondents employed in all three years)

Figure 1.7
Median Real Hourly Earnings of Wage and Salary Workers, by Age and Race, 1966, 1971, 1976 (respondents employed in all three years; 1976 dollars)

bers of these men. Cross sectional data for the age group of men 55 to 59 reveal a continuous increase in real income over the ten-year period that was especially pronounced for blacks. For whites the increase was 24 percent; for blacks, it was 58 percent.

The median annual wage and salary income shown in figure 1.8 reflects average hourly earnings and average number of hours worked per year. As a consequence the pattern of real earnings in annual terms is somewhat different from that in hourly terms: increases are considerably more moderate and decreases are sharper.

Attitudes toward work   A curious pattern of change in job satisfaction over the decade is displayed by the subset of the sample who remained at work during the decade (figure 1.9). The proportion of white men who reported high satisfaction with their jobs dropped by about 11 percentage points between 1966 and 1971—from 58 to 47 percent—but then returned to the earlier level by 1976. Although the magnitudes vary somewhat, the same V-shaped pattern prevails among all three age groups of white men. Blacks, on the other hand, reported little differ-ence in level of satisfaction in the two earlier years, but the proportion of very satisfied workers was highest in 1976. The reasons for these trends are not obvious. The men under con-sideration remained employed as wage and salary workers throughout the decade, at least as indicated by their status in the survey weeks of 1966, 1971, and 1976. In view of the in-verse relationship between job satisfaction and the likelihood of retiring,[38] and in view of the substantial decreases in labor force participation over the ten-year period, one can conclude that an analysis that included all those employed in any of the three years would probably show an even greater increase in the level of satisfaction between 1971 and 1976.

Given the substantial difference in the occupational distribu-tion of whites and blacks and the difference in their earnings, the small overall difference in job satisfaction is surprising and may reflect lower job expectations among blacks. In 1966 the difference was five percentage points in favor of the whites, but in the other two years slightly higher proportions of blacks than of whites expressed high satisfaction in their jobs.

In both 1971 and 1976 employed respondents were asked whether the fatigue they felt on the job had increased and

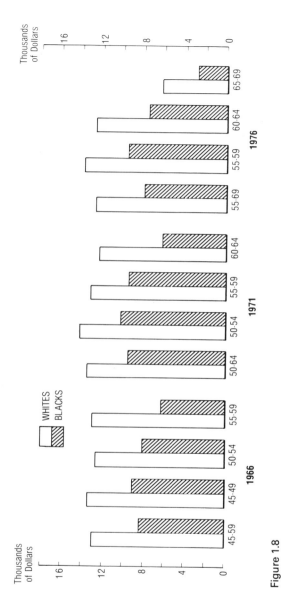

Figure 1.8
Median Real Annual Earnings of Wage and Salary Workers, by Age and Race, 1966, 1971, 1976 (respondents employed in all three years; 1976 dollars)

23

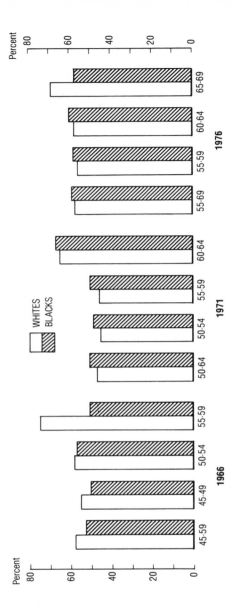

Figure 1.9
Percent of Wage and Salary Workers "Very Satisfied" with Jobs, by Age and Race, 1966, 1971, 1976 (respondents employed in all three years)

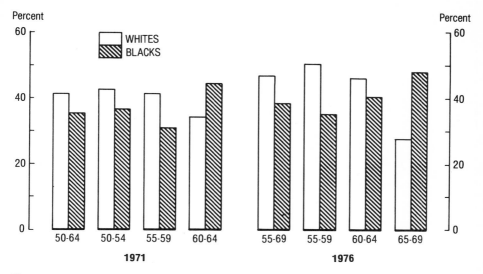

Figure 1.10
Percent of Wage and Salary Workers Reporting Increase in Fatigue on Job over Past Five Years,
by Age and Race, 1971, 1976 (respondents employed in both years)

whether they had perceived a change in their ability to keep
pace with their work. Figures 1.10 and 1.11 show the pattern of
responses. The results show that a substantial minority of men
in this age group feel the ravages of time over a five-year period.
Between 1966 and 1971, for instance, about two-fifths of the
whites and one-third of the blacks perceived an increase in
fatigue on the job. Nonetheless, 83 percent of the whites and 92
percent of the blacks reported no change in ability to keep pace
with their jobs. However, among men who remained employed
during the entire decade, there was relatively little change in the
pattern of these responses as they aged by five years. For
example, in each racial group there was an increase between
1971 and 1976 of only about five percentage points in the proportion reporting increased fatigue over the preceding five-year
period.

When the criterion is the perception of progress in the job
over the past five years, there is a perceptible difference between the two halves of the decade (figure 1.12). In 1971, 58
percent of the whites and 45 percent of the blacks reported progress over the preceding five years. By 1976 these proportions had
dropped to 46 percent and 32 percent. Not surprisingly, the decreases are most dramatic in the oldest age category. Appar-

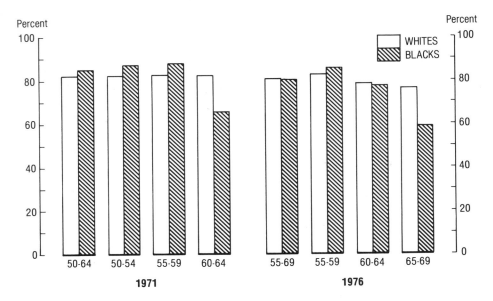

Figure 1.11
Percent of Wage and Salary Workers Reporting No Change in Ability to Keep Pace with Job, by Age and Race, 1971, 1976 (respondents employed in both years)

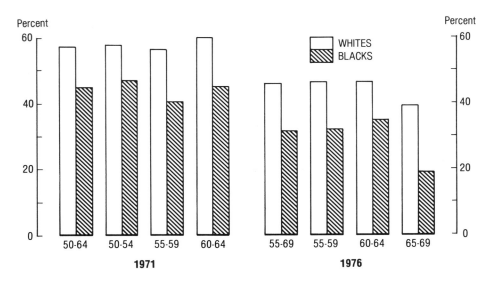

Figure 1.12
Percent of Wage and Salary Workers Feeling They Have Progressed in Job during Past Five Years, by Age and Race, 1971, 1976 (respondents employed in both years)

ently the decline is not only a function of the aging of the cohort but also the result of changes in external conditions, since cross-sectional data for the same age groups of men also show a drop in the proportions reporting progress. To illustrate, among white men 55 to 59 years of age, 56 percent in 1971 but only 46 percent in 1976 reported progress, while the corresponding proportions of blacks were 41 percent and 32 percent.

Income and Assets

We return now to the total group of respondents who were interviewed in all three years. Figure 1.13 shows median total family income expressed in 1976 dollars by race and age for 1966, 1971, and 1976. In each year there is an inverse relationship between income and age, and the relationship is most pronounced in 1976. The increasing differentials with age over time reflect the increasing proportions of the older age groups who are retired.

Within each age group and in each year median black family income is considerably lower than that of whites, but the ratio of black income to white income increases over the ten-year period. Part of this increase may reflect improvements in the labor market position of blacks over the decade, but some of it probably reflects the fact that the ratios of Social Security and pension benefits to prior earnings are higher for blacks than for whites.

For the total age cohort there is a deterioration in real family income over the decade, all of which occurs during the second half of the ten-year period. For white men the median increased from $15,600 in 1966 to $16,500 in 1971 and then declined to $14,300 in 1976. The evidence suggests that these trends are explained primarily by the declining income of the older age groups as a result of the increasing prevalence of retirements. For instance, cross-sectional data for men 55 to 59 in the three years indicate a continuous increase from 1966 through 1976, $3,500 for whites and $4,800 for blacks. Moreover, in the longitudinal data there are pronounced differences in the time trend depending on the age group. Among men 45 to 49 in 1966 real income rose between 1966 and 1971 for both blacks and whites; by 1976 it had dropped below the 1971 level but remained above the 1966 level, by 4 percent for whites and 10 percent for blacks. In contrast, among the men 55 to 59 in 1966,

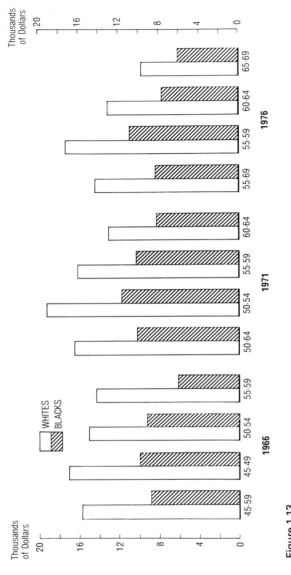

Figure 1.13
Median Real Total Family Income, by Age and Race, 1966, 1971, 1976 (1976 dollars)

real income declined by 32 percent between 1966 and 1976 for white men and remained virtually unchanged for blacks.[39]

Perhaps a better indicator of the economic welfare of these men is real family income per dependent (figure 1.14).[40] The burden of dependency decreased considerably over the decade, more so for whites than for blacks. As a consequence, there is a continuous improvement over the decade in income per dependent, more substantial for whites than for blacks. For the total age cohort real income per dependent rose from $5,200 for whites in 1966 to $11,000 in 1976, while the corresponding increase for blacks was from $2,500 to $5,300. Perceptible increases occurred for all the race-age groups.

The pattern of changes in assets over the period is shown in figure 1.15. By this criterion levels of welfare increased continuously over the decade for the cohort as a whole as well as for each age-race subgroup except the youngest group of blacks, although the rise was greater between 1966 and 1971 than during the second half of the ten-year period. Expressed in 1976 dollars, the median level of assets for the total age group of whites was $18,500 in 1966 and $31,300 in 1976. For the blacks the levels were only a fraction as high, rising from $1,300 in 1966 to $3,700 in 1976.

General Satisfaction with Life

In the 1976 survey respondents were asked for the first time how happy they were with their standard of living, leisure time activities, local area of residence, housing and health and with life in general (figure 1.16). Only small minorities expressed unhappiness in any of these contexts, and at least half reported that they were very happy in each dimension. Even for standard of living 51 percent of the whites reported that they were very happy, and an additional 27 percent said that they were somewhat happy, for a total of 78 percent. Among blacks the overall percentage was slightly lower (73 percent). Over 90 percent of white men and at least 80 percent of black men expressed happiness in response to each of the other questions.

The difference between whites and blacks is not nearly so large as would be expected if men were using the same standards to evaluate objective circumstances. The same is true of age differences. For example, although larger proportions of white men 65 to 69 than of those 55 to 59 report health prob-

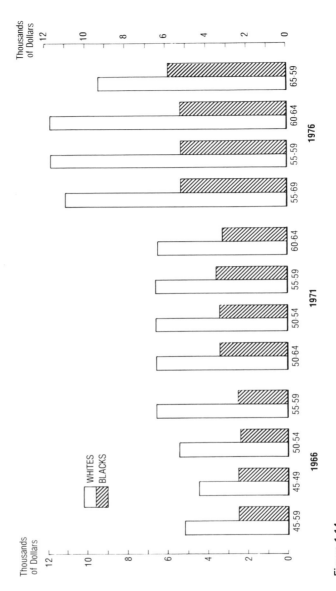

Figure 1.14
Median Real Per Capita Family Income, by Age and Race, 1966, 1971, 1976 (1976 dollars)

31

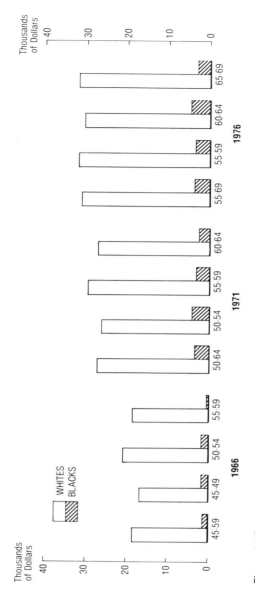

Figure 1.15
Median Real Total Family Assets, by Age and Race, 1966, 1971, 1976 (1976 dollars)

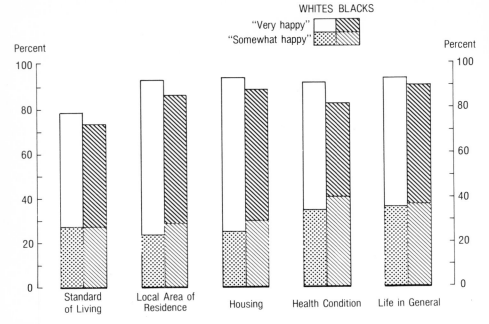

WHITES BLACKS
"Very happy"
"Somewhat happy"

Figure 1.16
Percent "Somewhat Happy" or "Very Happy" with Selected Aspects of Life, by Race, 1976

lems, identical proportions of the two groups say that they are happy with their health. Answers to the question about satisfaction with life in general (figure 1.17) revealed virtually no differences by age or race.

Summary

The National Longitudinal Surveys sample of men who were 45 to 59 years of age when the study began in 1966 shrank from its initial level of about 5,000 to slightly under 3,500 by the 1976 interview. Half of the 31 percent attrition rate was attributable to death, which does not affect the representativeness of the 1976 sample of men 55 to 69. The remainder of the attrition reflects primarily refusals of respondents to continue to be interviewed. Analysis of their characteristics leads to the conclusion that there is not likely to be significant nonresponse bias in analyses based on the 1976 data.

Major changes occurred in the lives of the respondents between 1966 and 1976. However one defines middle age, it is clear that a substantial fraction of the group moved out of that category during the ten-year period. Reflecting this aging pro-

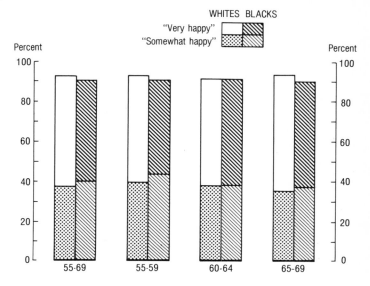

Figure 1.17
Percent "Somewhat Happy" or "Very Happy" with Life in General, by Age and Race, 1976

cess, the number of their dependents decreased, but health problems became more significant. From a labor market perspective the most dramatic manifestation was retirement. The proportion of the age group out of the labor force rose from the negligible level of about 5 percent in 1966, to almost two-fifths in 1976, and this fraction was as large as two-thirds among the men who were 65 to 69 in that year.

Among the majority of the men who remained at work more or less continuously over the decade, labor market experience appeared favorable by most criteria. Real hourly earnings of wage and salary workers were higher, on average, in 1976 than in 1966 for the entire age group. Only for those who were 65 to 69 in 1976 did this generalization not hold, reflecting the movement of many in this oldest age group into lower-paying post-retirement jobs. Even annual earnings in real terms were slightly higher at the end than at the beginning of the decade for white men (but not for black) who had not yet reached age 65, although for the oldest five-year age category they were only a fraction as high, again reflecting the prevalence of part-time postretirement jobs among this group.

In noneconomic terms, also, employment seemed to continue to reward those who remained at work. The proportions who reported that they were very satisfied with their jobs remained at the same high levels that has been recorded as of 1966—in the neighborhood of three-fifths. A substantial minority of the employed men acknowledged in 1976 that job pressures and feelings of fatigue had increased over the preceding five years, but the proportions were not much different from those that had been recorded five years earlier. Almost half of the white men and about one-third of the blacks felt in 1976 that they had progressed in their jobs during the preceding five years, and these proportions were only moderately lower than those reported by the same men five years earlier. Of course, in interpreting these data for the men who remained employed, one must remember that disproportionate numbers with less satisfactory experience had left the labor force.

Nevertheless, for the total sample there was little evidence of deterioration in average financial circumstances over the decade. Between 1966 and 1976 median real family income decreased by 8 percent for whites and 6 percent for blacks, but this decline occurred in the second half of the decade and was concentrated among the older ages in which retirements were most frequent. Because of the decrease in number of dependents, real income per family member showed a continuous improvement over the decade. Real assets were also higher in 1976 than in 1966 for the total cohort, as well as for all age-race subgroups except the youngest black men.

Table 1A.1
Noninterview Rate and Reason, 1976 Survey, by Selected 1966
Characteristics

1966 characteristics	Number of respondents, 1966[a]	Death rate, 1966–1976 (%)	Number potentially eligible for inter-view, 1976	Noninterview rate (%)		
				Refusal	Unable to locate[b]	Total
All respondents	5,020	16.8	4,179	12.4	4.2	16.6
Whites	3,518	14.7	3,001	14.4	3.3	17.7
Blacks	1,420	21.9	1,109	7.0	5.9	12.9
Age 45–49	1,835	11.3	1,627	13.2	4.3	17.5
Whites	1,306	9.6	1,180	14.9	3.2	18.1
Blacks	506	16.2	424	8.0	7.1	15.1
Age 50–54	1,724	16.7	1,436	12.0	3.4	15.4
Whites	1,206	15.0	1,025	14.1	2.9	17.1
Blacks	494	21.2	389	6.2	4.6	10.8
Age 55–59	1,461	23.6	1,116	11.8	4.9	16.8
Whites	1,006	20.9	796	13.8	3.9	17.7
Blacks	420	29.5	296	6.8	5.7	12.5
Educational attainment						
0–8 years	2,288	20.1	1,828	9.9	4.6	14.6
Whites	1,274	18.1	1,043	12.8	3.2	16.1
Blacks	971	22.2	755	5.8	5.8	11.7
9–11 years	941	16.2	789	15.0	3.0	18.0
Whites	709	14.8	604	16.6	2.5	19.0
Blacks	220	21.4	173	8.1	4.6	12.7
12 years	1,029	13.1	894	13.1	3.6	16.7
Whites	872	12.0	767	13.3	3.1	16.4
Blacks	144	20.8	114	13.2	5.3	18.4
13–15 years	342	12.0	301	15.0	4.3	19.3
Whites	298	10.4	267	16.1	3.4	19.5
Blacks	39	25.6	29	6.9	13.8	20.7
16–18 years	387	11.6	342	13.4	5.3	18.7
Whites	343	11.4	304	14.1	5.3	19.4
Blacks	35	17.1	29	3.4	6.9	10.3
Employed	4,595	14.6	3,924	12.6	3.8	16.4
Whites	3,277	13.2	2,846	14.4	3.1	17.5
Blacks	1,247	18.8	1,013	7.3	5.3	12.6
Unemployed	78	20.5	62	14.5	8.1	22.6
Whites	44	13.6	38	23.7	5.3	28.9
Blacks	32	25.0	24	0.0	12.5	12.5
Out of labor force	347	44.4	193	8.3	9.3	17.6
Whites	197	40.6	117	10.2	7.7	17.9
Blacks	141	48.9	72	5.6	11.1	15.7

1966 characteristics	Number of respondents, 1966[a]	Death rate, 1966– 1976 (%)	Number potentially eligible for inter- view, 1976	Noninterview rate (%)		
				Refusal	Unable to locate[b]	Total
Occupation						
White collar	1,497	13.6	1,294	15.1	3.7	18.8
Whites	1,310	13.5	1,133	15.1	3.5	18.6
Blacks	160	15.6	135	13.3	5.9	19.3
Professional	412	13.6	356	14.0	5.6	19.7
Whites	362	12.7	316	14.6	6.0	20.6
Blacks	41	24.4	31	6.4	3.2	9.7
Managerial	651	12.7	568	14.6	2.5	17.1
Whites	590	12.9	514	14.8	1.9	16.7
Blacks	49	12.2	43	9.3	9.3	18.6
Clerical	243	16.9	202	17.3	3.0	20.3
Whites	179	17.9	147	17.0	2.7	19.7
Blacks	60	15.0	51	17.6	3.9	21.6
Sales	191	12.0	168	16.7	4.8	21.4
Whites	179	12.8	156	15.4	4.5	19.9
Blacks	10	0.0	10	30.0	10.0	40.0
Blue collar	3,498	18.1	2,865	11.1	4.4	15.5
Whites	2,195	15.4	1,856	13.8	3.1	17.0
Blacks	1,249	22.7	966	6.1	5.9	12.0
Craft	1,078	14.7	919	14.1	2.7	16.9
Whites	877	14.6	749	15.9	1.9	17.8
Blacks	193	16.1	162	6.8	6.2	13.0
Operatives	1,028	16.6	857	12.2	4.9	17.2
Whites	631	14.7	538	15.4	3.9	19.3
Blacks	388	19.6	312	7.0	5.4	12.5
Laborers	498	23.9	379	8.7	5.8	14.5
Whites	174	22.4	135	13.3	3.0	16.3
Blacks	316	25.0	237	5.5	6.8	12.2
Service	403	25.1	302	9.9	7.3	17.2
Whites	189	19.6	152	11.8	7.9	19.7
Blacks	195	29.7	137	8.8	5.8	14.6
Farmer	324	11.7	286	6.3	2.4	8.7
Whites	257	10.5	230	7.4	2.2	9.6
Blacks	62	17.7	51	2.0	2.0	3.9
Farm laborer	167	26.9	122	1.6	5.7	7.4
Whites	67	22.4	52	3.8	3.8	7.7
Blacks	95	29.5	67	0.0	7.5	7.5

Table 1A.1 (continued)

1966 characteristics	Number of respondents, 1966[a]	Death rate, 1966–1976 (%)	Number potentially eligible for inter-view, 1976	Noninterview rate (%)		
				Refusal	Unable to locate[b]	Total
Annual income						
Less than $2,999	629	28.3	451	5.1	6.9	12.0
Whites	261	24.1	198	9.6	4.5	14.1
Blacks	360	30.8	249	1.6	8.0	9.6
$3,000–$3,999	2,120	16.9	1,761	11.1	3.7	14.8
Whites	1,417	16.6	1,182	12.4	2.7	15.1
Blacks	667	17.5	550	8.0	5.3	13.3
$10,000–$14,999	813	11.2	722	12.7	2.8	15.5
Whites	722	11.1	642	13.1	2.6	15.7
Blacks	85	12.9	74	8.1	4.0	12.2
$15,000–$19,999	238	9.2	216	13.9	6.0	19.9
Whites	211	9.0	192	14.6	5.7	20.3
Blacks	19	15.8	16	6.2	12.5	18.8
$20,000 or more	164	9.8	148	8.1	2.7	10.8
Whites	157	9.6	142	7.7	2.8	10.6
Blacks	6	16.7	5	0.0	0.0	0.0
Homeowner	3,418	14.6	2,920	14.0	2.0	16.0
Whites	2,683	13.6	2,318	15.0	1.9	16.9
Blacks	698	18.5	569	9.1	1.9	11.1
Renter	1,248	21.3	982	9.8	10.2	20.0
Whites	647	18.1	530	13.0	8.5	21.5
Blacks	562	25.1	421	6.2	11.4	17.6
No cash rent	222	21.6	174	2.3	5.7	8.0
Whites	108	16.7	90	4.4	6.7	11.1
Blacks	110	26.4	81	0.0	3.7	3.7
Other	131	22.1	102	9.8	6.9	16.7
Whites	79	21.5	62	16.1	6.4	22.6
Blacks	50	24.0	38	0.0	7.9	7.9
Married	4,376	15.4	3,702	12.7	3.4	16.1
Whites	3,167	13.9	2,727	14.5	2.8	17.3
Blacks	1,141	19.8	915	7.2	4.6	11.8
Not married	632	25.6	470	9.6	10.0	19.6
Whites	342	21.6	268	12.3	7.8	20.1
Blacks	276	30.1	193	6.2	11.9	18.1
Industry						
Agriculture	530	17.7	436	6.0	3.7	9.6
Whites	347	13.5	300	7.3	2.7	10.0
Blacks	172	26.2	127	3.1	4.7	7.9

1966 characteristics	Number of respondents, 1966[a]	Death rate, 1966–1976 (%)	Number potentially eligible for interview, 1976	Noninterview rate (%)		
				Refusal	Unable to locate[b]	Total
Mining	63	15.9	53	7.5	3.8	11.3
Whites	40	17.5	33	9.1	3.0	12.1
Blacks	23	13.0	20	5.0	5.0	10.0
Construction	578	17.1	479	11.7	6.3	18.0
Whites	388	17.8	319	14.7	4.4	19.1
Blacks	184	16.3	154	4.5	9.7	14.3
Manufacturing	1,459	15.9	1,227	13.5	2.7	16.2
Whites	1,049	14.8	894	16.1	2.7	18.8
Blacks	397	18.9	322	5.9	1.9	7.8
Transportation, communications, public utilities	497	19.3	401	11.7	3.5	15.2
Whites	335	17.6	276	12.7	1.8	14.5
Blacks	158	22.8	122	9.8	6.6	16.4
Trade	710	16.8	591	13.9	4.7	18.6
Whites	532	13.5	460	14.8	3.3	18.0
Blacks	158	27.8	114	9.6	10.5	20.2
Finance, insurance, real estate	167	17.4	138	15.9	4.3	20.3
Whites	133	14.3	114	17.5	3.5	21.0
Blacks	33	30.3	23	8.7	8.7	17.4
Services	676	18.5	551	7.2	7.2	20.3
Whites	454	15.0	386	6.2	6.2	21.0
Blacks	205	25.8	152	9.2	9.2	19.1
Public administration	330	10.9	294	1.7	1.7	15.6
Whites	235	8.9	214	1.9	1.9	17.3
Blacks	85	16.5	71	1.4	1.4	11.3

[a]Totals in each category include some men of races other than black or white.
[b]Includes a small number of cases in which the respondent was inaccessible to the interviewer even though his location was ascertained.

Notes

1. Neugarten (1968); Riley and Foner (1968).

2. Ross and Ross (1960). For a systematic examination of the labor market problems of older workers and a bibliography, see Sheppard (1979).

3. U.S. Department of Labor (1978), p. 186.

4. Ibid., p. 179.

5. These surveys have been designed by The Ohio State University Center for Human Resource Research under a contract with the Employment and Training Administration of the U.S. Department of Labor. The sample design, fieldwork, and the initial stages of data processing are the responsibility of the U.S. Bureau of the Census under a separate contract with the Employment and Training Administration. In addition to the sample of men on which the data of this volume are based, the National Longitudinal Surveys include samples of three other age-sex cohorts that have been under surveillance since the middle or late 1960s: women between the ages of 30 and 44, young men between the ages of 14 and 24, and young women between 14 and 24. In 1979 interviews were begun with a new sample of males and females between the ages of 14 and 21. For a complete description of the surveys see Center for Human Resource Research (1980).

6. The sample was drawn from the 235 Primary Sampling Units (PSUs) included in the experimental Monthly Labor Survey that was being conducted in the mid 1960s to test proposed changes in the Current Population Survey (CPS) interview schedule. Thus sampling procedures were analogous to those used in the CPS.

7. Exceptions are chapters 2 and 5, in which the regression analyses are based on unweighted data. Econometricians and survey analysts differ on whether it is more appropriate to use weighted or unweighted data in the kinds of analysis in this volume. Experience with the NLS data at the Center for Human Resource Research suggests that provided there is stratification by race, there is relatively little difference between the results of weighted and unweighted regressions. Authors of the papers in this volume were therefore encouraged to follow their individual predilections.

8. For a fuller description of the sample, field procedures, and the weighting system, see appendix B.

9. Additional telephone surveys were conducted in 1978 and 1980. The results of neither survey are available yet. A final face-to-face survey is planned for 1981.

10. For a detailed description of the information collected in the surveys, see Center for Human Resource Research (1980). Copies of the 1966 and 1976 schedules may be obtained from the Center for Human Resource Research.

11. In addition to the four comprehensive reports published as research and development monographs by the Employment and Training Administration of the Department of Labor (Parnes et al., 1970a, 1970b, 1973, 1975) there have been over 50 articles or monographs on specific topics based on the NLS surveys of men. For a bibliography, see Center for Human Resource Research (1980). This section draws heavily on the concluding chapters of Parnes et al. (1970a, 1975).

12. Parnes et al. (1970), pp. 127, 238.

13. Parnes et al. (1975), pp. 26, 237.

14. Parnes et al. (1970), p. 239.

15. Parnes et al. (1975), pp. 285–290, 212–213, 142.

16. Ibid., pp. 20–22.

17. Ibid., pp. 86–103.

18. Parnes et al. (1970), p. 27.

19. Parnes et al. (1975), pp. 175, 15, 285–290.

20. Ibid., pp. 285–290, 135, 137.

21. Ibid., pp. 62–73.

22. Ibid., pp. 11, 120.

23. Ibid, pp. 146, 104–111.

24. Ibid., pp. 162–169.

25. Ibid., pp. 187–190.

26. Ibid., pp. 13–15.

27. Ibid., p. 22.

28. Ibid., pp. 89, 99–103, 107.

29. In each comparison made in this chapter an identical group of men is being compared at the several points in time. In other words, in each case we have confined the analysis to men who were interviewed and who provided the relevant information in *every* year. Moreover, where attention centers on men in a particular status (such as wage and salary earners), the figures relate only to men who were in that status at all three times.

30. The actual death rate for the cohort is undoubtedly higher than this, since some of those who left the sample for other reasons may have died by 1976. If the death rate among this group was the same as for the remainder of the sample, the total number of deaths would be greater by 116, and the actual mortality rate would have been 19.1 percent rather than 16.8 percent. By the same token, the number of original sample members still alive in 1976 would have been 4,063 rather than 4,179, and the proportion of this group not interviewed would have been 14.2 percent rather than 16.6 percent.

31. A large majority of the remaining 17 percent (12 percent) refused to continue their participation in the study sometime after the initial survey, and the rest could not be located in two successive years or in 1976.

32. We cannot compare responses in 1971 with those of 1966 and 1976, since the question on health was worded slightly differently in the 1971 survey.

33. See Parnes et al. (1975), p. 162.

34. Walker (1976).

35. Confining the sample to those employed at all three dates results in a highly select group of men, particularly in the oldest five-year age group. Only a minority of men who were 64 to 69 in 1976 were still employed in that year, and some of these were in postretirement jobs. The group is therefore not representative of the total five-year age cohort who were employed in 1966 and/or 1971, but is likely to overrepresent those who had strong work commitments, enjoyed good health, and were in the most desirable jobs. A fairly dramatic example is provided in the following table, which compares the 1966 data for all 55- to-59-year-old men who were employed in that year with the more restricted group of that cohort who were also employed in 1971 and 1976:

Group	Whites		Blacks	
	Number of sample cases	Percentage employed as professionals or managers, 1966	Number of sample cases	Percentage employed as professionals or managers, 1966
Men 55–59 employed in 1966	897	29	347	5
Men 55–59 employed in 1966, 1971, 1976	154	43	59	21

36. When men who never reported themselves retired were excluded from the universe (in a tabulation not shown here), weekly hours in 1976 were 41 rather than 33 for the 65- to 69-year-old white men and 42 rather than 34 for the blacks.

37. U.S. Department of Labor (1978), p. 265.

38. See Parnes et al. (1975), p. 191.

39. When the sample is confined to men who had never reported themselves retired, median real family income is higher in 1976 than in 1966 for both blacks and whites and, within each racial group, for every age category except white men 50 to 54 years of age in 1966, among whom there was a 2 percent decline.

40. "Dependent" in this context is defined to include both the respondent and his wife. It therefore differs from the measure used in figure 1.1.

References

Center for Human Resource Research. 1980. *The National Longitudinal Surveys handbook.* Columbus, Ohio: The Ohio State University.

Neugarten, B. L. 1968. The awareness of middle-age. In B. L. Neugarten, ed., *Middle age and aging.* Chicago: The University of Chicago Press.

Parnes, H. S., Adams, A. V., Andrisani, P., Egge, K., Fleisher, B. M., Kohen, A. I., Miljus, R. C., Nestel, G., Schmidt, R. M., and Spitz, R. S. 1970a, 1970b, 1973, 1975. *The pre-retirement years: a longitudinal study of the labor market experience of men,* vols. 1–4. U.S. Department of Labor, Manpower Administration, Manpower R&D Monograph 15. Washington, D.C.: U.S. Government Printing Office.

Riley, M. W., and Foner, A. 1968. *Aging and society, vol. 1: An inventory of research findings.* New York: Russell Sage Foundation.

Ross, A. M., and Ross, J. N. 1960. Employment problems of older workers. In *Studies in unemployment.* Prepared for the Special Committee on Unemployment Problems, U.S. Senate, 86th Congress, 2nd session. Washington, D.C.: U.S. Government Printing Office.

Sheppard, H. L. 1979. Employment-related problems of older workers: a research strategy. U.S. Department of Labor, Employment and Training Administration, R&D Monograph 73.

U.S. Department of Labor. 1978. *Employment and training report of the President, 1978.* Washington, D.C.: U.S. Government Printing Office.

Walker, J. W. 1976. Will early retirement retire early? *Personnel* 53 (January-February): 33–39.

Chapter 2

Changes in
Black-White
Labor Market
Opportunities,
1966–1976

Thomas N.
Daymont

The period 1966 to 1976 was one of intensified effort on the part of government as well as many private groups to eliminate, or at least reduce, racial discrimination. This chapter attempts to assess the success of these efforts in improving the labor market opportunities of older black men. The studies of this issue have reached no consensus on the success of antidiscrimination efforts. Some observers have argued that the labor market opportunities of blacks have improved substantially relative to those of whites during the last few years, largely because of government antidiscrimination programs.[1] Others have countered that such improvements have been minimal.[2] Skeptics also assert that studies showing improvement in relative black opportunities have frequently failed to account adequately for the effects of changes in economic conditions and the effects of a reduction in racial differences in individual characteristics that affect labor market success.[3] This analysis explicitly considers both economic changes and the reduction in racial differences in individual characteristics. It exploits the rich panel data of the National Longitudinal Surveys to assess recent changes in the opportunities of older black men as measured by pay and employment security.

Antidiscrimination
Efforts

Civil rights organizations, struggling for racial equality for more than a century, attained some success by the 1940s and 1950s. It was not until the 1960s that the legislative and executive branches of the federal government showed much interest in their cause. During this decade the Equal Employment Opportunity Commission (EEOC) and the Office of Federal Contract Compliance (OFCC) were established to help reduce racial inequities in the labor market and other social institutions. Although these programs helped focus attention on the issue of racial discrimination and probably had some direct positive impact on opportunities for blacks, a growing body of literature suggests that their impact during the first half decade of their existence was minimal.[4] It appears that the limited effectiveness of these programs during the late 1960s was due largely to their lack of enforcement powers or, in the case of the OFCC, to the failure to exercise such powers.[5]

I would like to thank Herbert S. Parnes, Stephen M. Hills, Ronald J. D'Amico, Russell W. Rumberger, Lois B. Shaw, Woo Cho, David Shapiro, and Henry M. Levin as well as the other authors of this volume for many helpful comments.

Few civil rights initiatives were made during the early 1970s. However, progress was made in improving the enforcement capabilities of existing programs. For example, in 1972 the Equal Employment Opportunity Commission was empowered to bring legal action against discriminators on behalf of victims of discrimination,[6] and federal appropriations to the EEOC increased sevenfold between 1969 and 1976. To the extent that these greater enforcement capabilities and increased expenditures were effective, we would expect to see increases in the relative opportunities of blacks through the 1970s.

Most indicators of labor market success show that blacks have improved their positions relative to whites in recent years.[7] The ratio of mean earnings for black males to mean earnings for white males increased from 0.51 to 0.68 between 1959 and 1974.[8] Most closely related to this investigation is the recent finding that the black-white earnings ratio for men aged 51 to 60 rose monotonically between 1967 and 1974, from 0.53 to 0.61.[9] In general, improvement in indicators of labor market success such as these can result from changes in racial differences in skills and other individual characteristics important for labor market success and from changes in the relative opportunities open to blacks and whites with the same characteristics.

There is disagreement, however, on how these trends are to be interpreted. Some investigators have concluded that even after changes in individual characteristics such as education and social background have been accounted for, there has been a trend toward improvement in the relative opportunities of blacks.[10] Others have argued that these studies have failed to account adequately for the changing economic conditions through the 1960s and 1970s or have failed to control adequately for the changes in racial differences in all relevant individual characteristics.

Most of the relevant studies have not used data that extended through the middle 1970s.[11] Since the labor market positions of blacks are more sensitive than those of whites to cyclical fluctuations in economic conditions,[12] it is possible that the improvement in relative black opportunities during the 1960s was primarily a function of generally favorable economic conditions and that this improvement ceased when economic conditions deteriorated in the 1970s.

The second criticism is that studies with positive findings at best overstate any improvement in the relative opportunities of blacks because they failed to control all relevant human capital factors. Smith and Welch (1977, 1978) assert that the major cause of the reduction in black-white earnings ratios has been a convergence of black-white differences in earnings-producing characteristics such as socioeconomic background and the quantity and quality of education. They further conclude that "the effect of government on aggregate black-white income ratios is apparently quite small, and the popular notion that government pressures have driven these recent changes has little empirical support."[13] They hypothesize instead a "vintage," or cohort, effect. They argue that because the relative quality of schooling has improved substantially, more recent black cohorts have begun their job experiences with larger initial stocks of human capital than previous cohorts. According to their indicators, improvement in schooling quality began about 1920— about the time that the oldest members of our sample finished elementary school.

Thus there remains considerable uncertainty about the degree of change in the relative earnings opportunities of blacks, even though several studies have addressed the issue. The evidence on changes in the relative employment security of blacks is even less satisfactory. The ratio of the unemployment rate for older black men to the unemployment rate for older white men decreased from 1966 to 1970 but then increased through the 1970s.[14] However, we know of no study examining changes in employment security that has controlled for business cycle fluctuations and changes in racial differences in human capital factors.

Analytical Strategy

We examine two dimensions of labor market success: hourly rate of pay and the amount of unemployment experienced by the individual. For each dimension we use two regression models. The first is designed to assess changes in labor market success attributable to changes in labor market opportunities over time net of those attributable to changes in human capital factors. The NLS data are especially well suited for making this distinction, for they provide longitudinal data on a representative sample of older men as well as a rich array of individual characteristics. The second model attempts to distinguish between the effects of the civil rights movement and changing economic conditions as factors producing changes in the relative labor market opportunities of blacks.

The basic sample consists of observations for all black and white men who did not report being retired at the time of the survey in the reference years 1966, 1967, 1969, 1971, 1973, 1975, and 1976. To exploit the panel nature of these data, we pooled all the observations into one data file.[15] Thus this file includes up to seven observations for each respondent. However, since rates of pay for the respondent's job were not ascertained in all years, only observations for the years 1966, 1969, 1971, and 1976 were included in the analysis for log hourly earnings.[16]

In the first model each of two dimensions of labor market success—the natural logarithm of hourly earnings (in 1976 dollars) and the number of weeks unemployed in the year prior to the survey—were expressed as a function of (1) a series of dummy variables representing the year in which the dependent variable was measured and (2) a series of variables measuring human capital characteristics of the individual. These human capital variables include measures of the individual's educational, civilian labor force, and military experience; an indicator of the skill level of the respondent's longest job prior to 1966; an indicator of whether the respondent's health limited his ability to work; and three variables measuring the local labor market in which the respondent resided.[17]

Most of the variables included in this model are fairly standard. One exception may be the indicator of the skill level of the respondent's longest job prior to 1966. This variable was included to control for some of the effects of labor market discrimination prior to the time covered by this study. Labor market discrimination in the early part of the career is expected to have exacerbated the channeling of blacks and whites into different career paths with different opportunities to develop skills and other marketable characteristics. Thus even among men with the same level of the other characteristics in the model, blacks and whites are expected to have had different levels of opportunities to develop occupational skills before the initial year of the survey. The respondent's longest job is probably the best single readily available indicator of his career before the initial survey. The General Education Development (GED) from the *Dictionary of Occupational Titles* (DOT), measured in terms of numbers of years, was used as an indicator of skill level, since it is specifically designed to be an estimate of the education level needed to perform adequately in an occupation.[18] To allow the effects of variables in our model to differ between blacks and whites, we estimated each equation separately for each race.

In the second model we replace the dummy variables representing specific years with two explanatory variables designed to capture the particular reasons that temporal effects are thought to be important. First, as a measure of general labor market conditions, we include the unemployment rate for males aged 20 and over for the year of interview.[19] Second, as a measure of the public's commitment to reducing discrimination we include the combined appropriations to three federal agencies whose primary purpose is to combat discrimination—the Equal Employment Opportunity Commission, the Office of Federal Contract Compliance Programs, and the Commission on Civil Rights.[20]

In the second model we also include two indicators of the relative quality of black schools to other schools for the year when the respondent was 12 years old.[21] The inclusion of these variables improves our ability to control for the cohort effects that Smith and Welch have emphasized.

Findings

The first two columns of table 2.1 show the expected levels of hourly earnings, expressed in dollars of constant purchasing power, for a typical white and black for each year.[22] For example, the figure for 1966 in the first column means that a white man who was average in terms of measured characteristics earned $5.24 in that year, expressed in 1976 dollars. Although the expected rate of pay of older whites increased by 14 percent from 1966 to 1971, it actually decreased by 1 percent during the next five years. In contrast, the expected rate of pay of older

Table 2.1
Changes in Expected Values for Whites and Blacks and Relative Black Opportunities across Time: Real Hourly Earnings (1976 dollars)

Year	Expected values[a]		Black-white ratios of expected values	Relative black opportunities[b]
	Whites	Blacks		
1966	$5.24	$3.30	.63	.84
1969	5.72	3.73	.65	.86
1971	5.96	3.97	.67	.88
1976	5.91	4.18	.71	.94

[a]These values represent the expected level of hourly earnings for a typical white or black for each year.
[b]See note 25 and related material in the text for further information.

Table 2.2

Changes in Expected Values for Whites and Blacks and Relative Black Opportunities across Time: Weeks Unemployed in Last Year (WUNLY)

Year	Expected values of WUNLY[a]		White-black difference in expected values	Relative black opportunities[b]
	Whites	Blacks		
1965	0.93	2.15	−1.22	−0.76
1966–67	1.04	1.85	−0.81	−0.35
1968–69	0.95	1.73	−0.78	−0.32
1970–71	1.02	1.92	−0.90	−0.44
1972–73	1.13	1.61	−0.48	−0.02
1974–75	1.83	2.32	−0.49	−0.03
1975–76	2.30	3.33	−1.03	−0.56

[a]These values represent the expected level of weeks of unemployment for a typical white or black for each year.
[b]This indicator represents an estimate of how many more or fewer weeks of unemployment a typical black would have experienced had his level of unemployment been determined by the process that governed whites.

blacks increased during both halves of this decade, by 20 percent and 5 percent, respectively. As a consequence, the black-white ratio of expected rates of pay improved from 0.63 in 1966 to 0.71 in 1976.

These racial differences in pay may be the result of racial differences in income-producing characteristics such as those measured here and differences in the earnings opportunities of blacks and whites with the same measured characteristics. To ascertain the degree to which the trends were attributable to changes in the second factor, we calculated the expected black-white ratio of hourly earnings for men with the same characteristics.[23] On this basis, the relative opportunities of blacks improved steadily throughout the period. For example, the pay disadvantage of blacks relative to whites with the same characteristics improved from 0.84 in 1966 to 0.94 in 1976.

The first two columns of table 2.2 show the expected levels of weeks unemployed during the previous year for a typical white and black for each year.[24] For whites the number of weeks unemployed increased only slightly between 1965 and 1972–73 but then doubled by 1975–76. The relative black opportunities as measured by the expected white-black differences in weeks unemployed for men with the same characteristics (the black means) are shown in column 4 of table 2.2.[25] According to these indicators, the relative opportunity of blacks improved during the period, although the improvement was uneven.

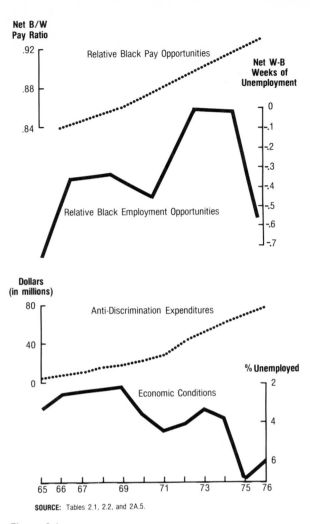

SOURCE: Tables 2.1, 2.2, and 2A.5.

Figure 2.1
Relative Black Opportunities, Economic Conditions, and Governmental
Expenditures on Antidiscrimination Programs, 1965–1976

How do these trends in relative black opportunities relate to
changes in the economic and social environment over the ten
years under consideration? The assessment of this relationship
is facilitated by looking at the profiles in figure 2.1.[26] The top two
profiles show the changes in relative black opportunities. The
third profile shows changes in the public commitment to reducing discrimination as measured by government expenditures on
antidiscrimination programs. The bottom profile shows changes

in economic conditions as measured by the unemployment rate (inverted) of males aged 20 and older. Focusing on employment security first, we see that the relative opportunities of blacks seem to be quite sensitive to short-run fluctuations in economic conditions. Black employment opportunities improve when economic conditions improve. However, even though economic conditions over the decade deteriorated, the underlying trend in relative black opportunities improved. This improving trend seems to correspond quite closely with the increased government expenditures on antidiscrimination programs. The improvement in the relative earnings opportunities of blacks also corresponds closely with the increased government expenditures on antidiscrimination programs. The relationship between the relative earnings opportunities of blacks and economic conditions is less clear; however, any such relationship appears to be dominated by an effect of a public commitment to reduce discrimination.

Our second model was designed to accomplish two tasks. First, we wanted to model the relationships summarized in figure 2.1 more explicitly. Second, we wanted to allow for possible vintage effects due to changes in school quality, as hypothesized by Smith and Welch. To accomplish the first task, we replaced our dummy variables representing specific years with indicators of the unemployment rate (UNEMP), as a measure of economic conditions, and government expenditures on antidiscrimination programs (GVEXP). To accomplish the second task, we included two indicators of the relative quality of black schools during the year when the respondent was 12 years old. The school quality indicators are the same as those used by Smith and Welch (1978, table 6) and Welch (1974). The first one is the ratio of the average number of days attended per pupil in black Southern schools to the same measure of all schools in the United States. The second indicator is a comparable ratio for the number of pupils enrolled per classroom teacher. The pattern of both of these indicators suggests that the quality of black schools relative to white schools improved between the times when the oldest and the youngest members of our sample were in elementary school (table 2.3). Thus without proper controls the changes in the relative quality in black schools could produce a bias toward overestimating the improvement in relative black opportunities over time.

Table 2.3
Changes in the Relative Quality of Black Schools in the South Relative to All Schools in the United States, 1918–1934

Year	Days attended per pupil	Pupils enrolled per classroom teacher
1918	.58	1.74
1919–20	.66	1.66
1921–22	.64	1.67
1923–24	.64	1.56
1925–26	.69	1.54
1927–28	.68	1.51
1929–30	.68	1.46
1931–32	.71	1.44
1933–34	.76	1.41

The estimated effects of government antidiscrimination expenditures and of economic conditions on relative black opportunities from our second model are obtained by calculating the racial differences in their effects (table 2.4). These effects were calculated so that a larger value would indicate an improvement in the relative opportunities of blacks.[27] The results for employment security indicate that the relative opportunities of blacks were adversely affected by the level of unemployment and positively affected by the civil rights movement. To estimate the magnitude of these effects, we calculated the change in relative black opportunities implied by the amount of change in the two explanatory variables between the first and last years of the study (row 5 of table 2.4). These calculations imply that the increases in government expenditures for antidiscrimination programs between 1966 and 1976 had the effect of reducing the black-white unemployment differential over the period by 1.11 weeks. This expected change, with economic conditions controlled, is much greater than the change of 0.20 weeks measured by our first model,[28] which implies that the improvement in the relative employment opportunities of blacks would have been substantially greater had it not been for the general deterioration in economic conditions during the period. The change in the relative employment opportunities of blacks implied by the combined changes in antidiscrimination expenditures and economic conditions (1.11 − 0.86 = 0.25) is quite close to the change implied by model 1. This suggests that the addition of the school quality variable had little effect on our estimate of the changes in relative black employment opportunities.

Table 2.4
Effects of Government Expenditures on Antidiscrimination Programs and Economic Conditions on Relative Black Opportunities

Sample or calculation	Dependent variable			
	(Log) hourly earnings		Weeks unemployed last year	
	Expenditures on antidiscrimination programs	Unemployment level	Expenditures on antidiscrimination programs	Unemployment level
Whites	−0.00391	0.0029	0.0169	0.139
Blacks	−0.00261	0.0028	0.000224	0.416
Racial difference[a]	0.00130	−0.0001	0.0167	−0.277
Change in explanatory variable between first and last year	69.2	3.40	66.3	3.10
Implied change in relative black opportunities[b]	0.84 to 0.92	trivial	1.11	−0.86

[a]So that a larger value indicates a greater effect on relative black opportunities, it was calculated as the black effect−white effect for log hourly earnings and the white effect−black effect for weeks unemployed last year.
[b]For weeks unemployed, the implied change is simply the product of the racial difference in the coefficients and the change in the level of the explanatory variables between the first and last years. For hourly earnings the implied change of government expenditures was calculated as follows. First, we substituted the value for government expenditures in 1966 (8.8) and the means for all other variables into the black and white regressions for model 2 to get the expected level of log hourly earnings for blacks and whites with the characteristics of a typical black given the level of government expenditures in 1966. The black-white ratio of the antilog of these values was calculated to be 0.84. We repeated the calculation of expected log hourly earnings except that we now substituted the value of government expenditures in 1976 (78.0). The black-white ratio of the antilog of these values was 0.92. Thus with all other measured variables controlled, the change in government expenditures between 1966 and 1976 implied a change in the black-white earnings ratio from 0.84 to 0.92. Since the racial difference in the coefficient for unemployment rate was practically zero, the change in economic conditions implied only a trivial change in the black-white earnings ratio.

The results for model 2 indicate a favorable effect of the civil rights movement on the relative earnings opportunities for blacks. The increase in government expenditures over the period implies a change in the black-white earnings ratio from 0.84 to 0.92, which is only slightly smaller than the change measured by model 1.[29] This, in conjunction with the negligible influence of economic conditions, suggests that omitting the school quality variables leads to a slight overestimation of the degree of change in the relative earnings opportunities of older black men. In addition, it suggests that the relative earnings opportunities of blacks would be about the same even if economic conditions had not deteriorated.

The evidence produced by this study strongly refutes the hypothesis of Smith and Welch that there has been little improvement in the underlying labor market opportunities for blacks relative to whites, once "vintage effects" are taken into account.[30] To the contrary, controlling for these effects as well as for human capital characteristics and the character of the labor market, we have found a substantial improvement between 1966 and 1976 in the relative opportunities of older black men as measured by both rates of pay and employment security.

Of course, these results do not necessarily mean that all the measured improvement was a direct result of government expenditures on antidiscrimination programs. Instead, the estimated effects of this variable should be interpreted as reflecting the total effects of the civil rights movement. Studies that have attempted to focus on the direct effects of government programs such as the EEOC and the OFCCP on relative black opportunities have yielded different results, depending on the data and methods of analysis.[31] However, in a critical review of this literature, Butler and Heckman (1977) concluded that on balance there is no evidence that government programs have had any impact on black-white wage differences. Even if one accepts this verdict, it is not clear whether it reflects the actual absence of any effect or merely the failure of studies to detect it. We suspect that the second explanation is more likely correct. There are at least two reasons for believing that previous studies may have failed to detect an effect of antidiscrimination programs. First, most studies with negative findings have been designed to assess only specific types of effects, such as those that show up when firms or industries covered by the program are compared with those that are not. This approach ignores the indirect effects that these programs are likely to have by increasing the awareness of the racial equity issue among employers and employees. Such indirect effects may show up by improving black opportunities in noncovered as well as in covered establishments. They may also result in greater investments in the human capital of blacks, by themselves and by employers, in anticipation of greater opportunities for blacks.

Second, the periods covered by previous studies may have been too early to detect a positive effect. Many of them analyzed data from the late 1960s, and none analyzed data later than 1974. Thus most assessed the impact of federal programs during a period when the EEOC and OFCC were especially limited in their effectiveness. However, during the 1970s the enforcement capabilities of these programs improved. As data for the late 1970s become available, we suspect that there will be increasing evidence that federal antidiscrimination programs are having a positive impact on the relative opportunities of blacks.[32]

Given the present state of the art of social science, it would be extremely difficult, if not impossible, to disentangle empirically the underlying relationships between such programs and other aspects of a public commitment to racial equity such as political action, judicial decisions, and more favorable attitudes of whites toward blacks. The several aspects of this process are, of course, complementary and mutually reinforcing. However, were such an analysis possible, it seems likely that one would find that government antidiscrimination efforts played an important role in this process of social change.

Conclusions

This study has examined changes in the relative labor market opportunities of older black men between 1966 and 1976. As measured by employment security, the relative opportunities of blacks were quite sensitive to fluctuations in economic conditions, improving in good times and falling in bad. On the other hand, the relative earnings opportunities of blacks appeared to be unrelated to changes in economic conditions.

The most important finding was that net of the influence of changing economic conditions, the relative opportunities of blacks improved during the decade 1966 to 1976 as measured by earnings and by employment security.[33] In terms of earnings opportunities this improvement was substantial. Controlling for education and other factors affecting productivity increased the black-white earnings ratio from 0.84 to 0.94. The actual improvement in relative employment opportunities was less impressive, but the evidence suggested that the improvement would have been greater had it not been for the decline in economic conditions during the period. In addition, there was a close correspondence between the improvement in both the earnings and employment opportunities of blacks and the amount of government expenditures on antidiscrimination programs, which was used as an indicator of the public commitment to eliminating discrimination. Thus our results indicate progress in improving the relative opportunities of middle-aged and older black men and suggest that government efforts have had an impact.

They also show, however, that racial equity for this group of men is still unattained and thus lead to a recommendation that government antidiscrimination efforts be continued and intensified. In particular, attention should be given to making these efforts more effective, such as by increasing the enforcement powers of government agencies and changing the organization of these agencies so that programs can be coordinated more effectively.[34]

Table 2A.1
Determinants of Log Hourly Earnings: Model 1

Explanatory variables[a]	Whites		Blacks	
	Coefficient	t-value	Coefficient	t-value
YR69	0.0885	4.72	0.123	8.63
YR71	0.129	10.84	0.183	10.12
YR76	0.121	5.89	0.235	7.86
SKLJ	0.0427	11.65	0.0156	3.03
ED	0.0312	8.95	0.0102	2.50
EX	−0.00505	−2.72	−0.00841	−3.21
MILT	−0.00453	−1.08	0.112	1.69
HLTH	−0.0377	−3.91	−0.0297	−1.88
SMSA	0.147	8.55	0.305	11.12
SIZELF	0.0306	4.62	0.0341	2.84
SOUTH	−0.0959	−5.47	−0.228	−8.19
FATHOCC	0.000827	2.00	−0.000256	−0.26
FARM15	−0.124	−6.54	−0.0449	−1.81
CONSTANT	0.945	10.12	1.224	9.55
Number of respondents	2,678		1,130	
Number of observations	7,311		3,103	
R^2(adj)	0.30		0.36	
ρ	0.74		0.65	

[a]See Glossary for definitions of variables.

Table 2A.2
Determinants of Weeks Unemployed Last Year: Model 1

Explanatory variables[a]	Whites		Blacks	
	Coefficient	t-value	Coefficient	t-value
YR67	0.105	0.89	−0.300	−1.24
YR69	0.0178	0.13	−0.421	−1.57
YR71	0.0865	0.20	−0.232	−0.76
YR73	0.200	1.22	−0.538	−1.53
YR75	0.897	4.77	0.165	0.41
YR76	1.374	6.77	1.181	2.73
SKLJ	−0.0952	−3.31	−0.0317	−0.53
ED	−0.147	−5.45	−0.146	−3.00
EX	−0.0125	−0.86	−0.037	−1.18
MILT	−0.0104	−0.32	−0.068	−0.86
HLTH	0.666	6.54	0.764	3.60
SMSA	−0.160	−1.13	0.217	0.66
SIZELF	−0.132	2.33	0.145	0.97
SOUTH	−0.286	−2.03	−0.518	−1.51
FATHOCC	0.00214	0.65	0.00635	0.55
FARM15	−0.457	−3.07	0.443	1.48
CONSTANT	4.085	5.56	4.582	3.01
Number of respondents	3,269		1,265	
Number of observations	16,447		6,157	
R^2 (adj)	0.02		0.01	
ρ	0.26		0.28	

[a]See Glossary for definitions of variables.

Table 2A.3
Determinants of Log Hourly Earnings: Model 2

Explanatory variable[a]	Whites		Blacks	
	Coefficient	t-value	Coefficient	t-value
UNEMYR	0.00288	0.68	0.00279	0.39
GVEXP	−0.00391	−9.01	−0.00261	−3.81
SQDA	0.439	1.35	0.898	1.80
SQPT	−1.660	−9.44	−1.647	−6.46
SKLJ	0.439	12.01	0.0195	3.79
ED	0.0652	17.27	0.037	8.41
EX	0.033	12.19	0.0318	7.85
MILT	0.0343	7.98	0.0505	7.27
HLTH	−0.0381	−3.93	−0.0289	−1.82
SMSA	0.149	8.66	0.302	11.03
SIZELF	0.0307	4.64	0.0363	3.02
SOUTH	−0.0912	−5.21	−0.220	−7.92
FATHOCC	0.000868	2.10	−0.000228	−0.23
FARM15	−0.125	−6.60	−0.0498	−2.01
CONSTANT	1.520	3.80	1.430	2.43
Number of respondents	2,678		1,130	
Number of observations	7,311		3,103	
R^2(adj)	0.30		0.35	
ρ	0.73		0.64	

[a]See Glossary for definitions of variables.

Table 2A.4
Determinants of Weeks Unemployed Last Year: Model 2

Explanatory variable[a]	Whites		Blacks	
	Coefficient	t-value	Coefficient	t-value
UNEMYR	0.139	2.39	0.416	3.42
GVEXP	0.017	2.53	0.000224	0.02
SQDA	−3.956	−1.35	0.981	0.15
SQPT	0.740	0.38	2.907	0.78
SKLJ	−0.0956	−3.32	−0.0371	−0.61
ED	−0.193	−4.80	−0.188	−3.04
EX	−0.0617	−1.67	−0.955	−1.39
MILT	−0.0633	−1.39	−0.129	−1.35
HLTH	0.661	6.49	0.740	3.50
SMSA	−0.160	−1.13	0.217	0.66
SIZELF	0.131	2.32	0.146	0.98
SOUTH	−0.290	−2.06	−0.529	−1.53
FATHOCC	0.00227	0.70	0.00639	0.56
FARM15	−0.454	−3.05	0.453	1.51
CONSTANT	7.347	2.07	0.692	0.09
Number of respondents	3,269		1,265	
Number of observations	16,447		6,157	
R^2 (adj)	0.02		0.01	
ρ	0.26		0.27	

[a]See Glossary for definitions of variables.

Table 2A.5
Economic Conditions and Government Expenditure on Antidiscrimination Programs, 1965–1976

Year	Economic conditions (unemployment rate)	Antidiscrimination expenditures (in millions of dollars)
1965	3.2	5.4
1966	2.5	8.8
1967	2.3	11.9
1968	2.2	16.4
1969	2.1	18.5
1970	3.5	23.5
1971	4.4	29.3
1972	4.0	40.8
1973	3.2	51.2
1974	3.8	61.2
1975	6.7	68.8
1976	5.9	78.0

Notes

1. See, for example, Freeman (1973); Levin (1979).

2. See, for example, Smith and Welch (1977, 1978).

3. Kniesner et al. (1978); Smith and Welch (1977, 1978).

4. Burman (1973); Adams (1972); Ashenfelter and Heckman (1978); Kaufman and Daymont (1978).

5. Burman (1973); Levitan et al. (1975).

6. Levitan et al. (1975) outlines some other important changes in antidiscrimination public policy in the early 1970s. The 1972 amendment to the Civil Rights Act extended its coverage to smaller organizations, state and local governments, and educational institutions. In February 1970 the OFCC issued new orders requiring federal contractors to establish affirmative action goals, timetables for filling the goals, and procedures for collecting data to document their progress. Two Supreme Court decisions were of particular importance. First, *Griggs* v. *Duke Power Company* proscribed "not only overt discrimination but also practices that are fair in form but discriminatory in operation." Second, *Robinson* v. *Lorillard* established the principle of monetary relief to victims of discrimination in class action suits, making substantial settlement costs possible.

7. See, for example, Johnson and Sell (1976); Hauser and Featherman (1974); Farley (1977); Freeman (1973); Smith and Welch (1978).

8. Farley (1977).

9. Smith and Welch (1978).

10. Johnson and Sell (1976); Hauser and Featherman (1974); Freeman (1973); Farley (1977).

11. The studies that look at changes through the 1970s are of limited relevance for this analysis. In the portion of his analysis that shows improved relative opportunities for blacks, Farley (1977) restricts his sample to men under 55. Other studies, such as Smith and Welch (1978) and Kniesner et al. (1978), observe changes in racial differences in returns to schooling. Although the return to schooling is an important parameter of labor market processes, there is no direct logical correspondence between changes in racial differences in returns to schooling and changes in relative black opportunities as conceptualized in this chapter.

12. Freeman (1973); Wohlstetter and Coleman (1972); Kosters and Welch (1972); Vroman (1974). One exception to this is Ashenfelter (1970). However, he points out that the period covered by his study (1950–1966) was characterized by less severe cyclical fluctuations than earlier and subsequent periods.

13. Smith and Welch (1978), p. ix.

14. U.S. President (1977).

15. In a pooled data set such as this it is unreasonable to believe that there is no association among the residual terms within individuals. When such an association is allowed in models such as ours, ordinary least squares is not efficient (Maddala, 1971). Therefore we used the generalized least-squares procedure outlined by Avery and Watts (1977) to estimate our two-component models with missing observations.

16. The criteria for determining whether to include a given observation in the analysis were as follows. For the analysis of the number of weeks unemployed during the year prior to the survey, an observation was excluded if the respondent was not in the civilian labor market during the survey week or if there was no information on the dependent variable. An observation was excluded from the analysis of log hourly earnings if

the respondent had not worked within the six months prior to the survey, if there was no information on rate of pay, if the hourly rate of pay was calculated to be less than $0.50, or if the respondent was self-employed. In addition, an observation was excluded from both analyses if data were missing on age, education, or the occupation of the respondent's longest job prior to 1966. For missing data on other variables observations were assigned a race-specific mean or modal value.

17. Formally, the following equation was estimated separately for both races and for both aspects of labor market success (LMS):

$$LMS_{it} = a_0 + \Sigma_t \, b_t \, YR_t + a_1 \, SKLJ_i + a_2 \, ED_i + a_3 \, EX_{it} + a_4 \, MILT_{it}$$
$$+ a_5 \, HLTH_{it} + a_6 \, SMSA_{it} + a_7 \, SIZELF_{it} + a_8 \, SOUTH_{it}$$
$$+ a_9 \, FATHOCC_i + a_{10} \, FARM15_i + u_i + v_{it}.$$

YR_t is a dummy variable representing the year of interview (YR_{66} was the omitted variable). $SKLJ_i$ is the skill level (measured by the General Education Development (GED)) of the respondent's longest job prior to the initial survey (1966). ED_i is the educational attainment of the respondent as measured by the number of years of regular schooling completed, except that specific values are assigned for specific attainments. For example, a person who received a bachelor's degree but no additional schooling is coded as having 16 years of education regardless of how long it took him to obtain his degree. $MILT_{it}$ is the number of years the respondents served in the armed forces. EX_{it} is civilian labor force experience and is calculated as ($Age_{it} - ED_i - MILT_{it} - 6$), except that a respondent could not be given credit for civilian labor force experience that occurred before the age of 12. $HLTH_{it}$ is a dummy variable coded one if the respondent reported a health problem that limited his ability to work. $SMSA_{it}$ is a dummy variable coded one if the respondent resided in a Standard Metropolitan Statistical Area in year t. $SIZELF_{it}$ is an indicator of the size of the local labor market for the respondent's area of residence in year t. $SOUTH_{it}$ is a dummy variable coded one if the respondent resided in the South in year t. $FATHOCC_i$ is the occupational status (measured by the Duncan SEI score) of the respondent's father. $FARM15_i$ is a dummy variable coded one if the respondent resided on a farm when he was 15. u_i is an individual-specific residual term, and v_{it} is an individual-year-specific residual term.

18. Fine (1968); U.S. Employment Service (1965). The conversion of GED to a years-of-schooling metric was done by Eckaus (1964). In some preliminary analyses Specific Vocational Preparation (SVP) was also included, but it added very little explanatory power to the model once GED had been included.

19. U.S. President (1977), p. 221. We chose this population so that our indicator would reflect changes in the demand for labor rather than changes in the supply of labor.

20. U.S. President, the Budget of the United States Government; U.S. President, Catalogue of Federal Domestic Assistance. Since most interviews were conducted at about the middle of the year, one of our two dependent variables (weeks unemployed last year) refers to the period roughly from the middle of the year prior to the year of interview to the middle of the year of interview. Thus for this dependent variable these two explanatory variables capturing temporal effects were scored as the average for the year prior to the interview and the year of interview. One exception is that the 1966 interview asked about weeks unemployed during the calendar year 1965; thus for these observations the values for these two explanatory variables refer to 1965.

21. The first indicator measures the ratio of average number of days attended per pupil in black Southern schools to the same measure for all

schools in the United States. The second indicator is a comparable ratio for number of pupils enrolled per classroom teacher.

22. The phrase "typical white (black)" refers to an individual with the white (black) mean for all variables except the year dummies. The regression results used to make these calculations are shown in table 2A.1.

23. To do this we substituted mean values for blacks in the white regressions and compared the resulting level of earnings with the corresponding levels from the black regressions (column 4 of table 2.1). The indicator represents an estimate of how much lower (in relative terms) a typical black's pay was because blacks were compensated on a less favorable basis than whites. Compared with these indicators, relative black opportunities evaluated at the white means are lower in each year, but a similar pattern of improvement over time is discernible.

Since there were no interaction terms involving the year (YR) variables and the other variables in the race-specific regressions, the change in relative black opportunities over the period is constrained to be the same for all levels of individual characteristics. We experimented with more complicated models involving a number of interaction terms (in particular, terms involving the year variables and the occupational skill level of the respondent's longest job prior to 1966). Not surprisingly, we ran into some severe multicollinearity problems. Nevertheless, the results from these more complicated models suggested no need to modify the findings produced by either model 1 or model 2.

24. The regression for results used to make these calculations are shown in table 2A.2. Both models have very little power in explaining the within-race variation in weeks unemployed (see the low R^2's in tables 2A.2 and 2A.4). This is fairly consistent with the results of other studies in which standard human capital variables have had limited power in explaining unemployment. However, the models do explain a significant degree of the racial difference in weeks unemployed. This is apparent when we observe the substantial reduction in black-white unemployment experience when we control for racial differences in these explanatory variables (compare the last two columns in table 2.2).

25. Whereas our indicator of the relative earnings opportunities of blacks was calculated as a black-white ratio, our indicator of the relative employment opportunities was calculated as a white-black difference. This was done so that an increase in either indicator would imply an improvement in relative black opportunities.

26. The specific values for government expenditures and economic conditions for each year are shown in table 2A.5.

27. Thus, in measuring the effects of government expenditures on log earnings, we subtract the coefficient for this variable in the white equation from the corresponding coefficient in the black equation. Where weeks of unemployment is the dependent variable, the coefficient in the black equation is subtracted from that in the white equation.

28. This measure is obtained by subtracting the value for 1975–76 from the value for 1965 shown in the last column of table 2.2.

29. See note b in table 2.4 for the method of calculating this implied change.

30. These results do not address the issue of whether cohort or vintage effects, broadly defined, influence the changing patterns of racial differences in important dimensions of labor market success. The framework we have adopted in this analysis makes it clear that we believe such

cohort effects are fundamentally important. That is, we have attempted to ascertain changes in relative black opportunities by controlling for several factors (for example, father's occupation, farm residence, quantity and quality of education, and the labor market environment of the region of residence) for which one might expect racial convergence in succeeding cohorts. Because of the restricted age range of our sample, cohort effects are not likely to be substantial. Nevertheless, to the extent that they exist, the richness and the panel nature of the NLS data have provided an excellent opportunity to control for them.

31. Adams (1972); Ashenfelter and Heckman (1978); Beller (1974); Burman (1973); Goldstein and Smith (1976); Heckman and Wolpin (1976); Kaufman and Daymont (1978); Smith and Welch (1977, 1978); Vroman (1974).

32. Nothing in this discussion should be taken as in indication of a belief on our part that there have not been problems with these programs. For example, we agree with the observation of Wallace (1975) that the effectiveness of the EEOC would be improved by increased resources and by greater political and legal power.

33. These results may reflect a sample selection bias due to racial differences in the process of retirement. The men in our sample aged from 45 to 59 in 1966 to 55 to 69 in 1976. Largely as a result of this aging process, there was a substantial increase during the period in the proportion of men who were not included in the analysis because they had retired or were otherwise not working.

To examine the possible effects of this nonrandom sample selection process, we performed some additional analyses in which two strategies were used to control for sample selection bias. The first strategy was to restrict the sample to men aged 54 to 60 in the year of interview. This produced a sample in which the age composition changed little from year to year. We also used the strategy proposed by Heckman (1976, 1979) and others that models sample selection bias as an omitted-variable problem. In this two-equation approach the first equation was the basic equation used in this chapter and described in note 17. (We also included school quality indicators in the equation. In addition, we estimated the equation in which government expenditures and the unemployment rate were substituted for the year dummies.) The second equation was a probit equation in which the binary dependent variable indicated whether the observation was included in the subsample on which the first equation was estimated. The explanatory variables in this sample selection equation included all the explanatory variables in the first equation plus variables (such as family assets, social security eligibility, marital status, and the number of dependents) believed to influence the individual's ability to finance retirement or otherwise affect the relative desirability of retirement versus working.

The Heckman strategy of treating sample selection bias as an omitted-variable problem makes strong assumptions (in particular, that the errors in the two equations have a bivariate normal distribution), and little is known about the robustness of the approach to violations of these assumptions. In addition, due to a substantial degree of collinearity among the explanatory variables, the parameter estimates appear to be somewhat unstable. Thus only the most general conclusions can be drawn from these results, and even those must be viewed with caution.

With these qualifications in mind, we can report that the results support the conclusion that the relative earnings opportunities of blacks improved significantly during the period. So far as employment security is concerned, the results suggest that government expenditures had a positive impact on the relative opportunities of blacks but that this was counterbalanced by a negative effect of the declining economic conditions. The results were ambiguous as to whether the relative employment opportunities of blacks stayed about the same or improved during the period.

34. U.S. Commission on Civil Rights (1977), pp. 329–330.

References

Adams, A. V. 1972. Toward fair employment and the EEOC: a study of compliance procedures under Title VII of the Civil Rights Act of 1964. Washington, D.C.: Equal Employment Opportunity Commission.

Ashenfelter, O. 1970. Changes in labor market discrimination over time. *Journal of Human Resources* 5 (Fall): 403–429.

Ashenfelter, O., and Heckman, J. J. 1978. Measuring the effect of antidiscrimination programs. In O. Ashenfelter and J. Blum, eds., *Evaluating the labor market effects of social programs*, pp. 46–89. Princeton, N.J.: Princeton University Press.

Avery, R., and Watts, H. W. 1977. The application of an error components model to experimental panel data. In H. W. Watts and A. Rees, eds., *Labor supply responses.* Vol. 2 of *The New Jersey income-maintenance experiment.* New York: Academic Press.

Beller, A. H. 1974. The effects of title VII of the civil rights act of 1964 on the economic position of minorities. Ph.D. diss., Columbia University.

Burman, G. R. 1973. The economics of discrimination: the impact of public policy. Ph.D. dissertation, The University of Chicago.

Eckaus, R. S. 1964. Economic criteria for education and training. *Review of Economics and Statistics* 48 (May): 181–190.

Farley, R. 1977. Trends in racial inequalities: have the gains of the 1960s disappeared in the 1970s? *American Sociological Review* 42 (April): 189–207.

Fine, S. A. 1968. The use of the *Dictionary of occupational titles* as a source of estimates of educational and training requirements. *Journal of Human Resources* 3 (Summer): 363–375.

Freeman, R. B. 1973. Changes in the labor market for black Americans, 1948–1972. *Brookings Papers on Economic Activity* 1 (Summer): 67–131.

Goldstein, M. and Smith, R. S. 1976. The estimated impact of the antidiscrimination program aimed at federal contractors. *Industrial and Labor Relations Review* 29 (July): 523–543.

Hauser, R. M., and Featherman, D. L. 1974. White-nonwhite differentials in occupational mobility among men in the United States, 1962–1972. *Demography* 11 (May): 247–265.

Heckman, J. J. 1976. The common structure of statistical models of truncation, sample selection, and limited dependent variables, and a simple estimator for such models. *Annals of Economic and Social Measurement* 5 (Fall): 475–492.

————. 1979. Sample bias as specification error. *Econometrica* 47 (January): 153–162.

Heckman, J. J. and Wolpin, K. 1976. Does the contract compliance program work? An analysis of Chicago data. *Industrial and Labor Relations Review* 29 (July): 544–564.

Johnson, M. P., and Sell, R. R. 1976. The cost of being black: a 1970 update. *American Journal of Sociology* 82 (July): 182–190.

Kaufman, R. L., and Daymont, T. N. 1978. Racial discrimination and the social organization of labor markets. Paper presented at the American Sociological Association meetings, San Francisco.

Kosters, M., and Welch, F. 1972. The effects of minimum wages by race, age, and sex. In A. H. Pascal, ed., *Racial discrimination in economic life,* pp. 103–118. Lexington, Mass.: Lexington Books.

Kniesner, T. J., Padilla, A. H., and Polachek, S. W. 1978. The rate of return to schooling and the business cycle. *Journal of Human Resources* 13 (Spring): 264–277.

Levin, H. M. 1979. Education and earnings of blacks and the *Brown* decision. In Michael Namorato, ed., *Have we overcome?* pp. 79–119. Jackson, Miss.: University Press of Mississippi.

Levitan, S. A., Johnston, W. B., and Taggart, R. 1975. *Still a dream: the changing status of blacks since 1960.* Cambridge, Mass.: Harvard University Press.

Maddala, G. S. 1971. The use of variance components models in pooling cross-section and time-series data. *Econometrica* 38 (March): 341–358.

Smith, J. D., and Welch, F. R. 1977. Black-white male wage ratios: 1960–1970. *American Economic Review* 67 (June): 323–338.

————. 1978. *Race differences in earnings: A survey and new evidence.* Santa Monica, Calif.: Rand Corporation.

U.S. Commission on Civil Rights. 1977. *The federal civil rights enforcement effort—1977.* Washington, D.C.: U.S. Commission on Civil Rights.

U.S. Employment Service. 1965. *Dictionary of occupational titles.* 2 vols., 3rd ed. Washington, D.C.: U.S. Government Printing Office.

U.S. President. 1977. *The economic report of the President.* Washington, D.C.: U.S. Government Printing Office.

————. Selected years. *Catalogue of federal domestic assistance.* Washington, D.C.: U.S. Government Printing Office.

————. Selected years. *The budget of the United States government.* Washington, D.C.: U.S. Government Printing Office.

Vroman, W. 1974. Changes in black workers' relative earnings: evidence for the 1960s. In G. M. von Furstenberg, A. R. Horowitz, and B. Harrison, eds., *Patterns of racial discrimination*, vol. 2, pp. 167–187. Lexington, Mass.: D.C. Heath and Co.

Wallace, P. A. 1975. A decade of policy development in equal opportunities in employment and housing. Working paper No. 767–75, Massachusetts Institute of Technology.

Welch, F. 1974. Education and racial discrimination. In O. Ashenfelter and A. Rees, eds., *Discrimination in labor markets*, pp. 43–81. Princeton, N.J.: Princeton University Press.

Wohlstetter, A., and Coleman, S. 1972. Race differences in income. In A. H. Pascal, ed., *Racial discrimination in economic life*, pp. 3–82. Lexington, Mass.: Lexington Books.

Chapter 3

Job Loss among Long-Service Workers

Herbert S. Parnes,
Mary G. Gagen,
and
Randall H. King

A middle-aged man is less likely than a younger man to become unemployed. Yet, once unemployed, older men generally have greater difficulty in finding new jobs. This chapter focuses on a subsample of the men who were involuntarily separated from the jobs they held at the time of the first survey in 1966 and assesses the impact of the separation on their subsequent work lives and attitudes. Do many men lose their jobs late in their careers? Does such job loss occur more or less randomly, or is it more likely among men with certain characteristics? What happens to a man in his middle or later years when he loses a job in which he has built up a substantial equity? How long is he likely to remain unemployed? If and when he does find other work, how does the new job compare with the one he has lost? What impact does the total experience have on his economic position and his well-being?[1]

There have been numerous previous analyses of the experience of "displaced" workers, but this study and an earlier version by Parnes and King (1977) are the first to our knowledge to be based on a national sample of individuals who have suffered such displacement.[2] An added value of this study is its focus on men over 45, because previous research suggests that older workers are among those who have the most severe readjustment problems after job loss.[3] Moreover, the longitudinal data provide an opportunity to observe the characteristics and attitudes of the men before their job separations and to follow them for a minimum of one year after they have lost their jobs. Finally, we use a multivariate framework to compare the 1976 characteristics of the displaced workers with those of men who suffered no such separations, and we are thus in a good position to identify the effects of the job separations.

We have identified all wage and salary workers who at the time of the initial (1966) survey had been with their current employers for at least five years, who were permanently separated from those employers between 1966 and 1975, and who were interviewed in the 1976 survey. From this group we excluded men employed in agriculture or construction in 1966 because of the tenuous employment relationship in those industries. Our purpose is to focus on workers for whom a permanent involuntary separation would be regarded as a traumatic event rather than an occurrence which, either because of low seniority or the characteristics of the industry, would be regarded as reasonably commonplace and therefore not unexpected.[4]

Table 3.1
Distribution of Displaced Workers, by Time Period of Job Loss

Time period	Number displaced	Unweighted percentage
Total	117	100
1966–1969	48	41
1969–1971	36	31
1971–1975	33	28

The evidence of a permanent displacement in each case is the report by the respondent of an involuntary separation from the 1966 employer at the time of interview in 1967, 1969, 1971, 1973, or 1975. Of all the men interviewed in 1976, there were 117 who met these criteria. Approximately two-fifths of these men had lost their jobs between the 1966 and 1969 interviews, another one-third between the 1969 and 1971 interviews, and the remaining three-tenths between the 1971 and 1975 surveys (table 3.1).

To ascertain whether men who suffer involuntary job separations differ from the total population at risk,[5] we first perform a multiple classification analysis in which the dependent variable is the likelihood of displacement and the explanatory variables are a series of demographic, labor market, and attitudinal characteristics of the sample as of 1966.[6] To analyze the consequences of displacement, we employ a series of multiple classification analyses. In each analysis the dependent variable is some 1976 characteristic—labor force and employment status, average hourly earnings of those employed, number of weeks of unemployment in the previous 12 months, health condition— and the explanatory variables are a series of control variables[7] plus a variable indicating whether the individual suffered job displacement.[8] In effect, these analyses permit us to ascertain whether the status of the displaced group of men differed in 1976 from that of otherwise comparable men who had suffered no involuntary separation from their 1966 employers, hereafter referred to as the control group. Since other relevant factors are statistically controlled, any such differences that are found may be attributed to displacement.

Likelihood of Displacement

As of the 1976 survey 1,679 men in the sample represented the population at risk. These sample cases represented about 6.3 million men in the total population in that year who ten years previously had held wage and salary jobs outside agriculture and

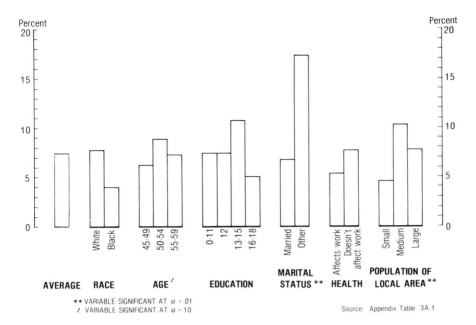

Percent
20

15

10

5

0

Percent
20

15

10

5

0

White
Black

45-49
50-54
55-59

0-11
12
13-15
16-18

Married
Other

Affects work
Doesn't
affect work

Small
Medium
Large

AVERAGE   RACE   AGE /   EDUCATION   MARITAL
STATUS **   HEALTH   POPULATION OF
LOCAL AREA **

** VARIABLE SIGNIFICANT AT α = .01
/ VARIABLE SIGNIFICANT AT α = .10

Source: Appendix Table 3A.1

Figure 3.1
Likelihood of Displacement, by Demographic Characteristics

construction and who in 1966 had worked for their employers
for at least five years. Of that total group, 7.4 percent—
approximately half a million men—had experienced an involuntary separation between 1966 and 1975. Figures 3.1 and 3.2
show the extent to which that percentage varies according to
selected demographic, economic, and attitudinal characteristics
of the sample.[9]

There is little difference between whites and blacks in the
likelihood of displacement. When other factors are controlled,
the displacement rate among blacks was actually 3.8 percentage
points lower than among whites, but this difference is not
statistically significant. Apparently race has little or no bearing on
the likelihood of continued employment once a person has
gained a measure of seniority.[10] Moreover, the risk of displacement does not differ systematically among the three five-year
age categories of men in this sample. Differences among the
categories by length of service are small, although men with
20 or more years of seniority are somewhat less likely than
shorter-service workers to have experienced an involuntary separation. There is also surprisingly little difference in the incidence

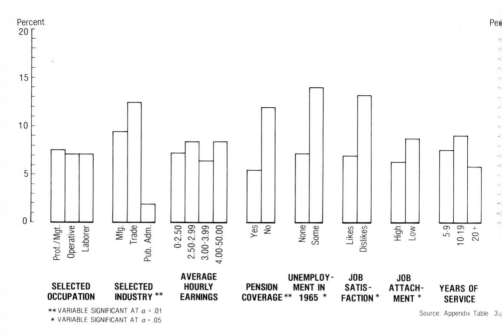

Percent   Pe█

20

15

10

5

0

| Prof./Mgt. | Operative | Laborer | | Mfg. | Trade | Pub. Adm. | | 0-2.50 | 2.50-2.99 | 3.00-3.99 | 4.00-50.00 | | Yes | No | | None | Some | | Likes | Dislikes | | High | Low | | 5-9 | 10-19 | 20 + |

| SELECTED OCCUPATION | SELECTED INDUSTRY ** | AVERAGE HOURLY EARNINGS | PENSION COVERAGE ** | UNEMPLOY-MENT IN 1965 * | JOB SATIS-FACTION * | JOB ATTACH-MENT * | YEARS OF SERVICE |

** VARIABLE SIGNIFICANT AT $\alpha = .01$
 * VARIABLE SIGNIFICANT AT $\alpha = .05$

Source: Appendix Table 3█

Figure 3.2
Likelihood of Displacement, by Characteristics of and Attitude toward 1966 Job

of displacement by educational attainment or among the major occupational groups. For example, nonfarm laborers were no more likely than professional, technical, and managerial workers to have suffered displacement. On the other hand, there are pronounced and statistically significant differences by industry. The incidence of involuntary separation is higher in trade and in manufacturing than in other industries and almost nonexistent in public administration. The differences in the incidence of displacement among labor market areas of different population size are difficult to account for. The displacement rate was highest in labor market areas of intermediate size and lowest in small areas.

There is a significant difference in the incidence of displacement among marital status groups. Men who in 1966 were married and living with their wives had displacement rates less than half as great as other men. This may indicate that personality traits relating to behavior on the job differ between the two groups, or it could indicate that employers take marital status into account when making layoff decisions, or both. The observed relationship could also reflect a tendency of unmarried men to accept less secure jobs. There is little difference in the incidence of displacement depending on health condition. If anything, the rate may have been somewhat higher among men who reported no health limitation in 1966.

Even though no occupational differences in displacement rates have been found, the likelihood of displacement was greater among men whose 1966 jobs were less favorable in terms of stability and conditions of employment. For example, the displacement rate was nearly twice as high among those who in 1965 experienced some unemployment as among those who had experienced none. The same kind of relationship prevails between the incidence of displacement and pension coverage, although there is no corresponding systematic relationship with average hourly earnings. Probably reflecting these objective differences is the finding that men who were ultimately displaced had less favorable attitudes toward their 1966 jobs than those whose employment continued to be stable. For example, the rate of displacement was almost twice as great among men who expressed some dislike for their jobs in 1966 as among those who reported liking their jobs somewhat or very much. Those who registered high job attachment in 1966 by indicating that they would not take another job at any conceivable wage rate were less likely ultimately to be displaced than men with lower degrees of job attachment.

Despite these differences, the 1966 jobs held by the men who were ultimately to be displaced appeared as important to their total careers as those of their more fortunate counterparts (table 3.2). For example, almost identical proportions of displaced workers and the remainder of the population at risk—somewhat over four-fifths—reported that the jobs they held in 1966 were the longest of their careers. Similar proportions had moved up the occupational prestige ladder from the time they first entered the labor market until 1966, and about two-thirds of each group saw their 1966 occupational assignment as the best in their career. The same proportion of the two groups, about 72 percent, reflected strong commitment to the work ethic by indicating that they would continue to work even if they were somehow able to live comfortably without doing so.

To summarize, in terms of conventional human capital characteristics there is little variation in the likelihood of involuntary displacement within the population at risk. Evidently, once men have gained a moderate measure of tenure in a job,

Table 3.2
Selected Characteristics of 1966 Jobs: Comparison of Displaced Workers with Workers Who Retained Their Jobs (percentage distributions)

Characteristic	Displaced workers	Nondisplaced workers
Was 1966 job longest of career?		
Number of respondents	117	1,553
Total percentage	100	100
Yes	84	86
No	16	14
Was 1966 occupational assignment best of career?[a]		
Number of respondents	117	1,548
Total percentage	100	100
Yes	67	66
No	33	34
Degree of work commitment[b]		
Number of respondents	117	1,554
Total percentage	100	100
High	72	73
Low	28	27
Occupational mobility between first job and 1966 job[c]		
Number of respondents	113	1,531
Total percentage	100	100
Upward	65	67
No change or lateral	16	16
Downward	19	17

[a]Respondent's perception.
[b]Respondents who reported that they would continue to work even if they somehow acquired enough money to live comfortably without working are classified as having "high commitment."
[c]Mobility is measured in terms of the first digit of the Duncan Index of Socioeconomic Status. See *occupational status* in appendix A.

the risk of displacement is insensitive to many characteristics that would normally influence labor market outcomes, such as occupation or educational attainment. The men who were subsequently displaced were, even in 1966, not doing as well as their counterparts in terms of employment stability and other job characteristics. Nevertheless, on the basis of their total career patterns these 1966 jobs were as important to the men who ultimately lost them as those of the population at risk in general, and the loss of such jobs was not viewed lightly.

We assess the impact of displacement on subsequent labor market status by comparing the 1976 circumstances of the displaced workers with those of members of the population at risk who suffered no involuntary separation from their 1966 employers. In making this comparison by means of multiple classification analyses, we control for all the 1966 characteristics that have been used in analyzing the incidence of displacement. For this reason we feel justified in referring to the nondisplaced members of the population at risk as the control group.

For all members of the sample at least one year had to elapse between the displacement and the 1976 interview. For approximately one-third of the group that interval was at least five years, and for an additional two-fifths it was at least seven years. To reveal the extent to which time alters the impact of displacement, table 3.3 and figures 3.3–3.6 allow comparisons not only between the total group of displaced workers and the control group but also among the three categories of displaced workers classified according to the time of their involuntary separations (1966 to 1969, 1969 to 1971, and 1971 to 1975).[11]

Duration of Unemployment

We attempt to ascertain how long the displaced workers were without work before finding other jobs and then calculate the cumulative number of weeks of unemployment from the time of displacement to the date of the 1976 survey. Only rough estimates can be made in either case because of gaps and ambiguities in the detailed work histories.[12] Even with these limitations, the distributions shown in table 3.3 yield several reliable and noteworthy generalizations.

First, in over one-half of the displacements that occurred between 1966 and 1969 and in one-third of those between 1969 and 1971, the displaced men suffered no unemployment, although the records suggest that a small number of these individuals retired immediately. Even so, a sizable number of the displaced workers were able to move immediately into other jobs. Another one-third of the men who had lost their jobs between 1966 and 1971 experienced fewer than 13 weeks of unemployment.

Second, there are very pronounced differences in this pattern depending on time of displacement. Men who were displaced during the relatively favorable labor market conditions of 1966 to

Table 3.3
Number of Weeks of Unemployment following Displacement,[a] by Date of Displacement (unweighted percentage distributions)

Number of weeks	Until reemployment or withdrawal from the labor force				Until 1976 survey			
	Total, all displaced men[a]	Displaced 1966–1969	Displaced 1969–1971	Displaced 1971–1975[a]	Total, all displaced men[a]	Displaced 1966–1969	Displaced 1969–1971	Displaced 1971–1975[a]
Number of respondents	116	48	35	33	117	48	36	33
Total percentage	100	100	100	100	100	100	100	100
0[b]	45	54	34	42	32	44	22	27
1–4	12	17	14	3	10	12	17	0
5–13	18	21	11	21	18	15	14	27
14–26	7	2	17	3	12	12	17	6
27–52	12	6	23	9	16	15	22	12
More than 52	6	0	0	21	11	2	8	27
Mean number of weeks	12.2	4.8	12.4	22.5	19.0	10.8	20.9	28.4

[a]See note 12.
[b]Includes five cases in which respondent immediately withdrew from the labor force.

1969 had the highest proportion with no unemployment and an average duration of under 5 weeks. At the other extreme, those displaced between 1971 and 1975 suffered from the less favorable labor market conditions and from the fact that they were on average somewhat older. As a consequence, even according to conservative estimates, they had the highest proportion of very long unemployment (over 26 weeks) and an average duration of 22 weeks.

Third, the time it takes to find another job is only part of the burden of unemployment. When one takes into account all the unemployment experienced by the displaced workers to the time they were interviewed in 1976, including that produced by layoffs from their low-seniority postdisplacement jobs, the average number of weeks of idleness increases substantially, and fewer of the men escaped unemployment entirely. However, the pattern among the several groups of displaced workers is the same as when only the spell of unemployment directly following displacement is considered. Despite their much greater exposure, the men who were displaced in the 1966–1969 period experienced considerably fewer weeks of unemployment on average than those who lost their jobs between 1971 and 1975.

Labor Market Status in 1976

In the survey week of 1976 there was little difference in the employment rate of the displaced workers and the control group (figure 3.3). The adjusted percentages differed by five percentage points in favor of the men who had not suffered displacement. Among the displaced workers employment rates varied inversely with the recency of displacement. These differences, although apparently systematic, are not statistically significant. Substantially the same pattern is revealed by data on the number of weeks worked in the 12-month period preceding the 1976 survey.

The proportion of the two groups who were unemployed at the time of the 1976 survey differed more substantially. Ten percent of the displaced group were unemployed, in contrast to only 2 percent of the control group. There were large differences in the extent of unemployment among the displaced workers depending on the period in which they lost their jobs—2 percent of those displaced between 1966 and 1969, 7 percent of those displaced between 1969 and 1971, and 25 per-

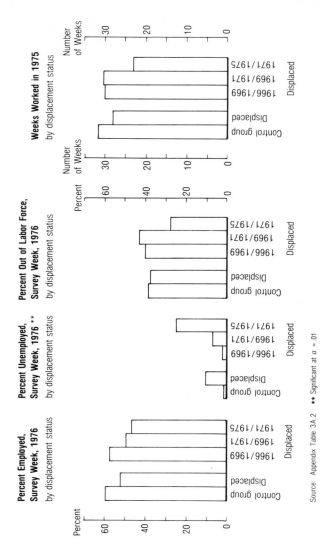

Figure 3.3
Postdisplacement Labor Market Activity

Source: Appendix Table 3A.2   ** Significant at α = .01

cent of those separated between 1971 and 1975. These figures probably reflect both the increasing probability of reemployment with the passage of time and the substantially more depressed economic conditions during the most recent of the three periods.[13] The men who lost their 1966 jobs between 1971 and 1975 operated in much less favorable labor markets and would therefore be expected to have more difficulty finding and keeping jobs. Moreover, the mean age at the time of displacement was 57 years for this group, compared with 52 and 55 years for the first and second groups. While these differences are not very large, the greater proximity to customary retirement age may have made this group less attractive to employers than those who had lost their jobs in earlier periods.

The difference between the displaced workers and the control group in the proportion who were out of the labor force is small and not statistically significant. Since the cohort was between 55 and 69 by 1976, retirements would be expected. One might also expect displacement to hasten or precipitate retirement, as a reflection of the "discouraged worker" phenomenon. Contrary to this expectation, however, the displaced workers were no more likely than the control group to withdraw from the labor market. Of course, the less favorable economic circumstances of the displaced men probably made retirement financially less feasible.

Characteristics of 1976 Jobs

There is considerable evidence that for the majority of men employed in 1976 displacement had resulted, on average, in a substantial slide down the occupational ladder (figure 3.4). When other factors are controlled, the proportion of displaced workers in professional, technical, and managerial positions was lower than among the control group by about 7 percentage points. Second, with the occupational status of the 1966 job controlled, the displaced workers averaged nine points lower than the control group on the Duncan Index of Socioeconomic Status. Third, about 45 percent of the displaced workers were in jobs of lower status in 1976 than in 1966, compared with only 26 percent of the control group.[14] On the other hand, in a number of cases displacement improved occupational status. Overall, 23 percent of both the displaced workers and the control group moved upward, and there is no systematic difference in this regard de-

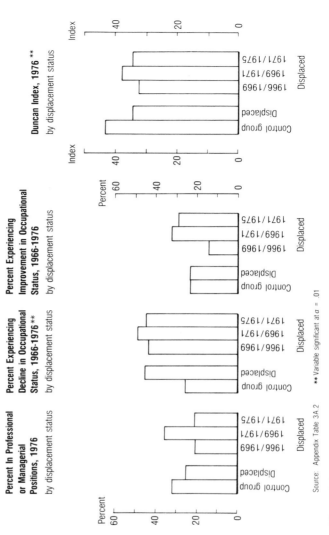

Figure 3.4
Postdisplacement Occupational Assignment

pending on the time of displacement. The earliest group and the latest group of displaced workers have adjusted Duncan Index scores somewhat lower than those of men displaced between 1969 and 1971.

The data on average hourly earnings are perhaps the most dramatic and concrete evidence of the long-term losses suffered by the displaced workers (figure 3.5). As a group, those who had been displaced had an adjusted 1976 average hourly wage more than one-fifth below that of the control group ($5.50 compared with $7.09). This differential was largest for the men who lost their jobs most recently (1971–1975). The pattern of annual earnings from wage and salary employment was similar, although the difference between the displaced workers and the population at risk was smaller.

Some Prototypical Cases

We may make more real these generalizations by highlighting the experiences of a few individuals. A small minority of displaced workers actually improved their positions as the result of their job loss, at least in the limited sense of having a higher real income in 1975 than in the year preceding their separation.[15] One example was a 52-year-old mechanic with a high school education. In 1966 he had nine years of service with a firm in the miscellaneous paper and pulp products industry, and his earnings were $7,800. He lost his job sometime between 1967 and 1969 and found another in the same occupation and industry with no intervening unemployment. With this new employer he experienced no layoffs and regular increases in earnings up to the time of the 1976 survey. His 1975 earnings were $13,900, 7 percent greater in real terms than they had been at the time of his separation.

Another example is a 53-year-old dispatcher with a high school education. After losing his job of 24 years, he was unemployed for one month but finally found a job as a truck driver. Although his earnings had dropped from the 1968 level of $9,300 to $8,000 in 1970 because of the spell of unemployment, by 1972 his earnings were $13,000 at his new occupation, and by 1975 they had grown to $17,000 in spite of a six-week absence from the labor force. This represented an 18 percent increase over what he had been earning at the time of

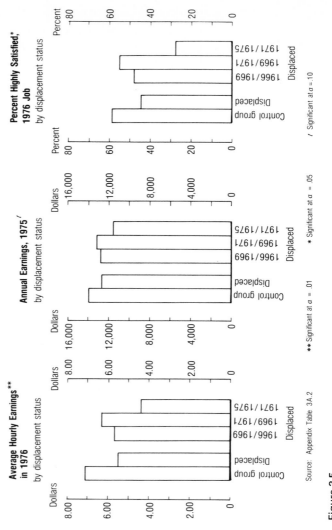

Figure 3.5
Postdisplacement Earnings and Job Satisfaction

displacement, even after adjusting for changes in the cost of living.

Illustrative of a more complex and less favorable experience in which the ultimate outcome is still unclear is the case of a 53-year-old industrial engineer with a college education. By 1969 he had accumulated 25 years of service with a manufacturer of fabricated metal products and had moved into the ranks of management at an annual salary of $16,000. He was displaced from that job between 1969 and 1971 and suffered 25 weeks of unemployment. He then found a job as a labor relations worker with a financial institution at a higher salary. After quitting this job because of dissatisfaction with working conditions, his subsequent employment was irregular. He took another job in labor relations with a trucking firm but was unemployed when interviewed in 1973 and reported 30 weeks of unemployment in the previous 12 months. As a consequence, his 1972 earnings were only $12,000, well below what they had been prior to his separation from the manufacturing company. By the time of the 1975 interview he had worked a full year for an office machine manufacturing company and reported earnings of $16,300 in 1974, slightly higher than his 1969 earnings, but in inflated dollars. When last interviewed in 1976, he had been unemployed for 4 months. His total earnings for 1975 were $17,700, 25 percent below his predisplacement salary in real terms.

More typical were cases in which the individual suffered reductions in both occupational status and income. For example, a 53-year-old man with only 10 years of education had worked his way up from a laborer to an operative and ultimately to an engineering technician during the course of 14 years with his employer. His salary had advanced from $5,800 in 1965 to $8,000 in 1972, an increase of 38 percent in current dollars but only 4 percent in real terms. He lost that job late in 1974 and remained unemployed for 13 months before finding a job as a delivery man at which he was employed at the time of the 1976 survey. He reported no earnings for 1975.

In another instance a 50-year-old man with a high school education lost his managerial position in an electrical machinery firm where he had been employed for 17 years. His annual earnings prior to his separation, which occurred between 1969 and 1971, were $13,000. In the 1971 interview this man reported 44 weeks of unemployment during the preceding 12 months but was then working as a salesclerk in a retail store. In 1973 he was doing clerical work for a farm machinery store, where his annual earnings were $8,500. Two years later he was unemployed and had worked only 22 weeks in the previous year, as a farm manager with earnings of $4,500. By the time of the 1976 survey he had apparently given up; after 42 weeks of unemployment during the preceding 12 months he finally ceased looking for work. By this time his health, which had deteriorated over the preceding three years, prevented him from working entirely.

These narratives do not capture the full personal costs of displacement. The process of seeking a job can be expensive materially and psychologically. Thus the full impact of disruption of this heretofore stable group of workers can only be surmised.

Attitudes and Outlook

The adversities suffered by displaced workers and the deterioration in the quality of the jobs of those who were employed in 1976 are reflected in their attitudes. For example, almost three-fifths of the control group but less than half of the displaced workers who were working in 1976 were highly satisfied with their jobs, and the proportion was considerably lower among the men whose displacement had occurred most recently (figure 3.5). Similarly, the proportion of displaced workers who felt that they had "progressed" over the five-year period 1971 to 1976 was lower than the comparable fraction of the control group—about 31 percent versus 40 percent (figure 3.6). Not surprisingly, those whose displacement occurred in the 1971–1975 period had the lowest proportion who thought that the five-year period had been good to them—only 18 percent.

The displaced workers were also somewhat more likely than members of the control group to perceive themselves as victims of age discrimination, although the differences in this case are not large. Only very small proportions of both groups viewed age discrimination as a problem. Overall, nearly 11 percent of the displaced workers perceived age discrimination, compared with 7 percent of the control group. Among the displaced the likelihood of reporting age discrimination increases monotonically with the recency of the separation. There is a significant difference between the displaced workers and their employed counterparts in the overall level of happiness they report.[16] Forty-seven percent of the displaced men characterized

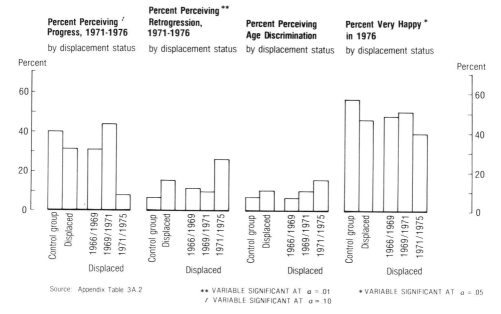

Percent Perceiving /
Progress, 1971-1976

by displacement status

Percent Perceiving **
Retrogression,
1971-1976

by displacement status

Percent Perceiving
Age Discrimination

by displacement status

Percent Very Happy *
in 1976

by displacement status

Source: Appendix Table 3A.2

** VARIABLE SIGNIFICANT AT α = .01
/ VARIABLE SIGNIFICANT AT α = .10

* VARIABLE SIGNIFICANT AT α = .05

Figure 3.6
Postdisplacement Attitudes

themselves as "very happy," compared with 57 percent of the
control group. Again, the proportion was lowest among the
most recent job losers.

There is also some evidence that the displaced workers were
likely to experience a sense of powerlessness and a loss of
initiative. This interpretation is based on the highly significant difference (at the 1 percent level) between the displaced and control groups in their 1976 scores on an abbreviated version of the
Rotter I-E (internal-external) scale, which is designed to measure
the extent to which an individual perceives success to be con-
tingent on personal initiative (table 3A.2). At one extreme are the
internals, who believe that success is the result largely of their
personal conduct and effort; at the other are the externals, who
believe that a person's experiences are governed largely by
forces beyond his control.[17] The higher scores of the displaced
men indicate their greater externality.

This evidence is not conclusive, since the displaced men may
have been more external in 1966 as well. However, the large
number of demographic, socioeconomic, and attitudinal control
variables in the multiple classification analysis provides some

degree of assurance that this is not the case. Moreover, the Rotter scale was administered in 1969, and it is therefore possible to examine the predisplacement scores of those men who lost their jobs after that date. When the 1969 Rotter score is used as a dependent variable in a multiple classification analysis for this group, the men who later lost their jobs actually displayed slightly higher internality than the control group (20.9 percent versus 22.0 percent), a difference that narrowly misses statistical significance at the 0.10 level.[18]

Summary and Conclusions

The loss of a job after the accumulation of some substantial seniority is likely to be psychologically unsettling and to produce economic hardship under any circumstances. When such an involuntary separation from a long-service job occurs during a man's fifties or sixties it can be calamitous. Although such displacements are not common, they happen often enough to constitute a social problem. Among men who were 55 to 69 years of age in 1976, one of 14 had lived through such an experience during the preceding decade. This represents over half a million persons.

This disruption of work career happens indiscriminately to men in all occupational categories and irrespective of educational background. Such displacement is much more likely in the private than in the public sector and is also considerably more common in some major industry divisions, notably trade and manufacturing. Even very long seniority does not provide immunity from such displacement. The overall displacement rate is 7.4 percent, while the rate is as high as 5.9 percent, controlling for other factors, among men with 20 or more years of service.

The incidence of displacement is uneven from other points of view. It is much higher among nonmarried than among married men, and men whose jobs had manifested some lack of stability even before 1966 were more likely to suffer an involuntary separation sometime over the next decade. Displacement was considerably less likely from establishments with pension plans than from those without them. Nevertheless, there is no evidence that the 1966 average hourly earnings of the men who were ultimately displaced differed systematically from those of men who were not. Despite the objective evidence of some qualitative difference in the security and amenities of their 1966 jobs, the men who were later displaced were just as likely as their more fortunate counterparts to have reported that their 1966 jobs were the longest and best of their careers.

As many as two-fifths of the displaced workers were apparently able to move immediately into new jobs. On average, the duration of postdisplacement unemployment was 12.2 weeks, but this varied considerably depending on labor market conditions at the time of displacement—from 4.8 weeks for those displaced in the buoyant economy of 1966 to 1969 to 22.5 weeks for those whose job loss occurred in the relatively depressed period of 1971 to 1975.

By 1976, 10 percent of the displaced men but only 2 percent of the control group were unemployed, reflecting the fact that some of the recently displaced men had not yet found work as well as the greater susceptibility to unemployment (because of low seniority) of those who had found postdisplacement jobs. Significantly, among men whose displacement had occurred at least seven years before 1976 in the relatively tight labor market of 1966 to 1969, the proportion unemployed in 1976 was almost indistinguishable from that of the control group. Contrary to what might have been expected, the displaced men were no more likely than their more fortunate counterparts to have left the labor force by 1976. Thus any greater tendency they may have had to retire because of discouragement was offset by their lesser financial ability to do so.

The major long-term economic impact of displacement appears to be a substantial deterioration in earnings and occupational status. Average hourly earnings in 1976 were 22 percent lower for the displaced men than for the control group. Over two-fifths of the displaced workers were in jobs of lower status in 1976 than in 1966, compared with only one-fourth of the control group. There is no evidence that this adverse impact softens with time, at least over the decade that we have examined. In addition to these economic losses, there is evidence of concomitant psychological penalties. The displaced workers not only were less satisfied with their jobs and less happy with life in general than members of the control group but also appear more likely to have developed a sense of alienation, with possible adverse effects on initiative.

Case studies of plant shutdowns have generally called attention to the need for advance notice of such closings and of special services for the displaced workers. Where displacement results from the closing of an entire plant, the problem is obviously exacerbated by the large number of individuals who are simultaneously thrown on the labor market, and unemployment may be an even more pervasive and persistent problem in that context than is suggested by this study. However, while efforts to prevent and to minimize the duration of unemployment are clearly important, our evidence demonstrates that unemployment is often only the most immediate and dramatic cost of displacement among men in their middle or later years. Even after they find other work, many individuals continue to suffer the consequences of their job loss through less attractive occupational assignments, lower earnings, and some damage to their psychological well-being.

Table 3A.1
Likelihood of Displacement, by 1966 Characteristics

1966 characteristic	Number of respondents	Unadjusted mean (%)	Adjusted mean (%)	F-Ratio	T-Ratio
Race				2.661	
Whites	1,222	7.6	7.8		1.587
Blacks	457	5.8	4.0		−1.525
Age				1.682	
45−49	666	6.6	6.2		−1.492
50−54	583	8.9	8.9		1.679†
55−59	430	6.9	7.3		−0.121
Education				2.379*	
0−11	944	8.0	7.5		0.021
12	427	6.7	7.5		0.027
13−15	139	10.8	10.8		1.683†
16−18+	163	4.1	5.1		−1.090
NA	6	0.0	—		−2.044*
Marital status				9.444**	
Married	1,543	6.7	6.8		−3.946**
Other	134	17.8	17.3		4.142**
NA	2	0.0	—		−0.878
Tenure				2.707†	
5−9	319	8.1	7.6		0.112
10−19	640	9.1	9.1		2.043*
20−60	720	5.7	5.9		−2.024*
Occupation				0.622	
Professional/managerial	388	6.5	7.6		0.107
Clerical/sales	206	5.4	5.5		−1.140
Craft	381	7.8	7.9		0.391
Operatives	445	8.5	7.1		−0.282
Service	126	10.4	11.3		1.385
Laborers (nonfarm)	132	7.6	7.1		−0.125
Farm	1	0.0	—		−0.316
Industry				6.006**	
Manufacturing	739	9.2	9.4		2.470*
Transportation, communication, public utilities	262	4.5	4.3		−2.062*
Trade	219	13.7	12.4		3.040**
Service	235	5.1	4.3		−1.851†
Public administration	189	0.1	1.9		−2.948**
Other	35	4.1	6.6		−0.185
Labor market size				7.252**	
0−99,999	581	5.2	4.6		−3.269**
100,000−499,999	511	9.6	10.3		3.045**
500,000−5,000,000	587	7.9	7.8		0.448

1966 characteristic	Number of respondents	Unadjusted mean (%)	Adjusted mean (%)	F-Ratio	T-Ratio
Health				8.811**	
Limits/prevents work	285	5.3	5.4		−1.519
No restriction	1,387	7.8	7.7		0.963
NA	7	46.4	51.3		3.520**
Job attachment				3.220*	
High	679	5.9	6.3		−1.509
Other	892	9.1	8.8		2.203*
NA	108	2.8	3.2		−1.615
Job satisfaction				3.528*	
Likes job	1,540	6.8	7.0		−2.381*
Dislikes job	120	15.0	13.2		2.585**
NA	19	8.0	6.2		−0.183
Unemployment				2.008	
None	1,601	7.1	7.2		−1.930†
Some	73	14.8	14.0		1.879†
NA	5	23.9	13.0		0.463
Average hourly earnings				0.575	
0–2.49	434	9.4	7.3		−0.067
2.50–2.99	302	8.9	8.4		0.667
3.00–3.99	489	5.5	6.4		−1.109
Over 4.00	362	7.0	8.4		0.777
NA	92	8.1	6.0		−0.540
Pension coverage				11.822**	
Yes	1,085	5.2	5.5		−3.927**
No	534	12.6	12.0		4.361**
NA	60	5.0	4.5		−0.847

R^2 (ADJUSTED) = 0.063
**Significant at $\alpha = 0.01$
*Significant at $\alpha = 0.05$
†Significant at $\alpha = 0.10$

Table 3A.2
Consequences of Displacement

Occupational characteristic and displacement status	Number of respondents	(Grand mean) unadjusted	Adjusted mean	F-Ratio[a]	T-Ratio[b]
Percentage employed		(58.8)		3.705†	
Not displaced	1,562	59.4	59.4		1.847†
Displaced	117	52.0	51.9		
1966–1969	48	57.1	57.2		−0.281
1969–1971	36	48.5	49.2		−1.385
1971–1975	33	48.3	46.9		−1.657†
Weeks worked past year		(31.5)		3.704†	
Not displaced	1,557	31.8	31.8		1.822†
Displaced	117	28.5	28.2		
1966–1969	48	29.4	30.1		−0.513
1969–1971	36	30.6	30.4		−0.342
1971–1975	33	25.0	23.0		−2.454*
Percentage unemployed		(2.5)		36.358**	
Not displaced	1,562	1.8	1.8		−5.898**
Displaced	117	10.9	10.4		
1966–1969	48	2.4	2.5		0.019
1969–1971	36	7.2	7.4		2.005*
1971–1975	33	27.2	25.1		8.776**
Percentage out of labor force		(38.7)		0.069	
Not displaced	1,562	38.8	38.8		0.263
Displaced	117	37.1	37.8		
1966–1969	48	40.6	40.3		0.279
1969–1971	36	44.3	43.3		0.680
1971–1975	33	24.5	28.0		−1.501
Percentage professional/ managerial[c]		(31.6)		2.454	
Not displaced	918	32.3	32.0		1.495
Displaced	61	21.3	25.0		
1966–1969	28	17.8	20.7		−1.648†
1969–1971	17	27.3	35.6		0.477
1971–1975	16	21.1	21.0		−1.212
Duncan index[c]		(42.9)		18.097**	
Not displaced	916	43.6	43.4		4.031**
Displaced	61	32.6	34.6		
1966–1969	28	31.2	32.4		−3.428**
1969–1971	17	32.9	38.2		−1.203
1971–1975	16	34.8	34.6		−2.056*
Percentage upwardly mobile[c]		(23.3)		0.000	
Not displaced	915	23.2	23.3		−0.002
Displaced	61	25.0	23.4		
1966–1969	28	14.6	14.3		−1.208
1969–1971	17	33.5	32.4		0.953
1971–1975	16	33.8	29.2		0.599

Occupational characteristic and displacement status	Number of respondents	(Grand mean) unadjusted	Adjusted mean	F-Ratio[a]	T-Ratio[b]
Percentage downwardly mobile[c]		(27.2)		12.293**	
Not displaced	915	26.1	25.9		−3.356**
Displaced	61	42.6	45.3		
1966–1969	28	42.8	43.8		2.074*
1969–1971	17	47.0	48.8		2.086*
1971–1975	16	37.5	44.4		1.613
Average hourly earnings[c]		($6.98)		11.946**	
Not displaced	790	7.14	7.09		3.271**
Displaced	53	4.81	5.50		
1966–1969	24	5.09	5.68		−1.938†
1969–1971	15	4.95	6.30		−0.758
1971–1975	14	4.18	4.38		−2.917**
Annual earnings		($13,862)		2.809†	
Not displaced	1,006	14,078	13,949		1.506
Displaced	72	10.979	12,611		
1966–1969	30	11,723	12,756		−0.930
1969–1971	23	11,212	13,216		−0.452
1971–1975	19	9,459	11,671		−1.416
Job satisfaction[c]		(57.8)		4.780*	
Not displaced	919	58.9	58.7		2.090*
Displaced	61	42.6	44.8		
1966–1969	28	46.4	48.0		−1.061
1969–1971	17	47.0	55.2		−0.222
1971–1975	16	31.2	28.0		−2.424*
Percent progressed 1971–1976		(39.4)		3.175†	
Not displaced	1,158	40.3	40.0		1.732†
Displaced	92	28.4	31.3		
1966–1969	33	31.9	31.4		−1.019
1969–1971	30	39.2	43.7		0.511
1971–1975	29	13.4	18.2		−2.430*
Percentage felt "moved backwards"		(7.7)		8.823**	
Not displaced	1,158	7.0	7.0		−2.865**
Displaced	92	16.3	15.6		
1966–1969	33	12.1	11.7		0.859
1969–1971	30	10.0	9.8		0.437
1971–1975	29	27.6	26.0		3.675**
Percentage perceived age discrimination		(7.5)		1.807	
Not displaced	1,547	7.2	7.2		−1.298
Displaced	117	11.7	10.5		
1966–1969	48	7.2	6.7		−0.223
1969–1971	36	10.7	10.3		0.660
1971–1975	33	19.2	16.4		1.979*

Table 3A.2 (continued)

Occupational characteristic and displacement status	Number of respondents	(Grand mean) unadjusted	Adjusted mean	F-Ratio[a]	T-Ratio[b]
Percentage very happy		(56.1)		5.242*	
Not displaced	1,535	57.2	56.9		2.199*
Displaced	116	43.4	46.5		
1966–1969	47	45.8	48.2		−1.142
1969–1971	36	46.1	50.4		−0.712
1971–1975	33	37.3	39.8		−1.952†
Rotter score		(22.5)		7.770**	
Not displaced	1,373	22.4	22.4		−2.657**
Displaced	108	24.0	23.9		
1966–1969	43	24.0	24.2		2.079*
1969–1971	34	24.2	24.0		1.595
1971–1975	31	23.8	23.3		0.788

[a]F-ratios are from MCAs using dichotomous independent variable for displacement. They indicate the significance of the difference between the displaced and nondisplaced groups.
[b]T-Ratios are from MCAs using independent variable categorized by time-of-displacement. They indicate the significance of the difference between each time of displacement category and the grand mean.
[c]Universe restricted to those employed in 1976 survey week. For Duncan Index MCAs, the 1966 Duncan Index was used as the control variable, rather than one-digit occupational classifications.
**Significant at $\alpha = 0.01$
*Significant at $\alpha = 0.05$
†Significant at $\alpha = 0.10$

1. This chapter essentially replicates an earlier and more restricted study by Parnes and King (1977), in which the sample consisted of men with at least five years of service in their 1966 jobs (outside agriculture and construction) who had been involuntarily separated from those jobs by 1971. Our study uses a somewhat different method of analysis and has at least two advantages over the earlier version. First, the number of sample cases is larger, since men separated from their 1966 jobs between 1971 and 1975 have been added to the original group. Second, and of more importance, the variety of postdisplacement characteristics examined is greater in view of the more comprehensive interview schedule in 1976 (relative to that of 1973).

2. Previous analyses have generally been case studies based on the closing of a plant or firm. For a bibliography see Mick (1975), p. 204, notes 2–6. For a longitudinal study focusing on psychological and physiological effects of a plant shutdown see Cobb and Kasl (1977) and Slote (1969).

3. Mick (1975), p. 205.

4. For the same reason we have excluded six individuals whose involuntary job separation represented retirement under a mandatory retirement plan. For the experience of retirees see chapter 6.

5. We use the phrase "population at risk" to refer to the 1,679 men interviewed in 1976 who in 1966 were employed outside agriculture and construction and had a minimum of five years of service with their employer. In other words, this was the total group of men who could have been included in our sample had they suffered a permanent displacement.

6. Multiple classification analysis (MCA) allows one to calculate for each category of a particular explanatory variable (for example, blacks and whites) what the proportion of involuntarily displaced men would have been had the members of the category been average in terms of all the other variables entering into the analysis. Differences in these adjusted proportions among the categories of a given variable represent the pure effect of that variable on the likelihood of displacement, controlling for all the other variables in the analysis. The MCA formulation is more general than the more commonly specified multiple regression approach since it avoids the assumption of linearity between independent and dependent variables. The constant term in the multiple classification equation is the mean of the dependent variable. The coefficient of each category of every explanatory variable represents a deviation from this mean.

7. The control variables are identical to the explanatory variables used in the multiple classification analysis of the likelihood of displacement.

8. Actually, two versions of each MCA were run. In one a binary variable simply differentiated men who had suffered displacement from those who had not. In the second version the variable consisted of four categories: (1) those who had not suffered displacement, (2) those displaced between 1966 and 1969, (3) those displaced between 1969 and 1971, and (4) those displaced between 1971 and 1975. Using the results of both analyses for any given dependent variable allows us to see whether displacement (at any time) had an independent effect on the dependent variable and whether there were differences in that effect depending on the time of displacement.

9. In selecting the explanatory variables for this analysis we were guided by the findings of an earlier version of this study (Parnes and King, 1977). In that study the analysis of the effects of displacement was based on the comparison of the displaced workers with a control group of workers with stable employment who had been drawn from the total

population at risk and matched as nearly as possible with the displaced workers on seven characteristics: race, age, educational attainment, tenure in 1966 job, occupation in 1966, industry in 1966, and size of labor market area in 1966. When the displaced workers were compared with the control group in terms of other characteristics in 1966, a number of substantial differences were found. The variables that were found to differentiate between the two groups in the earlier study have been incorporated as explanatory variables in our analysis of the probability of displacement and also as control variables in our analysis of the consequences of displacement.

10. In a study of 1,701 white and 701 black male family heads who were employed in 1971 and 1972, Sorenson and Fuerst (1978) found that the probability of a layoff between 1971 and 1972 was almost twice as high among blacks as among whites. Age was found to be positively related to the probability of layoff for blacks but not for whites. Among both races married men were less likely than their nonmarried counterparts to have experienced a layoff.

11. The differences among these three groups may reflect not only the passage of time but also the character of the labor market at and subsequent to their displacement. The overall unemployment rate averaged 3.7 percent during the four-year period 1966 to 1969, 4.8 percent during the three-year period 1969 to 1971, and 6.1 percent during the five-year period 1971 to 1975.

12. In the 1973 and 1975 interview schedules respondents were asked only about the number of weeks of unemployment experienced during the preceding 12 months, leaving the first 12 months of the two-year interval since the preceding interview completely unaccounted for. Thus the data for men displaced between 1971 and 1975 are the least reliable and almost certainly understate the extent of their unemployment. Even in the other surveys it is not possible to conclude that all reported weeks of unemployment occurred immediately following the displacement. In one of the 117 cases there was no information on the number of weeks of unemployment, and in several additional cases it was not possible to distinguish the exact sequence of periods of unemployment and periods out of the labor force. Even where extended periods of unemployment are followed by clearly distinguishable periods out of the labor force, it may not always be realistic to exclude the latter from the period of unemployment, although this is what we have done.

13. The employment status (unweighted percentages) of the 1966–1969 displaced men and of the 1969–1971 displaced men in the survey week two years after displacement is revealing. Only 4 percent of the first group were unemployed, a percentage slightly greater than the rate for that group in 1976. Among the men who were displaced in the 1969–1971 period, 11 percent were unemployed in the survey week of 1973, in contrast to the 7 percent unemployed in 1976. These relationships demonstrate dramatically the advantages of a tight labor market for individuals who lose their jobs.

14. A job of lower status is defined as one whose Duncan Index score is lower by more than three points. For a description of the Duncan Index see *occupational status* in appendix A.

15. The individual's ultimate position even in these cases may have been less favorable than it would have been had he been able to remain in his 1966 job.

16. "Taking things altogether, would you say you're very happy, somewhat happy, somewhat unhappy, or very unhappy these days?"

17. For a fuller description of the Rotter Scale and an explanation of its interrelationships with labor market experience, see Andrisani and Nestel (1975).

18. In the earlier version of this study (Parnes and King, 1977) there appeared to be some evidence that displacement resulted in deterioration of health. However, no support for that conclusion has been provided by a careful examination of the data used in our study.

References

Andrisani, P. J., and Nestel, G. 1975. Internal-external control and labor market experience. In H. S. Parnes, A. V. Adams, P. J. Andrisani, A. I. Kohen, and G. Nestel, *The pre-retirement years*, vol. 4. U.S. Department of Labor Manpower R&D Monograph 15. Washington, D.C.: U.S. Government Printing Office.

Cobb, S., and Kasl, S. V. 1977. *Termination: the consequences of job loss.* NIOSH Research Report, U.S. Department of Health, Education, and Welfare. Washington, D.C.: U.S. Government Printing Office.

Mick, S. S. 1975. Social and personal costs of plant shutdowns. *Industrial Relations* 14: 203–208.

Parnes, H. S., and King, R. 1977. Middle-aged job losers. *Industrial Gerontology* 4: 77–95.

Slote, A. 1969. *Termination: the closing at Baker plant.* Indianapolis: Bobbs-Merrill.

Sorensen, A. B., and Fuerst, S. 1978. Black-white differences with occurrence of job shifts. *Sociology and Social Research* 62: 537–557.

Chapter 4

Impairment and Labor Market Outcomes: A Cross-Sectional and Longitudinal Analysis

Thomas N. Chirikos
and
Gilbert Nestel

Health status commands increasing attention in empirical research on labor force behavior, but the manner in which it influences labor market outcomes is not yet fully documented or understood. The state of health itself is an outcome conditioned by a complex web of medical, demographic, and socioeconomic relationships. Thus even under the best of circumstances individual variations in health levels are difficult to measure, and the health variable must be suitably controlled when used to predict labor force participation, hours of work, and wages. Researchers have so far been able to use only crude indicators of health status in such investigations. It is likely, therefore, that existing estimates of the impact of poor health on labor market behavior are inaccurate because they contain substantial measurement and specification errors.

Improved estimates of the effects of poor health on labor market outcomes are needed because such estimates play an important role in policy issues. They have assumed a pivotal position in evaluations of the effectiveness of income maintenance and social insurance programs. These evaluations turn on the extent to which poor health accounts for withdrawals from the labor market. A growing literature suggests that health status is a key determinant of male labor supply.[1] Nonetheless, some studies conclude that health may be less important than the inducements of Social Security retirement benefits and disability insurance payments in explaining decisions to leave the work force.[2] The evaluation of policy options in these areas would be well served by additional studies of health effects and the forces that shape their distribution across categories of workers.

This chapter examines the relationship between health and selected labor market outcomes of middle-aged and older men. Our aim is to estimate the effects of variation in health on hours and wages in both cross-sectional and longitudinal terms. The analysis departs somewhat from the earlier literature because of its longitudinal character and because it uses as the measure of health an index of impairment level (functional limitations). This approach was made possible by the collection of information on functional limitations for a portion of the sample in the 1971 survey and for all the men who were interviewed in the 1976 sur-

We wish to acknowledge the very able research assistance of Jeannette Fraser in the preparation of this chapter.

vey. These data permit a more sensitive test of the hypothesis that labor force participation, hours of work, wage rates, and (thereby) earnings are affected by an individual's health status. They also permit us to compare the performance of alternative measures of health status in such investigations.

Measuring Health Status

Alternative Approaches

Health may be defined as that bundle of physical and mental capacities affecting the ability to perform primary and secondary social role responsibilities.[3] Research on the relationship between health and labor force behavior has been hampered by the absence of a suitable measure of these capacities or abilities. What has not been fully considered in the literature is the manner in which available health measures have limited and perhaps biased research findings. Since the NLS data set affords a choice of health measures, and since such a choice may lead to different policy implications, we begin with a brief appraisal of the options for quantifying variations in health levels. Two classes of health measures are available: those that rely on clinical examination or patient self-reports to reveal disease, and those that observe behavioral consequences of ill health such as inability to sustain role activities and inability to leave bed.[4] What are the comparative advantages of these two classes of health measures in investigations of relationships between health and labor market status?

Measures that rely on behavioral evidence to identify diminished capacities or ill health are not well suited for this type of research. The most common of these measures are survey inquiries about whether a physical condition prevents the individual from working or limits the amount or kind of work.[5] Despite their popularity, these work limitation measures have fundamental flaws. First, since they are not necessarily comparable across members of the survey population, they do not provide unambiguous evidence of differences in health levels. Such comparability can be achieved only if the character of health conditions is taken into account and if adjustments are made for role (job) requirements. Health conditions per se, however, are unobserved in behavioral measures. Role responsibilities, moreover, are evaluated by the respondent by unknown means and in the absence of an explicit reference point.

A more significant flaw is that behavioral measures of health are not necessarily independent of the labor force behavior that they are supposed to explain because the primary role responsibility, at least in adult male populations, typically relates to working or looking for work. Thus the behavioral evidence used to document poor health or classify the population under study as "disabled" may be identical to the behavior to be explained, namely, reductions in labor supply. Behavioral measures of health status and measures of labor market status cannot be disentangled in meaningful ways. One implies or (at least) is measured by the other. If this is so, the use of such measures obscures the relationships under study and leads to biased results. Our hunch is that their tautological character tends to result in overestimating the magnitude of health effects.

Another flaw is that behavioral work limitation measures make no allowance for adaptive behavior and thus lead to a myopic view of the policy instruments available for dealing with the socioeconomic consequences of poor health. For instance, cross-sectional measurements include individuals who have just encountered both short-term (reversible) and long-term (non-reversible) health problems, those who are in the process of adapting to such problems, and individuals who have made a successful adaptation to the problem even though that adaptation requires a change in the amount and kind of work. Unless good health is defined as a singular point—all deviations measured from it—those who have made a successful adaptation to a health problem have a new health status reference point; they should be classified among the healthy population. Whether this happens is unclear from the literature, however. To the extent it does not, the relationships under study are obscured and the benefits stemming from vocational rehabilitation and other adaptive efforts underestimated.

Measures of the second general class attempt to gauge health levels more directly. In principle, they are designed to measure the capacities or attributes that contribute to or detract from health status. In practice, the measures range from subjective evaluations of health states to self-reported limitations in physiological or psychological function. These varied measures are classified together because they do not rely (nominally) on behavioral data in detecting variations in health levels. Published studies have used such measures to examine the relationship between health and labor market outcomes.

Although subjective self-reports ("I rate my health as excellent (good, fair, poor)")[6] are not defined in reference to behavioral criteria, they are subject to the same ambiguity. It is not clear that the measures are comparable over the population because the specific environmental factors that shape an individual's interpretation of his or her health are not included.[7]

Health effects have also been investigated with the use of functional limitation or impairment measures.[8] Since such data are obtained through a battery of very specific items by level or degree of severity, the responses appear to be fairly comparable across sample members and thus are less likely than other measures to be ambiguous. While some have behavioral characteristics, that "behavior" is closely aligned to pathological conditions such as the inability to sit or stand for long periods resulting from certain musculoskeletal conditions. As residual or chronic departures from normal physiological and psychological functioning, then, these indicators come closest to the ordinary, intuitive definition of health. More important perhaps is that they correspond in more plausible fashion to expected changes in labor market outcomes. For example, activity limitations signal possible diminutions in the ability to perform role responsibilities and should thus account for reductions in labor supply. If such attributes are valued in the market, limitations can be traced to reductions in marginal productivities and thereby wages.

This discussion suggests that impairment measures are better suited than other health measures to the research at hand. However, the use of these indicators thus far has not yielded fruitful results. In studies that have used them (for example, Berkowitz and Johnson, 1974), data were obtained only for individuals who first classified themselves as disabled. That is, a behavioral measure was used to divide the population into healthy and disabled strata, and impairment data were obtained only for the latter group. This procedure is clearly tantamount to using a behavioral measure. Our study avoids this difficulty as well as an additional technical problem that characterized the analysis of Berkowitz and Johnson.[9]

An Impairment Index

This study draws on the functional limitation data collected in the 1971 and 1976 surveys. The 1976 data, which are summarized in table 4.1, do not suffer from the limitations that have characterized impairment data in earlier studies, since impair-

Table 4.1
Prevalence and Severity of Impairment, by Type, 1976

Type of impairment	Prevalence[a] (percentage)	Total number	Percentage Partial	Percentage Complete
Activity limitation				
Walk	21	797	94	6
Stairs	22	825	87	13
Stand	28	1,027	67	33
Sit	15	520	74	26
Stoop	28	1,009	77	23
Lift, light	13	496	59	41
Lift, heavy	38	1,350	43	57
Reach	12	428	77	23
Hands	9	332	90	10
See	10	405	90	10
Hear	17	544	96	4
Deal with people	4	151	72	28
Other	1	55	58	42
Signs and symptoms				
Pain	20	789	b	b
Fatigue	24	886	b	b
Weakness	18	661	b	b
Aches	17	655	b	b
Fainting	8	350	b	b
Nerves	19	707	b	b
Breath	18	681	b	b
Other	2	77	b	b

[a]3,437 respondents
[b]Question not asked

ment information was collected for all sample members. A majority of men between the ages of 55 and 69 responded positively to at least one question in the battery of impairment questions.[10] In 1976, for instance, less than 40 percent of all respondents answered no to each such question. Not surprisingly, however, different conditions command different frequencies, and different individuals report the existence of different combinations of conditions or problems. The relative frequencies of impairments calculated with respect to the total sample (table 4.1) show a pattern of inverse relationships between severity of impairments and frequency of report. For example, moderate impairments such as difficulty in lifting or carrying heavy weights and in stooping were reported by 38 percent and 28 percent of the sample, respectively (or about two-thirds and one-half of the 2,118 individuals reporting at least one impairment). But more serious impairments such as poor vision and difficulty in dealing with people were reported by only 10 percent and 4 percent, respectively, of the respondents in the 1976 sample. Similarly, signs and symptoms such as tiring easily, were more commonly reported than relatively more severe signs such as shortness of breath or fainting spells and dizziness. Nonetheless, approximately 10 percent of the entire sample and 20 percent of those having at least one impairment reported problems with seeing; about 1 percent of the sample reported being totally sightless. Similar proportions of the total sample and the total impaired sample reported fainting spells or dizziness. Although the epidemiology of impairments in the general population is not well documented, these rates appear to be consistent with the scanty evidence that is available.[11]

The epidemiological information embedded in the frequencies is not easily interpreted, of course, because individuals report multiple impairments.[12] Accordingly, by methods akin to those used by other researchers and described fully in the appendix to this chapter, we have constructed an impairment index that measures the severity of the impairment(s) that the respondents suffer. The index values range between 1 and 2 for individuals with no impairments to about 15 for individuals reporting severe levels on all impairments. In the multivariate analyses we use this index in continuous form, but for the tabular presentations we have classified individuals into five categories according to the severity of their impairments. The distributions of respondents among these categories in 1971 and 1976 are shown in appendix table 4A.2.[13]

Impairment Status of Mature Males

This section describes the correlates of impairment status of older men and the changes in their health status over the period 1966 to 1976. We begin by examining the personal and labor market characteristics of the men interviewed in 1976 by their level of impairment in that year. We then explore the intertemporal stability of the health states of these men by comparing their responses to health-related questions in earlier survey years with their impairment status in 1976 and then by comparing, for a subset of the total sample, impairment states in 1971 and 1976.

Status in 1976

Slightly more than 60 percent of the men are classified as impaired by the criteria employed in this study. As might be expected, there are differences among the impairment categories in personal attributes such as age and educational attainment and in employment-related characteristics such as occupational assignment and labor force participation rates. An examination of table 4.2 suggests two patterns. First, the direction of the relationship between the impairment index values and the selected demographic and socioeconomic characteristics is in rough accord with a priori expectation. For instance, if we compare the profiles of the severely impaired against the nonimpaired, we see from a demographic perspective that the severely impaired are older and less likely to be married. They are more likely to reside in the South, to have been born in the United States, and to have completed fewer years of formal schooling. From an economic viewpoint these individuals tend more often to be self-employed and to hold blue-collar jobs in the primary or secondary sectors of the economy. They are, by a wide margin, less likely to be in the labor force or employed in 1976, and (if employed) to earn as much. They are, however, more likely to have high levels of disability-related income. While these descriptive profiles do not unravel the complex relationships that underlie them, they nonetheless alert us to the possibility that health problems will play themselves out differently across different socioeconomic groups.

The second noteworthy point is that a small proportion of nonimpaired individuals report work-limiting health problems and that even some severely impaired individuals continue to work. The percentage reporting work-limiting health problems increases (nonlinearly) with impairment level, rising from about 6 percent for men with no impairment to about 95 percent for men with severe impairment.

Intertemporal Changes

Sample members interviewed in 1976 may be conveniently classified into three groups. The first is a group of individuals who, under any of the self-rating or activity definitions of health encompassed by the data set,[14] never reported any health problems. This group consists of approximately 1,000 men, or

Table 4.2
Selected Characteristics, by Impairment Status, 1976

Characteristics	Impairment status					
	All	None	Minor	Moderate	Substantial	Severe
Number of respondents	3,437	1,319	630	747	401	340
Total percent	100	40	19	22	11	8
Personal characteristics						
Mean age	62	61	62	62	63	63
Median years of schooling	11	11	11	10	9	9
Married (%)	86	87	86	87	82	85
Residency non South (%)	68	71	69	67	66	55
Father's occupation, mean Duncan Index	28	29	30	27	25	21
Job characteristics						
Wage and salary workers (%)	80	82	81	79	79	76
White-collar workers (%)	37	44	40	34	28	19
Service industry workers (%)	16	18	17	14	12	11
Current labor force participation						
In labor force (%)	63	80	70	56	34	20
Employed (%)	60	77	66	54	32	19
Mean hours worked past 12 months	1,276	1,685	1,417	1,096	625	360
Mean hourly earnings ($)	6.36	6.72	6.21	6.00	5.04	4.98
Unemployed (%)	3	3	3	3	2	1
Mean weeks unemployed past 12 months	2	2	2	2	1	1
Out of labor force (%)	37	20	31	44	66	80
Retired (%)	28	19	27	35	39	33
Not having work-seeking intentions (%)	91	87	89	90	93	96
Health characteristics						
Prevents work (%)	17	1	5	19	50	71
Limits amount/kind of work (%)	23	5	29	41	41	24
Work accident (%)	19	15	15	20	21	26
Mean disability income (1975 dollars)	379	98	120	499	970	1,247

about one-fifth of the original cohort. The second is a group of individuals who, by any of the preceding definitions encompassed by the data, were continuously in poor health over the decade. We estimate this group to include between 200 and 300 individuals, or about 5 percent of the original sample. If one includes those who died over the decade and assumes that many of these individuals were in continuous poor health before

Table 4.3
Alternative Health Status Measures in Selected Periods 1966–1976 and Impairment Status 1971, by Impairment Status 1976 (percentage distributions)

Health status measure	1976 impairment status					
	Total	None	Minor	Moderate	Substantial	Severe
1966–1976						
Number of respondents	3,408	1,307	627	739	398	337
Total percent	100	100	100	100	100	100
Continuous good health	47	78	47	27	5	2
Continuous poor health	8	1	4	9	23	34
Health condition varies	45	22	49	64	72	64
1973–1976						
Number of respondents	3,437	1,319	630	747	401	340
Total percent	100	100	100	100	100	100
Health same	65	87	77	50	28	20
Health better	7	7	6	9	6	4
Health worse	28	6	17	41	66	76
1971 impairment status						
Number of respondents	961	109	103	120	153	476
Total percent	100	100	100	100	100	100
None	5	20	7	2	8	1
Minor	16	37	26	19	10	9
Moderate	19	21	32	30	21	12
Substantial	23	10	21	30	34	21
Severe	37	12	14	19	27	57

they died, this group is also about one-fifth of the original sample. By implication, the third group or about three-fifths of the cohort had some change in health condition over the decade 1966 to 1976.

The distribution of these three groups according to their impairment status in 1976 is shown in table 4.3. As expected, there is a pronounced relationship between current impairment levels and past health assessments. This table also shows that health conditions are fairly unstable for some individuals. The portion of table 4.3 that shows responses to questions whether health improved, worsened, or stayed the same over the past three years by level of impairment in 1976 suggests that deterioration as well as improvement in health may occur at both the highest and the lowest impairment levels.[15]

More light might be shed on these changes if it were possible to examine the extent to which impairment status itself changes

Table 4.4
Impairments, by Type, 1971–1976[a]

Type of impairment	Gamma (correlation) coefficient[b]	Percentage of longitudinal sample reporting	
		Change	No change
Activity limitation			
Walking	0.575	34	66
Using stairs or inclines	0.573	37	63
Standing for long periods of time	0.460	52	48
Sitting for long periods	0.362	39	61
Stooping, kneeling, crouching	0.467	47	53
Lifting or carrying weights up to 10 lbs	0.393	38	62
Lifting or carrying heavy weights	0.416	51	49
Reaching	0.528	31	69
Using hands and fingers	0.522	24	76
Seeing (even with glasses)	0.594	25	75
Hearing	0.705	23	77
Dealing with people	0.516	14	86
Signs and symptoms			
Pain	0.606	33	67
Tiring easily, no energy	0.533	36	64
Weakness, lack of strength	0.613	32	68
Aches, swelling, sick feeling	0.517	33	67
Fainting spells, dizziness	0.674	22	78
Nervousness, tension, anxiety, depression	0.587	32	68
Shortness of breath, trouble breathing	0.741	27	73

[a]Longitudinal sample

over time. Unfortunately this question can be approached only for a small set of the longitudinal panel, those who indicated a work limitation in 1971 and who were therefore asked the series of questions on impairment. For this subset of the sample table 4.3 cross-classifies impairment level in 1976 by impairment level in 1971.[16] Table 4.4 shows the degree to which individuals reported the same specific impairment in both years. These tables suggest not only that impairment status changes over time but also that such changes signal improvements in impairment level almost as frequently as they signal deteriorations.

These changes are most evident when we examine the 1971–1976 matrix of impairment index values (table 4.3). For instance, only about 20 percent of the men with no impairments in 1976 also reported the absence of an impairment in 1971. Of the most severely impaired respondents in 1976, 57 percent were in the same impairment category in 1971. In total, only about 42 percent of the longitudinal sample remained in the same impairment category over the five-year period 1971–1976, while about 28 percent moved to a more severe state and 30 percent moved into a less severe category. If we exclude from consideration movements to the next higher or lower category, we still find that 13 percent of the sample improved their impairment status over the period in question while 12 percent saw their impairment status deteriorate.

The extent of correlation between reports by respondents of the same specific impairments in the two years also suggests substantial changes over time in impairment status (table 4.4). While there is a relatively high degree of association (stability) in selected severe impairments (for example, hearing, seeing, shortness of breath), there are also relatively low associations (instability) in others (sitting for long periods, lifting light weights). These findings are interesting, although they appear to introduce some ambiguity in the use of impairment data as indicators of residual, long-term loss of function. It is possible, of course, that medical treatments restored functions, even in some of the more severe cases, for example, cataract surgery in the case of partial or complete sightlessness. It is also possible, however, that the apparent instability of impairment status is an artifact of the process used to collect and process the data.

The relationship between impairment state in 1971 and labor market status in 1976 is set out in table 4.5. The 1971 distribution of impairments is affected by the data collection procedure; the index values refer only to individuals reporting work-limiting health problems who, on average, would tend to be more impaired. This is evident in the classification of the median individual in 1971 as substantially impaired, while his counterpart in 1976 is categorized as having only minor impairments (table 4A.2). Nonetheless, the 1971 impairment values generally predict 1976 outcomes, including the mortality experience of the 1971 cross section. The mortality rate was more than twice as high for individuals with severe impairment levels as for those with only minor impairments. There is also a relationship between 1971 impairment status and 1976 labor market status.

Table 4.5
Labor Market Status in 1976, by Impairment Category in 1971[a] and Race

Status in 1976	Impairment status in 1971, all respondents					
	All	None	Minor	Moderate	Sub-stantial	Severe
Number of respondents	1,206	98	154	248	276	430
Percentage decreased	20	13	11	16	21	27
Number of respondents interviewed	961	84	134	210	218	315
In labor force (%)	44	65	60	56	44	22
Employed (%)	42	64	58	54	40	20
Mean hours worked	1,706	1,911	1,763	1,741	1,535	1,612
Mean hourly earnings ($)	5.60	6.38	5.78	5.73	5.05	4.91
Out of labor force (%)	56	35	40	44	56	78
Retired (%)	34	24	33	36	34	34

[a]Respondents reporting work-limiting health problems in 1971.

The relationship between the index values and 1976 hours and wages is perhaps most notable. The severely impaired in 1971 worked 300 fewer hours five years later than those with no impairments and earned almost $1.50 per hour less.

Multivariate Analysis

Our primary aim in this section is to test more formally the proposition that impairment status of older men is a robust predictor of labor market outcomes such as participation, hours of work, and wages and to compare the behavior of the impairment index with that of other health-related variables.

Hypotheses

Labor supply   Our first hypothesis is that the labor supply of mature males is inversely related to impairment level when conventional demographic and human capital characteristics are controlled. In the 1976 cross-sectional analysis labor supply is measured in terms of labor force participation during the survey week of 1976 and the number of hours worked in the 12-month period preceding the survey. It is also measured by self-reported disability or limitations in the amount or kind of work that the respondent can do. While this self-report measure differs from the more traditional participation or hours specification, its use here as an outcome variable is of interest in view of the significant statistical effects found in previous labor supply studies and given our contention that such measures have tautological characteristics. In each case the set of explanatory variables includes several (dummy) predictors representing particular clusters of occupational assignments as well as a set of terms that test for interactions between occupational assignment and impairment status.[17] These variables are used to assess whether impairments impose different penalties on different occupational groups.[18] To assess the differences in results attributable to differences in health measures, these cross-sectional labor supply models are run in a variety of ways: with and without the impairment index and with more traditional health measures replacing the impairment index.

Since it is difficult to trace the socioeconomic consequences of changes in health conditions in a cross-sectional framework, we also estimate a longitudinal labor supply model. This model examines changes in hours worked between 1971 and 1976 for a subset of respondents for whom impairment measures were obtained in both years.[19] The model includes as explanatory variables both impairment levels and changes in occupational and industrial status, residence, and a number of related factors.[20] As such, the model is designed to appraise the extent to which deterioration in impairment status translates into reductions in hours worked directly or indirectly through adjustments in job status (occupation, firm, industry). This test is particularly significant for older men because it gauges the extent to which there are alternative mechanisms for adjusting to chronic health problems. For instance, it should shed some light on the extent to which job requirements influence the degree of job disability, as well as on the extent to which occupational mobility serves as an alternative to leaving the labor market in response to the incidence or growing severity of an impairment.

Wages   Our second hypothesis is that wage rates are inversely related to the extent of impairment, again with a set of control variables similar to those used in the supply analysis.[21] An analysis of this relationship is needed primarily to evaluate average earnings losses associated with various levels of impairment. However, of interest in its own right is whether, all other things equal, impairment status influences the rate of pay. Clearly, this depends on the manner in which impairment affects other outcomes. For example, if impairments are accommodated simply by dropping out of the labor force, wage effects may not be substantial. If they are accommodated by job reassignment, the impact on wage rates may be considerable. The examination of this relationship also depends on the specification of the dependent variable and whether a cross-sectional or intertemporal relationship is estimated. Given the difficulties in estimating wage rates for self-employed workers and individuals outside the labor force, our wage model is estimated only for wage and salary workers with recent work experience. The use of this subsample permits us to use observed wage rates. It also allows for both cross-sectional and longitudinal wage equations, the former for all employed wage and salary workers in 1976 and the latter for the same individuals who also worked as wage and salary earners in 1971 and reported that their health affected their work. As before, the impairment index is either excluded or replaced by other health measures in the wage equations so as to appraise the differential impact of the various specifications.

Results

Cross-sectional estimates   Table 4.6 presents the results of regressions in which the dependent variables are labor force participation, annual hours of work, and the probability of having reported a work-limiting health problem for all respondents in 1976. It also presents hours and wage equations for employed wage and salary workers in 1976.[22] Since the regressions were run with alternative health measures (including one in which no health variable was entered), there are several estimates for each equation. For example, the 1976 cross-sectional participation equation was estimated with the set of controls and the impairment index (col. 1), with the impairment index and impairment-occupation interactions (col. 2), and with behavioral health measures replacing the impairment index (col. 3).

There is considerable evidence that impairment status influences the labor supply of older men. Indeed, there are statistically significant impairment effects on labor force participation, annual hours, and self-reported work limitations of the entire sample, as well as on hours worked by employed wage and salary workers. For instance, the regression coefficient for the impairment variable in column 4 indicates a reduction of approximately 185 hours per year for each point increase in the impairment index. Given the distribution of 1976 impairment (appendix table 4A.2) this translates into reductions of roughly

250 hours at the margin for movements between minor and moderate impairment and from moderate to substantial impairment categories. The marginal reduction in hours between the substantially and the severely impaired is greater than this; in fact, the estimates indicate clearly that the severely impaired, by our classification scheme, are not in the labor force.

Although impairment status affects labor supply, there is no clear evidence that these effects are more severe for individuals in more demanding occupations. In interpreting this evidence, recall that the analysis includes variables to control for the physical demands of different jobs and interactions between impairment level and occupational assignment.[23] Evidence that the labor supply of individuals at similar levels of impairment varies by the physical demands of the job is mixed. There are no differences in labor force participation, although there are slight variations in hours worked by individuals attached to different occupational groups (appendix table 4A.3). More important is the evidence of the interaction terms in table 4.6 that impairment effects do not differ substantially by occupation. The signs of the interaction coefficients are inexplicably opposite to those anticipated under the hypothesis that impairments have more severe consequences for men engaged in more physically demanding work.

The results of the wage equation shown in table 4.6 provide only weak evidence of an adverse effect of impairment on the average hourly earnings of employed wage and salary workers; the coefficient of the impairment variable narrowly misses statistical significance. Since the labor supply estimates are significant, it appears likely that health problems—especially impairments recently incurred—are accommodated by older men primarily by dropping out of the work place. Perhaps these adjustments obscure the effect of impairments on wages. However, the significance of the behavioral health measures in column 14 suggests that the results generally reported in the literature may be a function of the conventional measurement of health.

An examination of the specifications of the supply equations tends to support this proposition. In particular, the predictive power of the labor supply equation changes substantially when health variables are added or their specification changed. The proportion of variance explained by the equations (adj R^2) increases by about 10 percentage points when impairment status

Table 4.6
Health Status Effects on Labor Supply and Wages,[a] 1976 (t-values in parentheses)

Health status	Outcome variables and sample characteristics					
	All respondents, 1976					
	Labor force participation, 1976			Hours worked past 12 months, 1976		
	1	2	3	4	5	6
Impairment measures						
Impairment status	−8.85 (−18.57)	−10.52 (−11.23)		−185.00 (−17.35)	−232.55 (−11.10)	
Impairment × job requirements interaction						
Physically demanding jobs[b]		2.04 (1.87)			60.97 (2.49)	
Walking-standing jobs[c]		4.61 (2.32)			81.30 (1.83)	
Sitting-hand/eye jobs[d]		1.00 (0.47)			61.34 (1.27)	
Behavioral measures						
Health condition prevents work			−64.54 (−29.61)			−1,245.4 (−24.61)
Health condition affects work			−7.13 (−3.96)			−288.94 (−6.87)
R^2 (adj)	0.342	0.343	0.455	0.369	0.370	0.436

[a]See appendix tables 4A.3 and 4A.4 for complete estimated equations.
[b]OCC2
[c]OCC3
[d]OCC4

is taken into account (appendix table 4A.3). For instance, the variance explained in the labor force participation equations is about 24 percent without the impairment index but about 34 percent with it; the same statistics for the annual hours equation are 29 percent and 37 percent respectively. But these proportions increase even more when behavioral measures replace the impairment index. Perhaps because of their tautological nature, we find that the R^2's increase by 15 to 22 percentage points when behavioral measures are included in the hours and participation equations. We also observe some changes in the parameter estimation of these equations. Appendix table 4A.3 shows, for instance, that the statistical significance of the schooling variable changes substantially among the several regression runs. It is likely, of course, that these differences are artifacts attributable to the differences in the measurement of the health variable.[24]

Outcome variables and sample characteristics							
Employed wage and salary earners, 1976							
Self-reported work limitation, 1976		Hours worked past 12 months, 1976			(Log) Wages		
7	8	9	10	11	12	13	14
14.97	18.30	−41.83	−57.38		−0.008	−0.010	
(31.74)	(17.93)	(−3.06)	(−2.48)		(−1.62)	(−1.22)	
	−4.06		26.32			0.004	
	(−3.51)		(0.87)			(0.37)	
	−4.42		18.96			0.010	
	(−2.10)		(0.45)			(0.67)	
	−4.77		11.72			−0.024	
	(−2.51)		(0.17)			(−1.03)	
				−496.26			−0.124
				(−3.59)			(−2.47)
				−92.78			−0.044
				(2.48)			(−3.20)
0.377	0.380	0.324	0.323	0.329	0.439	0.439	0.445

Even though impairment status is a statistically significant predictor of the probability of reporting a work-limiting health problem, almost two-thirds of the variance in this dependent variable is left unexplained by the model. This clearly suggests that the alternative health measures do not capture the same underlying phenomena, nor can they necessarily be mapped onto each other very easily. It also implies that a number of factors impinge on such self-reports beyond matters relating to physiological or psychological functioning per se. We find that the probability of reporting a health problem is higher for men who are older, less well educated, who live in the South, are self-employed, and have higher "other family income." The magnitude of the other income variable, however, is not as great as the recent literature seems to suggest (appendix table 4A.3, cols. 9, 10).

Longitudinal estimates Table 4.7 summarizes the net effect of a change in health status on changes in wages and hours.[25] The regressions summarized in this table examine the factors associated with changes in hours and wages over the period

Table 4.7
Health Status Effects on Changes in Labor Supply and Wages,[a] 1971–1976 (t-values in parentheses)

	Outcome variables									
	Changes in hours worked					Change in (log) wages				
Health status	1	2	3	4	5	6	7	8	9	10
Impairment measures										
Impairment status, 1971	−8.10 (−0.50)					−0.018 (−1.59)				
Impairment status, 1976		−69.31 (−3.42)					0.006 (0.86)			
Impairment status, 1971–1976[b]										
Improved			170.72 (1.69)					0.135 (2.77)		
Worsened			−23.90 (−0.21)					0.035 (0.63)		
Behavioral measures										
Prevented work in 1971 and 1976				−173.25 (−0.91)					−0.142 (−1.71)	
Affected work 1971, no effect 1976				61.09 (0.31)					−0.138 (−1.58)	
No effect 1971, affected work 1976				−224.43 (−0.84)					−0.094 (−0.70)	
Health improved past three years					−52.34 (−0.32)					−0.057 (−0.58)
Health worsened past three years					−271.58 (−3.11)					−0.112 (−2.38)
R^2 (adj)	0.586	0.605	0.586	0.593	0.600	0.661	0.658	0.715	0.658	0.665

[a]See appendix table 4A.5.
[b]1976 impairment index values based on 1971 index weights and distribution of 1976 impairments.

1971 to 1976 for the subset of men for whom impairment information was collected in the earlier year. They include measures to control for change in family characteristics, such as marital status and number of dependents, as well as controls for changes in socioeconomic circumstances (receipt of training, occupational, industrial, residential, and interfirm mobility, and other family income). They also include both impairment and other health measures as well as the respondent's retirement status and race. The impairment variable is entered either as a dummy corresponding to whether impairment status improved or deteriorated over the period or in terms of its value at the beginning or at the end of the five-year period.[26] The alternative health measures include changes in self-reported work limitations and the respondent's report of whether his health has improved, worsened, or remained unchanged in the past three years.

The findings summarized in table 4.7 indicate that about 60 percent of the variance in change in labor supply and two-thirds of the variance in change in (log) wages over the period 1971 to 1976 is accounted for by the entire set of predictor variables in the longitudinal models. As expected, the values for hours and wages in 1971 tend to be significant predictors of their respective 1976 values. Factors such as changes in number of dependents and retirement are significant in the case of hours, and completion of training and change in employer in the case of wages. Contrary to expectations, few of the health measures are statistically significant. In the hours equations, for example, the behavioral health measures are not significant, and only respondents who report a worsening of health in the past three years significantly alter their hours of work (in this case downward) relative to those who report no change in health status in the five-year period. Impairment status in 1971 has no net effect on changes in number of hours worked, although the 1976 impairment index score is significant, a result that is not surprising. The level of impairment in 1971 should be related to the number of hours worked in 1971, but not necessarily to changes in hours over the ensuing five years.

More important perhaps is that neither improvements nor deteriorations in impairment status significantly affect changes in hours worked. Note, however, that improvement appears to have a more pronounced influence than deterioration; men who moved to a less severe impairment state averaged about 171 more hours of work annually than men who reported no change in impairment. The more pronounced impact of improvements in impairment status may be explained by the generally low health level of the longitudinal sample at the beginning of the five-year period and hence the greater leeway for upward adjustments in hours worked over the period.

This possibility may account for the statistically significant coefficient for improved impairment status in the equation relating to wage changes. None of the other impairment variables is a significant predictor of wage change over the period 1971 to 1976. Not even all the behavioral health measures have significant impacts on wage changes. Thus the longitudinal estimates are similar to the cross-sectional findings presented earlier in that they indicate only weak wage effects for different levels of impairment. The somewhat disappointing performance of the impairment variable in each of the variants of the longitudinal equations may be explained by the size and character of the subsample for which longitudinal impairment data were available. Further analysis of these relationships drawing on future survey information will be needed before more confident conclusions can be reached about the intertemporal consequences of health problems.

Summary

Impairment status, as we have measured it, appears to have an important effect on the decisions of older men relating to labor force participation and hours worked and, accordingly, cannot be ignored in any attempt to explain recent trends in the labor market behavior of the elderly. The cross-sectional estimates, for example, imply that an average blue-collar worker who is even moderately impaired reduces either his chances of being in the labor market or his hours worked by about 9 percent.[27] If well enough to be employed, this worker nonetheless works roughly 2 percent fewer hours and earns about 1 percent less per hour than a nonimpaired worker with identical skills and attributes. This translates into an earning loss of 2.5 percent to 12 percent of annual income.[28] Clearly, such loss is greater for individuals who are more seriously impaired or who have acquired less human capital. The estimated reduction in annual earnings associated with the most severe impairment levels ranges from 26 percent to 100 percent for white men and is even higher for black men. Consequently, policies aimed at reducing impairment levels or inequalities in the labor market can cushion individuals against the adverse economic effects of health problems.

Our results also indicate that calculations of the effects of health on labor market participation or on earnings are sensitive to the way in which health is measured.[29] In particular, the use of behavioral (work limitation) measures produces predictions of loss in annual earnings somewhat different from the estimates based on impairment values. The earnings loss of an average blue-collar worker (calculated in reference to the limitation measure and in a way comparable to the figures for the moderately impaired worker) is on the order of 9 percent to 18 percent of annual income. The estimate is higher because the behavioral measure produces predictions of both greater reductions in hours and greater wage loss than are produced by the impairment measure. Since figures such as these are frequently used as measures of potential benefits in planning and evaluation studies, further appraisal of methods for measuring health status appears to be required.

Although our findings generally support the effects of health on labor market outcomes, they fail to shed much light on several other important matters. First, there is little evidence that impairment profiles of older men are either static or simply growing more severe in time as a result of the "aging" process. Data on the longitudinal sample suggest considerable instability in impairment patterns. This is perhaps the most intriguing finding of the study, and one that warrants additional empirical and methodological investigation. Second, there is little evidence that occupational mobility is used as a mechanism for adjusting to changes in impairment status. Although we had supposed a priori that changes in wages and hours stemming from changes in health conditions were played out through shifts in occupational assignment, the data hint that older men are either unable or unwilling to adjust to health conditions in this fashion. Changes in impairment status, if severe enough, appear to be accommodated simply by dropping out of the labor market, at least by men in the age group under consideration. Finally, we did not find as strong a relationship between impairment and wages as has been found in studies using behavioral health measures. Some caution is required in evaluating this finding, because it is based on the subset of men who were healthy enough to be employed wage and salary workers in 1976. In our view the relationship between wages and impairments depends critically on the paths or mechanisms used to adjust to changes in impairment status. Since the analysis did not investigate these paths in highly detailed fashion, it may have obscured the measurement of wage effects. This is a matter, therefore, that also warrants high priority on the agenda of future research studies.

Construction of the Impairment Index

The large number of impairment items and the need to quantify the health status of the respondent led to a principal-components analysis of the impairment data. The solution vector, more specifically its components, was then used as the weight to aggregate the reported impairments and obtain an impairment index value. Linear indexes of health-related items have been used by Grossman and Benham and, more recently, by Nagi.[30] In both cases weights for the linear aggregation of items were obtained by statistical techniques. Grossman and Benham used principal-components analysis to weight self-rated health status and number of symptoms to obtain an index of ill health. Nagi used factor analysis to transform functional limitation items that are quite similar to those used in our study to obtain indexes of physical and emotional performance.

The data used in constructing the index consist of 12 activity limitation questions and 7 questions relating to the signs and symptoms of other types of health problems. The presence or absence of the activity limitations was requested from each respondent as well as an indication of the severity of that condition. The battery of questions on signs and symptoms asked for only a dichotomous response; that is, the presence or absence of the symptom was reported, with no indication of its severity. Bivariate contingency tables were prepared for each pair of impairments and a measure of the degree of association computed. The gamma statistic, rather than the more traditional Pearsonian r was selected as the summary measure for two reasons: first, because the impairment responses are ordinal in nature and, second, because concern has been expressed in the literature about using ordinal level data in principal-components analysis unless the measure of the degree of association is appropriate to the type of response reported.[31]

The gamma coefficients were then arrayed in a square matrix and analyzed by principal components. After the initial components were extracted, they were Varimax rotated, providing orthogonal components (factors) as the terminal solution. The resulting component weights measure the amount of residual variance in each component explained by that variable.

Impairment index weights were calculated from the factor-estimate matrix. The component scores associated with the highest loading component on each variable were included. The elements of the index were then formed as the product of the matrix of rotated component scores (ρ_i) and responses to the impairment items, the latter standardized to have zero means and unit variances ($\Sigma_{i=1}^{19} \rho_i \hat{IMP}_i$, where $\hat{IMP}$ are the normalized responses). A constant of 1.0 was added to each standardized value in the data set so that the range of values for each index would be positive.

The indexing is simply a means for reducing or transforming the data in linear fashion. The transformed data tell us little more than they do in their original form; they are just organized or arranged in a way that facilitates their use. Nonetheless, the results seem plausible from a substantive viewpoint because they reflect both the underlying epidemiological relationships and the rough (rank) ordering of the severity of the impairment items. This impression is supported by inspection of the specific component weights and standardized values of responses for the 1976 cross section given in columns 1–3 in table 4A.1. A priori, we might expect that (total) loss of hearing or of ability to deal with people would be less prevalent but weighted more heavily than, say, inability to lift heavy weights. Similarly, we might anticipate that signs and symptoms would count less than some activity limitations such as the loss of sight or hearing but (on clinical grounds) count somewhat more than activity limitations such as ability to reach or stoop. Of course, we cannot impute any real significance to the scalar differences between and among items except to say that they emerge from patterns embedded in the data and that a priori expectations are satisfied by the results. Ultimately, weighting schemes are imposed on the data in arbitrary fashion, in the hope that they provide workable results.

Since the principal-components method requires standardized responses, we constructed a set of impairment indexes, each index referring to a particular subsample of the total cohort of mature men. The primary subsample is the 1976 cross section; it includes all members of the cohort who were interviewed in 1976. An index was also constructed for the 1971 cross section, those individuals who reported a limiting health problem in the 1971 survey. The 1971 cross section included 1,014 men, or about one-quarter of the interviewed sample in 1971. For purposes of longitudinal analysis indexes were constructed for the subsample of individuals from whom we had both 1971 and 1976 data, that is, the subgroup of the 1971 cross section who were reinterviewed in 1976. We refer to this group as the longitudinal sample. Two impairment indexes were constructed for this sample, the cross sections in 1971 and in 1976. Since each index requires a gamma matrix, four such matrices were developed. These matrices, as well as a fifth which measures the degree of association between the 1971 and the 1976 impairment profiles of the longitudinal sample, are available from the authors on request.

An issue of some interest and importance to this study is whether the linear index weights change significantly from one subsample to another. The right-hand columns of table 4A.1 show the product of the principal component weights and standardized responses by impairment for the impairment indexes. As can be seen, the absolute values of the weights are reasonably similar for the 1971 cross section and the 1971–1976 longitudinal cross sections but are somewhat lower (relatively) than the 1976 cross section. The ordinal differences are less pronounced. For example, the rank order correlation coefficient is 0.811 between the 1971 and 1976 cross sections for the activity limitation weights; a similar calculation for the signs and symptoms is slightly higher. The rank order correlations for the two (longitudinal) cross sections is only 0.657. This is surprising, for the 1976 and 1971 cross section samples differ substantially while the longitudinal sample is defined for exactly the same individuals. Perhaps this can be explained by the aging process and by the fact that impairment characteristics appear to be transitory; that is, individuals who report some impairments in 1971 are equally likely to report fewer as to report more impairments in 1976. This instability may account for the shifting pattern of weights emerging from the principal-components analysis.

Construction of Occupation Dummy Variables

Principal-components analysis was used to cluster occupations with respect to the activity requirements of each occupation as reported by their incumbents. The resultant clusters were then entered into the multivariate analysis as dummy variables to control for variations in health-related job characteristics. More specifically, question 46 in the 1976 interview schedule asked employed respondents to describe the physical requirements of their occupations using the same array of activities on which the activity limitation impairments are based. The percentage of incumbents who reported that a particular activity was performed regularly on the job was computed for each occupation. A principal-components analysis of these percentages by occupation was then carried out. The occupation was the unit of analysis, and all occupations with more than two respondents were included. Occupations with two or fewer respondents were classified by hand by the researchers. Cluster assignments were then determined by the factor with the highest loadings for each variable.

One hundred seventeen occupations were analyzed. These occupations account for approximately 97 percent of the employed 1976 sample; the remaining 3 percent of the sample who were employed in 46 occupations were subsequently assigned by the researchers. After the Varimax rotation of the factor components, four clusters of occupations were identified. The cluster with the highest loading included 85 occupations with 1,194 incumbents. These tend to be traditional white-collar occupations—managers, watchmen, civil engineers, administrators—and tend generally to be sedentary in nature. This cluster is labeled OCC1 in the statistical analyses (see Glossary, Appendix A). The cluster of occupations with the second highest factor loading tend generally to be blue-collar and service jobs—carpenters, farm laborers, hospital attendants, bartenders, auto mechanics. These jobs require a wide range of physical activities including walking, lifting, and reaching, that is, general usage of all the extremities. Referred to as physically demanding jobs in the text and labeled OCC2, the cluster includes 59 occupations and accounts for 1,536 incumbents. One hundred sixty-five respondents in 14 occupations are included in the third occupational cluster (OCC3). These jobs tend to require walking or standing and use of the hands and are referred to in this fashion in the text; they include machinists, assemblers, mail carriers, and cooks. The final cluster (OCC4) includes 5 occupations with 199 incumbents. These occupations include bus, taxi and truck drivers, as well as cranemen and excavating operators. Their distinguishing characteristic is that all require sitting for long periods of time and a high degree of hand and eye coordination.

Table 4A.1
Principal Component Weights Used in Constructing Impairment Indexes[a]

Type of impairment	1976 cross-sectional index			Weights for other indexes		
	Weight	Component score	Value of standardized response	1971 cross-sectional index	1971 longitudinal index	1976 longitudinal index
Activity limitations						
Walking	0.399	0.08177	4.88	0.882	1.009	0.621
Using stairs or inclines	0.320	0.07330	4.37	0.581	0.956	0.578
Standing for long periods	0.237	0.06945	3.41	0.530	0.600	0.618
Sitting for long periods	0.853	0.17772	4.80	0.491	0.849	0.487
Stooping, kneeling, crouching	0.295	0.07921	3.73	0.583	0.598	0.607
Lifting or carrying weights up to 10 lbs	0.156	0.03526	4.42	0.410	0.933	0.793
Lifting or carrying heavy weights	0.326	0.12308	2.65	0.397	0.791	0.556
Reaching	0.008	0.00158	5.33	0.378	0.353	0.573
Using hands and fingers	1.127	0.16878	6.68	0.772	0.774	0.710
Seeing (even with glasses)	1.915	0.31033	6.17	1.309	1.203	1.516
Hearing	2.803	0.48582	5.77	1.793	1.671	2.076
Dealing with people	3.356	0.40234	8.34	1.545	1.561	2.466
Signs and symptoms						
Pain	0.522	0.18501	2.82	0.285	0.844	0.529
Tiring easily, no energy	0.446	0.16566	2.69	0.596	0.512	0.411
Weakness, lack of strength	0.384	0.12627	3.04	0.477	0.546	0.322
Aches, swelling, sick feeling	0.546	0.17902	3.05	0.305	1.180	0.604
Fainting spells, dizziness	0.558	0.14134	3.95	0.907	1.074	0.791
Nervousness, tension, anxiety, depression	0.339	0.11420	2.97	0.570	0.555	0.576
Shortness of breath, trouble breathing	0.549	0.18252	3.01	0.646	0.994	0.745

[a] Weights and standardized value are reported for the most severe response only.

Table 4A.2
Impairment Index Values, by Impairment Category, 1971, 1976[a]

Impairment category	Index value intervals	Number of respondents	Percentage
1971			
Total	1.177–11.861	1,206	100
None	1.177– 1.631	98	8
Minor	1.632– 2.123	154	13
Moderate	2.124– 3.034	248	15
Substantial	3.035– 4.442	276	25
Severe	4.443–11.861	430	39
1976			
Total	1.760–15.153	3,437	100
None	1.760	1,319	40
Minor	1.761– 2.562	630	19
Moderate	2.563– 4.162	747	22
Substantial	4.163– 5.762	401	11
Severe	5.763–15.153	340	8

[a]The index for the 1976 cross-section includes all members of the sample interviewed in 1976. The index for the 1971 cross section covers only those individuals who reported a work-limiting health problem in 1971.

Table 4A.3
Cross-sectional Estimates of Participation, Hours, and Work Limitation Equations, 1976[a] (t-values in parenthesis)

Independent variables	Dependent variables									
	PARTIC				HOURS				PROBLIM	
	1	2	3	4	5	6	7	8	9	10
Family and human capital characteristics										
AGE	-4.54	-4.08	-4.08	-3.69	-109.18	-99.31	-99.46	-92.62	0.940	0.944
	(-21.85)	(-20.86)	(-20.85)	(-20.66)	(-23.50)	(-22.56)	(-22.60)	(-22.15)	(4.57)	(4.61)
WHITE	-3.54	-2.07	-1.91	-0.67	-47.93	-14.58	-11.39	13.19	3.719	3.445
	(-1.10)	(-0.69)	(-0.64)	(-0.25)	(-0.67)	(-0.22)	(-0.17)	(0.21)	(1.72)	(1.59)
NONSOUTH	0.65	-1.33	-1.43	-1.52	58.07	16.83	15.60	5.39	-6.842	-6.777
	(0.34)	(-0.74)	(-0.80)	(-0.93)	(1.36)	(0.42)	(0.39)	(0.14)	(-3.64)	(-3.61)
MAR2	-6.12	-3.83	-3.68	-0.18	-240.96	-193.86	-189.79	-119.97	3.111	2.830
	(-2.15)	(-1.44)	(-1.38)	(-0.07)	(-3.80)	(-3.25)	(-3.18)	(-2.12)	(1.22)	(1.11)
MAR3	-4.95	-6.39	-6.25	-5.05	-205.83	-231.99	-229.60	-203.70	0.383	0.324
	(-1.03)	(-1.43)	(-1.40)	(-1.24)	(-1.90)	(-2.28)	(-2.26)	(-2.12)	(0.08)	(0.07)
SCHOOL	1.40	0.57	0.53	0.15	32.99	15.84	15.18	8.57	-0.660	-0.620
	(4.72)	(2.03)	(1.90)	(0.57)	(4.98)	(2.51)	(2.41)	(1.44)	(-2.37)	(-2.23)
TRN1	9.35	7.84	7.78	5.05	191.82	159.28	156.73	105.37		
	(3.62)	(3.25)	(3.23)	(2.30)	(3.33)	(2.94)	(2.90)	(2.05)		
TRN2	-5.10	-9.37	-9.43	-12.72	-55.08	-146.19	-147.87	-196.28		
	(-0.64)	(-1.25)	(-1.26)	(-1.87)	(-0.31)	(-0.88)	(-0.89)	(-1.25)		
OFINC	-0.001	-0.001	-0.001	-0.001	-0.024	-0.023	-0.023	-0.020	0.003	0.0003
	(-8.48)	(-8.78)	(-8.74)	(-8.05)	(-8.95)	(-9.29)	(-9.25)	(-8.49)	(1.96)	(1.94)
Job characteristics										
CLASS	-14.78	-15.31	-15.49	-13.72	-298.30	-311.56	-317.17	-303.17	-8.085	-7.837
	(-6.62)	(-7.35)	(-7.44)	(-7.21)	(-5.91)	(-6.57)	(-6.69)	(-6.73)	(-3.59)	(-3.49)
OCC2	-1.05	1.87	-3.85	0.51	-187.09	-124.89	-296.41	-151.14	-0.803	10.674
	(-0.50)	(0.95)	(-1.04)	(0.29)	(-3.98)	(-2.82)	(-3.59)	(-3.61)	(-0.38)	(2.71)

OCC3	-0.42 (-0.10)	0.97 (0.26)	-12.03 (-1.77)	-0.83 (-0.24)	-82.52 (-0.92)	-50.90 (-0.61)	-275.31 (-1.80)	-89.71 (-1.13)	-3.140 (-0.77)	9.01 (1.22)
OCC4	1.40 (0.34)	1.45 (0.38)	-1.01 (-0.14)	3.64 (1.05)	-207.36 (-2.24)	-203.87 (-2.34)	-371.17 (-2.24)	-155.20 (-1.88)	-1.380 (-0.36)	12.111 (1.76)
Health characteristics										
IMP	-8.85 (-18.57)	-10.52 (-11.23)			-185.00 (-17.35)	-232.55 (-11.10)			14.974 (31.74)	18.296 (17.93)
PREVENT				-64.54 (-29.61)				-1245.4 (-24.61)		
LIMIT				-7.13 (-3.96)				-288.94 (-6.87)		
IMP × OCC2			2.04 (1.87)				60.97 (2.49)			-4.055 (-3.51)
IMP × OCC3			4.61 (2.32)				81.30 (1.83)			-4.415 (-2.10)
IMP × OCC4			1.00 (0.47)				61.34 (1.27)			-4.768 (-2.51)
Intercept	351.7 (25.31)	357.1 (27.54)	361.9 (27.42)	320.7 (27.07)	8232.2 (26.49)	8334.6 (28.53)	8477.6 (28.54)	7683.9 (27.71)	-48.57 (-3.62)	-58.19 (-4.27)
R^2 (adj.)	0.244	0.342	0.343	0.455	0.286	0.369	0.370	0.436	0.377	0.380
Number of respondents	2318	2318	2318	2318	2275	2275	2275	2275	2157	2157

[a] All respondents

121

Table 4A.4
Cross-Sectional Estimates of Hours and Wage Equations, 1976[a] (t-values in parentheses)

Independent variables	Dependent variables							
	HOURS				LN WAGE			
	1	2	3	4	5	6	7	8
Family and human capital characteristics								
AGE	-14.60	-15.04	-15.21	-15.43	-0.002	-0.002	-0.002	-0.002
	(-3.16)	(-3.26)	(-3.29)	(-3.36)	(-1.27)	(-1.31)	(-1.27)	(-1.47)
WHITE	62.95	63.10	62.35	69.17	0.066	0.065	0.065	0.067
	(1.18)	(1.19)	(1.17)	(1.31)	(3.34)	(3.34)	(3.30)	(3.43)
MAR2	-105.45	-105.30	-106.92	-97.73	-0.053	-0.052	-0.052	-0.050
	(-1.97)	(-1.97)	(-2.00)	(-1.83)	(-2.67)	(-2.66)	(-2.65)	(-2.58)
MAR3	-14.11	-30.07	-27.96	-25.63	-0.197	-0.200	-0.200	-0.204
	(-0.13)	(-0.29)	(-0.27)	(-0.25)	(-5.28)	(-5.36)	(-5.35)	(-5.49)
RETIRE	-953.54	-929.31	-932.95	-919.17	-0.174	-0.169	-0.170	-0.158
	(-16.31)	(-15.82)	(-15.80)	(-15.51)	(-8.02)	(-7.76)	(-7.77)	(-7.20)
NONSOUTH	-37.19	-33.04	-33.05	-46.15	0.028	0.028	0.028	0.025
	(-1.06)	(-0.95)	(-0.95)	(-1.33)	(2.14)	(2.21)	(2.19)	(1.93)
SCHOOL	-5.27	-5.33	-5.41	-4.56	0.022	0.022	0.022	0.022
	(-1.00)	(-1.02)	(-1.03)	(-0.87)	(11.26)	(11.26)	(11.21)	(11.47)
TRN1	50.02	50.47	49.62	45.89	0.044	0.044	0.044	0.043
	(1.27)	(1.28)	(1.26)	(1.17)	(3.03)	(3.04)	(3.01)	(2.97)
TRN2	184.24	163.49	162.91	185.46	0.024	0.020	0.017	0.025
	(1.18)	(1.05)	(1.05)	(1.20)	(0.42)	(0.35)	(0.29)	(0.44)
OFINC	-0.001	-0.001	-0.001	-0.001				
	(-0.59)	(-0.56)	(-0.55)	(-0.36)				
Job characteristics								
UNION	-36.03	-37.88	-38.02	-34.72	0.100	0.101	0.100	0.100
	(-0.96)	(-1.02)	(-1.02)	(-0.93)	(7.34)	(7.33)	(7.27)	(7.29)

	(1)	(2)	(3)	(4)	(5)	(6)	(7)	(8)
TEN	3.81 (2.89)	3.62 (2.76)	3.53 (2.67)	4.14 (3.16)	0.003 (6.61)	0.003 (6.51)	0.003 (6.43)	0.003 (6.83)
JOBSAT	54.32 (0.90)	23.10 (0.38)	28.26 (0.46)	40.17 (0.67)	0.020 (0.93)	0.014 (0.64)	0.014 (0.62)	0.014 (0.66)
OCC2	−204.51 (−5.08)	−193.40 (−4.80)	−256.48 (−3.09)	−188.82 (−4.70)	−0.086 (−5.80)	−0.084 (−5.65)	−0.094 (−3.06)	−0.081 (−5.49)
OCC3	−99.78 (−1.55)	−86.71 (−1.35)	−131.01 (−1.07)	−87.52 (−1.37)	−0.083 (−3.57)	−0.081 (−3.47)	−0.107 (−2.39)	−0.079 (−3.42)
OCC4	−241.97 (−3.52)	−241.18 (−3.53)	−267.89 (−1.55)	−237.50 (−3.48)	−0.066 (−2.64)	−0.065 (−2.64)	−0.008 (−0.14)	−0.065 (−2.64)
Health characteristics								
IMP		−41.83 (−3.06)	−57.38 (−2.48)			−0.008 (−1.62)	−0.010 (−1.22)	
PREVENT				−496.26 (−3.59)				−0.124 (−2.47)
LIMIT				−92.78 (−2.48)				−0.044 (−3.20)
IMP × OCC2			26.32 (0.87)				0.004 (0.37)	
IMP × OCC3			18.96 (0.45)				0.010 (0.67)	
IMP × OCC4			11.72 (0.17)				−0.024 (−1.03)	
Intercept	3013.0 (10.32)	3162.3 (10.73)	3206.8 (10.69)	3075.5 (10.59)	2.506 (23.44)	2.534 (23.41)	2.539 (23.07)	2.535 (23.79)
R^2 (adj.)	0.319	0.324	0.323	0.329	0.438	0.439	0.439	0.445
Number of respondents	1082	1082	1082	1082	1066	1066	1066	1066

[a] Employed wage and salary workers.

123

Table 4A.5
Change in Hours and Wage Equations, 1971–1976 (t-values in parentheses)

Independent variable	Changes in hours worked					Change in (log) wages				
	1	2	3	4	5	6	7	8	9	10
HOURS 71	0.26	0.25	0.26	0.27	0.25					
	(3.95)	(3.82)	(3.98)	(4.05)	(3.83)					
LN WAGE 71						0.674	0.696	0.425	0.678	0.694
						(12.79)	(13.37)	(14.72)	(12.89)	(13.55)
TRN1	64.38	73.61	55.63	79.18	76.25	0.205	0.192	0.192	0.191	0.201
	(0.60)	(0.70)	(0.52)	(0.74)	(0.71)	(2.91)	(2.73)	(3.26)	(2.70)	(2.88)
TRN2	−202.24	−139.47	−193.35	−182.16	−182.19	0.052	0.057	−0.062	0.031	0.051
	(−0.68)	(−0.48)	(−0.66)	(−0.62)	(−0.63)	(0.17)	(0.19)	(−0.26)	(0.10)	(0.17)
DELMTL	134.68	197.97	157.70	136.70	157.36	0.063	0.073	0.015	0.074	0.061
	(0.75)	(1.12)	(0.88)	(0.77)	(0.89)	(0.80)	(0.91)	(0.19)	(0.93)	(0.78)
DELDEP	−217.34	−224.34	−226.94	−228.33	−225.69	−0.111	−0.103	−0.051	−0.109	−0.116
	(−2.51)	(−2.65)	(−2.63)	(−2.66)	(−2.65)	(−2.33)	(−2.16)	(−1.16)	(−2.26)	(−2.44)
DELOCC	2.90	52.90	13.82	27.77	31.94	0.027	0.135	0.008	0.025	0.026
	(0.03)	(0.59)	(0.15)	(0.31)	(0.36)	(0.54)	(0.27)	(0.18)	(0.49)	(0.53)
DELIND	−133.90	−88.63	−100.87	−126.87	−104.53	0.026	0.122	0.083	0.016	0.025
	(−1.30)	(−0.87)	(−0.97)	(−1.23)	(−1.02)	(0.45)	(0.21)	(1.69)	(0.27)	(0.45)
DELCJS	477.23	425.90	473.86	499.17	479.95	0.114	0.118	0.111	0.116	0.118
	(4.68)	(4.25)	(4.72)	(4.97)	(4.83)	(1.93)	(1.98)	(2.04)	(1.95)	(2.00)
DELRTS	−1,186.0	−1,119.3	−1,165.2	−1,147.4	−1,124.4	−0.234	−0.248	−0.226	−0.241	−0.227
	(−11.90)	(−11.28)	(−11.69)	(−11.44)	(−11.23)	(−2.94)	(−3.12)	(−3.28)	(−3.00)	(−2.86)
DELRES	75.90	71.21	65.20	106.25	75.07	0.299	0.307	0.146	−.304	0.302
	(0.53)	(0.51)	(0.46)	(0.74)	(0.53)	(3.13)	(3.19)	(1.92)	(3.15)	(3.18)
DELOFI	0.004	0.005	0.004	0.004	0.005					
	(0.88)	(1.11)	(0.91)	(0.84)	(1.07)					

	(1)	(2)	(3)	(4)	(5)	(6)	(7)	(8)	(9)	(10)
WHITE	202.50	175.54	179.90	222.56	206.08	0.053	0.056	0.058	0.068	0.063
	(1.08)	(0.96)	(0.97)	(1.20)	(1.12)	(0.99)	(1.04)	(0.73)	(1.25)	(1.19)
DELHTI				−173.25					−0.142	
				(0.91)					(−1.71)	
DELHT3				61.09					−0.138	
				(0.31)					(−1.58)	
DELHT4				−224.43					−0.094	
				(−0.84)					(−0.70)	
HL3YRI					−52.34					−0.057
					(−0.32)					(−0.56)
HL3YR2					−271.58					−0.112
					(−3.11)					(−2.38)
IMP71	−8.10					−0.018				
	(−0.50)					(1.59)				
IMP76		−69.31					0.006			
		(−3.42)					(0.86)			
DIMP2			−23.90					0.035		
			(−0.21)					(0.63)		
DIMP3			170.72					0.135		
			(1.69)					(2.77)		
Intercept	919.8	1,083.2	800.4	890.6	958.7	1.631	1.392	1.296	1.654	1.479
	(2.75)	(3.36)	(2.46)	(2.39)	(3.00)	(4.55)	(3.92)	(4.07)	(4.58)	(4.34)
R^2 (adj)	0.586	0.605	0.592	0.593	0.600	0.661	0.658	0.717	0.658	0.665
Number of respondents	253	253	253	253	253	182	182	182	182	182

Table 4A.6
Means and Standard Deviations of Variables in Cross-Sectional Labor Supply, Self-Reported Work Limitation (PROBLIM), and Wage Equations, 1976

Variables	HOURS OR PARTIC		PROBLIM		WAGES	
	Mean	SD	Mean	SD	Mean	SD
AGE	61.4	4.3	61.5	4.2	59.5	3.6
WHITE	0.912	0.284	0.695	0.460	0.901	0.299
NONSOUTH	0.680	0.467	0.593	0.491	0.697	0.460
MAR2	0.108	0.310	0.135	0.342	0.090	0.286
MAR3	0.034	0.181	0.032	0.176	0.023	0.149
SCH	10.6	3.6	9.7	3.9	11.0	3.5
TRN1	0.151	0.359			0.219	0.414
TRN2	0.012	0.108			0.001	0.097
OFINC	7,476	7,720	6,752	6,993	6,215	6,453
RETIRE					0.089	0.286
CLASS	0.811	0.392	0.822	0.383		
UNION					0.317	0.466
TENURE					16.1	12.2
JOBSAT					0.929	0.257
OCC2	0.470	0.499	0.539	0.499	0.399	0.490
OCC3	0.054	0.227	0.050	0.218	0.071	0.257
OCC4	0.054	0.226	0.062	0.241	0.065	0.246
IMP	2.98	1.77	3.11	1.87	2.40	1.13
PREVENT	0.159	0.366			0.012	0.110
LIMIT	0.238	0.426			0.211	0.408
IMP × OCC2	1.556	2.15	1.830	2.257	1.017	1.465
IMP × OCC3	0.159	0.804	0.149	0.792	0.181	0.782
IMP × OCC4	0.161	0.791	0.196	0.922	0.152	0.630
PARTIC	65.5	47.5				
HOURS	1,344.0	1,081.9			2,014.8	596.5
PROBLIM			42.7	49.5		
LN WAGES					2.736	0.239

Table 4A.7

Means and Standard Deviations of Variables in Longitudinal Hours and Wage Equations, 1971–1976

Variables	HOURS		WAGES	
	Mean	SD	Mean	SD
HOURS71	2,269.6	645.0		
LNWAGE71			6.192	0.497
TRN1	0.189	0.392	0.133	0.340
TRN2	0.020	0.140	0.005	0.074
DELMTL	0.943	0.233	0.905	0.294
DELDEP	0.586	0.494	0.526	0.501
DELOCC	0.592	0.492	0.597	0.492
DELIND	0.696	0.461	0.711	0.454
DELCJS	0.633	0.483	0.778	0.417
DELRET	0.395	0.490	0.104	0.306
DELRES	0.906	0.292	0.938	0.242
DELOF1	−5,084.7	9,453.6		
WHITE	0.948	0.223	0.742	0.438
DELHT1	0.637	0.482	0.585	0.494
DELHT3	0.267	0.443	0.284	0.452
DELHT4	0.044	0.205	0.043	0.204
HL3YR1	0.069	0.254	0.053	0.224
HL3YR2	0.444	0.498	0.364	0.482
IMP71	4.342	2.646	3.415	2.035
IMP76	3.472	2.177	5.474	3.169
DUMP2	0.264	0.441	0.238	0.427
DUMP3	0.454	0.499	0.477	0.501
HOURS76	1,475.2	1,002.2		
LNWAGE76			6.186	0.511

1. See, for example, Davis (1972, 1973); Berkowitz and Johnson (1974); Grossman and Benham (1974); Scheffler and Iden (1974); Luft (1975, 1978); Elesh and Lefcowitz (1977); Parsons (1977); and Kalachek, Mellow, and Raines (1978).

2. See, for example, Boskin (1977) and Campbell and Campbell (1976) on the relationship between retirement decisions and the social security system, and see Berkowitz, Johnson, and Murphy (1976) and chapter 5 in this volume on the impact of disability transfers.

3. See the authors' working paper (1978) for a discussion of the theoretical grounding of the health variable.

4. See Sullivan (1966).

5. They, or some variant thereof, have been employed in studies by Scheffler and Iden (1974); Luft (1975, 1978); Elesh and Lefcowitz (1977), and NLS researchers.

6. See, for example, studies by Grossman and Benham (1974) and by Parsons (1977). In the first case, these self-ratings were combined with reported number of chronic conditions into an index of ill health; in the latter, they were introduced as a set of dummy predictors per se.

7. For example, "I rate my health as excellent, assuming that I maintain my white-collar office job and am not required to do strenuous physical labor." Since self-report measures are not usually adjusted in this fashion, they probably produce a misleading picture of differences in health status.

8. Berkowitz and Johnson (1974), for example, incorporated self-reported difficulties in physical function (difficulties in walking, stooping, reaching) and several indicators of psychological functioning into labor force participation equations.

9. Specifically, Berkowitz and Johnson introduced the impairments (difficulty in walking, reaching,) as individual dummy predictors into labor outcome equations. Inspection of the estimated regression coefficients suggests that this procedure yields inappropriate results. In particular, a number of the coefficients had the "wrong" algebraic signs or were insignificant, a result no doubt caused by substantial multicollinearity among the predictors.

10. Impairment items are limited to items in questions 47a and 47b. We choose to refer to functional limitations as impairments not only because this term is less cumbersome but also because we wish to measure postpathogenic consequences of illness or injury episodes. Functional limitations such as the inability to walk or handle heavy objects are proxies of residual impairments in physiological or psychological function. It is these residual impairments, of course, that are of importance from a conceptual viewpoint. For some background on this nomenclature see Nagi (1969) and Haber (1967).

11. Compare Nagi (1976).

12. Respondents who reported at least one impairment in 1976 averaged 3.75 activity limitations and 2.36 signs or symptoms, for a total of 6.11 impairments. A descriptive account of the clustering of these multiple impairments is cumbersome; moreover, given the development of the impairment index later in this chapter, it is not an altogether fruitful exercise.

13. The primary subsample is the 1976 cross section, which includes all members of the sample who were interviewed in 1976. The index for the 1971 cross section covers only individuals who reported a work-limiting health problem in 1971, for only these respondents were asked the questions relating to impairments.

14. The relevant questions, in addition to those relating to impairment, are of two types: (1) self-rating of health status available from the 1966 survey and (2) responses to work limitation questions asked in the 1966, 1971, and 1976 surveys.

15. Derived from question 47h in the 1976 interview schedule.

16. Problems associated with the data normalization procedures that have been used preclude a straightforward comparison. We have used the 1971 index scores (weights) and the 1976 impairments to categorize the respondents in 1976, which permits comparisons to be made in the metric of the 1971 results. See the appendix to this chapter for a fuller discussion of the problem.

17. Our method of classifying occupations was made possible by a question in the 1976 survey that obtained data from employed workers on activities performed on the job. These activities are identical to the items requested in the activity limitations question. Consequently, the 1976 survey permits the identification of the demand for and the supply of activities of respondents and thus the degree to which the market values health-related attributes or penalizes individuals who are unable to perform particular tasks. These data are clustered by principal-components analysis in a manner similar to the construction of the impairment indexes. The clusters and general procedure used in obtaining them are set out in the appendix to this chapter. For a discussion of need to include interaction terms in an analysis of this kind, see our working paper (1978) as well as Luft (1978).

18. In more formal terms, the cross-sectional models are specified as

$$\text{Outcome} = \alpha_0 + \alpha_1 \text{ IMP} + \sum_{j=1}^{3} \alpha_{2j} (\text{IMP} \cdot \text{OCC}_j) + \sum_{k=3}^{K} \alpha_k X_k + U,$$

where x_k is an element of the vector X of control variables. See appendix tables 4A.3 and 4A.4 for the specific variables included in the control set and see the glossary in appendix A for a complete description of each variable. All tests of hypotheses, unless otherwise indicated, are one-tail tests at an $\alpha = 0.05$ level of significance. The parameters of all equations are estimated by ordinary least squares.

19. We acknowledge that the characteristics of the sample of older men are not exactly suited for these purposes. One reason is that a sizable proportion of the individuals retired during the period in question, and changes in labor supply and wage accompanying partial or complete retirement decisions are likely to obscure the relationship under study. Another reason is that the longitudinal subsample is almost certainly in poor health at the beginning of the period, since it includes only individuals who reported a work-limiting health problem in 1971. Moreover, we have difficulty in comparing impairment index values at different points in time. For all these reasons, hypotheses about the longitudinal implications or consequences of impairments are not easily tested.

20. We can summarize the longitudinal models of changes, or first differences, among the outcome variables as

$$\text{Outcome } 76 = \beta_0 + \beta_1 \text{ Outcome } 71 + \sum_{l=2}^{L} \beta_l y_l + \epsilon$$

where the y_l's are elements in a Y vector of change variables. See appendix table 4A.5 for the variables included in the Y vector, and see the Glossary (appendix A) for a complete description of each variable.

21. See appendix tables 4A.3 and 4A.4.

22. Table 4.6 focuses only on parameters of special interest; the full set of parameter estimates is given in appendix tables 4A.3 and 4A.4,

while the means and standard deviations are given in appendix table 4A.6.

23. In interpreting this evidence, recall that the four occupational categories were derived by means of a principal-components analysis of the physical activities reported by the incumbents of each occupation. In the regressions the omitted category includes the most sedentary occupations, while the included categories are more demanding in physical terms.

24. They may also be attributable to the specifications of the models. Preliminary regressions testing the "drift" hypothesis (Harkey, Miles, and Rushing, 1976) suggest that the impairment status of older men is affected by their early socioeconomic conditions, including educational attainment.

25. The complete equations are given in appendix table 4A.5; the means and standard deviations of the variables are found in table 4A.7.

26. These specifications were necessitated by the problems involved in taking the difference between two impairment indexes with different distributions. The change-in-impairment dummy variables were constructed by weighting 1976 impairments by 1971 index weights so that changes in categories based on the 1971 impairment status distribution could be ascertained. Improvement in impairment status is defined as any state less severe in 1976 than in 1971; status deterioration is defined as any change to a more severe category over this period. The omitted or reference group consists of men whose impairment status category did not change between 1971 and 1976.

27. These estimates are based upon the regression coefficients reported in columns 2 and 6 of appendix table 4A.3. They assume that the individual is average in the sense that he is (a) slightly more than 61 years of age (the sample mean); (b) white; (c) married; (d) resides outside the South; (e) has completed 12 years of formal schooling; (f) has a mean level of other family income; (g) is a wage and salary worker; and (h) is in a blue-collar occupation demanding a reasonable amount of physical activity (OCC_2). The calculations compare proportional changes in dependent variables between men with no impairments and those with moderate impairment.

28. These predictions are based on the regression coefficients reported in columns 2 and 6 of appendix table 4A.4 and the assumed characteristics of the average worker given in note 28. The lower bound of earnings loss is defined as the proportional reduction in predicted wages times predicted hours between men with no impairments and those who are moderately impaired. The upper bound is obtained by adjusting for the predicted labor force participation rate. Since the estimates are presented simply as illustrations of the empirical results, we ignore the set of bounds formed by the standard errors of the estimate.

29. To achieve comparability, we used the PROBLIM function (column 7 of table 4.6) to predict the impairment value at which the odds favor a blue-collar worker with the average characteristics (note 28) reporting a work-limiting health problem. This value falls at the lower bound of the moderate impairment category; it was used in the predictions of outcome differences using the impairment equations. The predictions reported here, consequently, have been prepared on the basis of the coefficients given in table 4.6, columns 11 and 14, and adjusted for the labor force participation rate predicted from column 3 in that table.

30. Grossman and Benham (1974) and Nagi (1976).

31. Kendall and Lazarsfeld (1950).

References

Berkowitz, M., and Johnson, G. 1974. Health and labor force participation. *Journal of Human Resources* 9 (Winter): 117–128.

Berkowitz, M., Johnson, W. G., and Murphy, E. H. 1976. *Public policy toward disability*. New York: Praeger Publishers.

Boskin, M. 1977. Social security and retirement decisions. *Economic Inquiry* 15 (January): 1–25.

Campbell, C. D., and Campbell, R. G. 1976. Conflicting views on the effect of old-age and survivors insurance on retirement. *Economic Inquiry* 14 (September): 369–388.

Chirikos, T., and Nestel, G. 1978. Impairment, work disability, and labor supply. Mimeographed. Columbus, Ohio: The Ohio State University, Center for Human Resource Research.

Davis, J. M. 1972. Impact of health on earnings and labor market activity. *Monthly Labor Review* 95 (October): 46–49.

————. 1973. Health and the education-earnings relationship. *Monthly Labor Review* 96 (April): 61–63.

Elesh, D., and Lefcowitz, M. J. 1977. The effects of health on the supply of and returns to labor. In H. W. Watts and A. Rees, eds., *The New Jersey income-maintenance experiment. vol. 2: Labor-supply responses*, pp. 289–319. New York: Academic Press.

Grossman, M., and Benham, L. 1974. Health, hours, and wages. In M. Perlman, ed., *The economics of health and medical care*, pp. 205–233. New York: Halsted Press.

Haber, L. 1967. Identifying the disabled: concepts and methods in the measurement of disability. *Social Security Bulletin* 30 (December): 17–34.

Harkey, J., Miles, D., and Rushing, W. A. 1976. The relation between social class and functional status: a new look at the drift hypothesis. *Journal of Health and Social Behavior* 17 (September): 194–204.

Kalachek, E., Mellow, W., and Raines, F. 1978. The male labor supply function reconsidered. *Industrial and Labor Relations Review* 31 (April): 356–367.

Kendall, P., and Lazarsfeld, P. F. 1950. Problems of survey analysis. In R. K. Merton and P. F. Lazarsfeld, eds., *Continuities in social research*, pp. 133–196. Glencoe, Ill.: Free Press.

Luft, H. S. 1975. The impact of poor health on earnings. *Review of Economics and Statistics* 67 (February): 43–57.

————. 1978. *Poverty and health*. Cambridge, Mass.: Ballinger.

Nagi, S. 1969. *Disability and rehabilitation*. Columbus, Ohio: Ohio State University Press.

————. 1976. Epidemiology of disability among adults in the United States. *Milbank Memorial Fund Quarterly* 54 (Fall): 439–467.

Parsons, D. O. 1977. Health, family structure, and labor supply. *American Economic Review* 67 (September): 703–712.

Scheffler, R. M., and Iden, G. 1974. The effect of disability on labor supply. *Industrial and Labor Relations Review* 28 (October): 122–132.

Sullivan, D. F. 1966. Conceptual problems in developing an index of health. *Vital and health statistics: data evaluation and methods research*. Washington, D.C.: U.S. Department of Health, Education, and Welfare.

Chapter 5

Black-White
Differences
in Labor Force
Participation
of Older Males

Donald O. Parsons

Racial differences in earnings are an issue of considerable interest to economists and the public.[1] A number of economists, most notably Welch (1973) and Smith and Welch (1977), have noted recent trends in the racial inequality of income among males which suggest that the inequality is diminishing at a measurable if not dramatic rate. The main evidence for this conjecture is the increasing black-white relative wage ratios among young workers. One troublesome labor market trend that has run counter to the trend toward racial equality of income has been the decline in labor force participation among older blacks. While a secular decline in labor force participation among white males also seems to be occurring, the rate of decline and the absolute level of nonparticipation in the labor force are higher for blacks.

The magnitude of the problem is illustrated in figure 5.1, in which nonparticipation levels of black and white males are graphed for three age groups over the period 1954 to 1976. The most dramatic increases in nonparticipation have occurred among those 55 to 64 (figure 5.1, panel c). For blacks in this age group nonparticipation in the labor force has risen from 17 percent to 30 percent while for whites nonparticipation has risen from 11 percent to 22 percent. Some of the increase in this age group represents voluntary retirement; however, similar trends exist for younger male cohorts in which retirement as traditionally conceived is likely to be rare. Black male nonparticipation has risen from 7 percent to 15 percent in the 45–54 age group (panel b) and from 3 percent to 9 percent in the 35–44 category (panel a) over this 22-year span. White male nonparticipation has only risen from 3 percent to 7 percent in the 45–54 age range and from 2 percent to 3 percent in the younger group. The majority of the nonparticipators did not work at all in the preceding year; thus the magnitude of the potential resource losses becomes even more apparent.

As in many other areas of economic inquiry, cross-sectional analyses of the labor force participation of prime-age males give few clues to the determinants of these secular trends. Bowen and Finegan (1969), for example, identify marital status, race, education, and more tentatively health status as major determinants of participation in this age group.[2] Most of the factors identified, unfortunately, had secular trends that would have increased labor force participation. The fraction of married males in these age groups has generally increased, and education

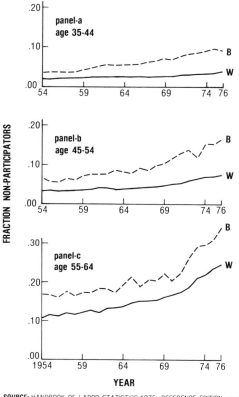

SOURCE: HANDBOOK OF LABOR STATISTICS 1975 REFERENCE EDITION, pp. 34-35
AND HANDBOOK OF LABOR STATISTICS 1977, pp. 30-31

Figure 5.1
Rates of Nonparticipation in the Labor Force of Older Males, by Age and
Race, 1954–1976

levels and health condition have improved, all of which would
tend to raise participation.

One factor that has risen substantially over the period is the
availability of transfer income for those who do not work. It
seems reasonable to suppose that the presence of an increasingly attractive social insurance or social assistance benefit as an
alternative would reduce the work effort of those who would
otherwise earn low incomes in the labor market. Given that
blacks are disproportionately among the low income earners,
this transfer income factor would also explain the differentially
greater decline among blacks. This general issue, of course, is of
considerable interest to a number of economists, particularly
with reference to the negative income tax debate, although ef-

133

forts to date do not suggest any consistently strong effects on work effort of such subsidies.[3] Nonetheless, the working hypothesis of this study is that the secular increase in nonlabor force participation results from the rise in potential transfer income relative to market earnings and that racial differences in labor force participation can be fully explained by the relatively poor market position of blacks.

Labor Force Participation

U.S. Census Data

The transfer income hypothesis implies that groups with the lowest incomes should have the highest and most rapidly growing levels of nonparticipation. Published census data tend to support this implication. Education levels are used as the principal measure of the economic position of these older males, since income itself obviously depends on labor force participation.

Figure 5.2 shows labor force participation rates by educational level and race for three age groups of males. The graphs illustrate the strong relationship between education and nonparticipation. In the group aged 55 to 64, for example, the nonparticipation rate for both blacks and whites varies from 30 percent of those with 0 to 7 years of schooling to 10 percent of those with 16 years or more of schooling. Similar systematic differences, although of smaller magnitude, exist for the younger age cohorts.

Some behavioral differences between blacks and whites are evident in the census data. Because blacks aged 55 to 64 have substantially less schooling than whites, one would predict lower rates of labor force participation for them even if they had similar education-participation relationships, given the positive relationship between schooling and participation. The data graphed in figure 5.2, however, indicate that participation rates for blacks are somewhat lower than for whites with the same level of education.

The rate of increase in nonparticipation also depends strongly and negatively on education level. The change in participation by education level between 1960 and 1970 is charted in figure 5.3. For all age-race groups the rate of participation of those with 16 or more years of schooling was unchanged over the decade of the 1960s. The largest decrease in the participation of 55- to 64-year-old males (from 5 percent to 7 percent), occurred

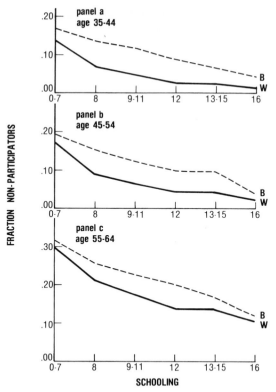

SOURCE: EMPLOYMENT STATUS AND WORK EXPERIENCE, 1970 CENSUS
SUBJECT REPORT PC(2)-6A, 98-101.

Figure 5.2
Rates of Nonparticipation in the Labor Force of Older Males, by Age,
Race, and Years of Schooling, 1970

among the group with fewer than 8 years of schooling. Similar
patterns hold in the lower age intervals.

The transfer income argument suggests that the participation
rate of a group of workers should be inversely related to the
fraction of workers in that group with potential incomes low
enough to make transfer payments an attractive alternative to
work. Figure 5.4 illustrates the relationship between nonparticipation and the fraction of full-time workers in each schooling
group with incomes less than $3,000 in 1970. The results sug-
gest a consistent linear relationship between these two measures. A rise of one-tenth (0.10) in the fraction of full-time
workers with incomes less than $3,000 is associated with a rise

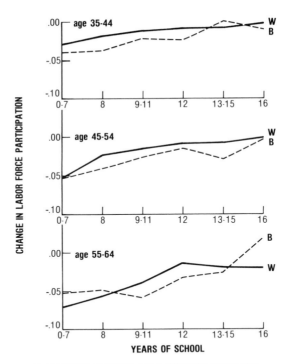

SOURCE: EDUCATIONAL ATTAINMENT, 1960 CENSUS REPORT PC(2)-5B, 54-57.
EMPLOYMENT STATUS AND WORK EXPERIENCE, 1970 CENSUS REPORT PC (2)-6A, 98-101.

Figure 5.3
Change in Labor Force Participation Rates of Older Males, by Age, Race, and Years of Schooling, 1960–1970

of 0.20 in the fraction of the age-race group who are nonparticipators in the market.

That the behavioral relationship is similar for blacks and whites is apparent from figure 5.4, where data points for blacks are denoted by a square and for whites by a circle. They appear to fall on the same imaginary line. The only possible outlier is the point for blacks with 0 to 8 years of schooling, who are in the market to a greater extent than would be suggested by their concentration in the low income range. If a linear function were fitted to the other data points, the predicted nonparticipation rate from that function would be almost 40 percent for black males 55 to 64 with eight or fewer years of schooling rather than the observed 30 percent.

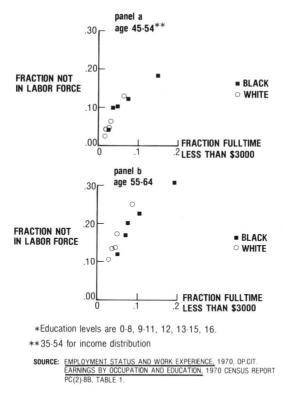

panel a
age 45-54**

.30

.20

FRACTION NOT
IN LABOR FORCE

.10

.00

0   .1   .2

FRACTION FULLTIME
LESS THAN $3000

■ BLACK
○ WHITE

panel b
age 55-64

.30

.20

FRACTION NOT
IN LABOR FORCE

.10

.00

0   .1   .2

FRACTION FULLTIME
LESS THAN $3000

■ BLACK
○ WHITE

*Education levels are 0-8, 9-11, 12, 13-15, 16.

**35-54 for income distribution

SOURCE: EMPLOYMENT STATUS AND WORK EXPERIENCE, 1970, OP.CIT.
EARNINGS BY OCCUPATION AND EDUCATION, 1970 CENSUS REPORT
PC(2)-8B, TABLE 1.

Figure 5.4
Nonparticipation of Older Males in the Labor Force as a Function of
Proportion of Full-Time Workers Earning Less than $3,000 per Year, by
Age, Race, and Years of Schooling, 1970

NLS Data

The NLS surveys provide a somewhat richer data base that is
useful in disentangling the complex interaction of health and
economic conditions influencing the labor force participation decision. Previous analyses of this data set suggest the important
role of health in the labor force participation decision.[4] Few older
males who report themselves to be in good health are out of the
labor force. The participation rate of whites with no health problem was 99.5 percent in 1966 and 96.2 percent in 1971 (when
the cohort was five years older); the corresponding rates for
blacks were 99.7 percent and 97 percent.[5] Health differences by
education are reported in figure 5.5. Clearly, health problems
could go far toward explaining differences in labor force partici-

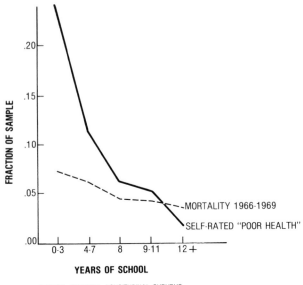

SOURCE: NATIONAL LONGITUDINAL SURVEYS

Figure 5.5
The Incidence of Poor Health and Mortality among Older Males, by
Years of Schooling, 1966

pation by education. The percentage of individuals who report
themselves in poor health falls from 24 percent for males 45 to
59 with 0 to 3 years of education to 2 percent for those with 12
or more years. The three-year mortality rate (1966 to 1969) follows a similar if less dramatic pattern. More than 7 percent of
those with 0 to 3 years of schooling died between 1966 and
1969, while less than 4 percent of those with 12 or more years
died during the same period.

The simple health relationship, however, cannot explain the
declining labor force participation of older males, since health (as
measured, for example, by age-specific mortality rates) has
modestly but consistently improved over time in the United
States. Thus the role of health in the decline of the participation
rate of this group over time is not straightforward. Apparently
the decline, to the extent that it is health related, must involve a
reduction in the rate of participation for a given health condition.
Social security programs that ease the burden of nonparticipation in the labor force among males with health problems could
be expected to induce such reductions. Apparently it is necessary to undertake a multivariate analysis if the forces affecting
labor force participation are to be identified.

Income Levels
and Sources for
Older Males Out
of the Labor Force

In a predominately market economy, indeed in most economies, the principal source of family income and market consumption activities is the labor earnings of family members, particularly the adult male. The question arises whether and how the family can afford to have the adult male out of the labor force. Is consumption correspondingly reduced? Are the earnings of other family members increased through their reduced leisure and home activities? Do transfer programs largely compensate for the reduced earnings?

Comparing the sources and magnitude of income for older males out of the labor force with the incomes of those who remain in makes it possible to develop a crude measure of the economic penalties paid by different racial and schooling groups for withdrawal from the labor force. One would assume that the withdrawal is related to the size of the income penalty. The analysis will also give some indication of the factors—family earnings, types of transfer programs—whose institutional characteristics are most important to include in the formal model.

Table 5.1 shows NLS data on the mean total family incomes in 1965 by race for males in and out of the labor force. Since few older males with more than 12 years of schooling were out of the labor force, and since those who were had very different characteristics (high pension and asset income), the analysis is limited to men with 12 or fewer years of schooling. The evidence from other surveys suggests that transfer income is typically underreported, no doubt reducing the reported income of

Table 5.1
Mean Total Family Income in 1965, by Labor Force Status in Survey Week, 1966, Educational Attainment, and Race[a] (respondents with 12 or fewer years of schooling)

Labor force status, 1966	Total or average	Years of schooling				
		0–3	4–7	8	9–11	12
Whites						
In	$9,196	$5,776	$7,222	$8,183	$9,785	$10,847
Out	4,065	4,114	3,378	3,950	4,605	4,835
Blacks						
In	5,615	3,858	5,139	5,874	7,078	8,157
Out	2,399	2,040	2,710	1,798	3,405	2,407

[a]The sample sizes are 2,197, 150, 1,007, and 106 respectively for whites in and out of the labor force and blacks in and out of the labor force.

Table 5.2
Ratio of Total Family Income: Men out of the Labor Force to Men in the Labor Force, by Educational Attainment and Race (respondents with 12 or fewer years of education)

Race	Total or average	Years of education				
		0–3	4–7	8	9–11	12
Whites	.44	.71	.47	.48	.47	.45
Blacks	.43	.53	.53	.31	.48	.30

Source: Table 5.1.

males out of the labor force relatively more than the income of other males.

The data in table 5.1 suggest that total family income is more than 50 percent lower for families with older males out of the labor force (56 percent for whites and 57 percent for blacks). The proportional reduction in income does not appear to be systematically related to schooling attainment for either racial group, as is indicated in table 5.2. The absolute decline in earnings increases dramatically with schooling, however. The income of whites and blacks with 3 or fewer years of formal schooling is only about $1,800 lower if the older male is not in the labor force. For those with 12 years of schooling income is about $5,500 or $6,000 lower. Indeed for males out of the labor force, total family income rises hardly at all with schooling. The direct link between family income and male schooling is, of course, broken when the worker leaves the labor force, but apparently the more highly educated nonparticipant cannot find methods of augmenting transfers or other family earnings when he withdraws. The economic penalty for withdrawal for more highly skilled workers is therefore correspondingly greater.

Although the older male has withdrawn from the market, family earnings are not zero. The importance of earnings sources for the different racial and labor force participation groups is reported in table 5.3. As one might expect, the older males' earnings as a share of total income drop from about 75 percent for those in the labor force during the survey week to 13 percent for whites out of the labor force and 6 percent for blacks out of the labor force.

The insubstantial annual earnings of the older male who is out of the labor force during the survey week imply that withdrawal from the labor force is a long-term decision. This impression is reinforced by consideration of the weeks spent in the labor force

Table 5.3
Source of Total Family Income in 1965, by Race and Labor Force Status in Survey Week, 1966 (percentage distributions)

Source of income	Whites		Blacks	
	In	Out	In	Out
Number of respondents	2,197	150	1,007	106
Total percentage	100	100	100	100
Respondent's earnings	75	13	74	6
Other family earnings	19	33	22	25
Rent, interest, dividends	3	13	1	2
Pensions	1	4	—[a]	2
Unemployment compensation	1	—[a]	—[a]	1
Disability transfers	1	29	1	48
Welfare	—[a]	4	1	10
Other	1	2	1	6

[a]Percentage is 0.5 or less.

during the preceding year by men who were in and out of the labor force during the survey week of 1966. The distribution of weeks in the labor force for each group is illustrated in figure 5.6. Clearly, the decision to participate in the labor force is at least semipermanent for this age group of men.

This phenomenon may be partly the result of the institutional structure of disability transfer programs. Eligibility for Social Security disability benefits requires proof of "the inability to engage in any substantial gainful activity." Indeed, during the early years of the program, earning as little as $100 per month was deemed sufficient to disprove such inability, while earning $50 to $100 was felt to be ambiguous. There is also an investment aspect to eligibility under this program since there was a six-month waiting period before benefits were paid. (Currently there is a five-month waiting period.)

The earnings of other family members as a share of total family income are 19 percent and 22 percent for whites and blacks, respectively, who are in the labor force, as compared with 33 percent and 25 percent for whites and blacks who are out of the labor force. The income categories that suggest voluntary retirement—pensions, rent, interest, dividends—represent less than 19 percent of the earnings of whites out of the labor force and 4 percent of blacks. Labor force withdrawal in 1966 by this age group of men does not appear to have been explained to any substantial degree by voluntary early retirement.

Social transfer programs account for 33 percent of the family

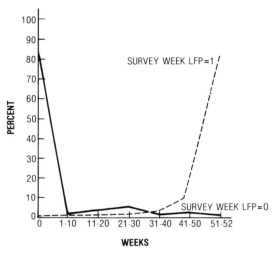

Figure 5.6
Number of Weeks in Labor Force in 1965, by 1966 Survey Week Labor
Force Status (percentage distributions)

income of whites out of the labor force and 59 percent in the
case of blacks. Of these, disability payments are the largest part,
accounting for 29 percent and 48 percent of family income for
whites and blacks respectively. Public assistance accounts for 4
percent and 10 percent of the family income of the two groups.
Most such programs, of course, have been specifically designed
to preclude payments to families with healthy, working-age
males present. Since disability programs provide so much of the
income of this group of men, it is useful to indicate in more detail the specific programs involved. The percentage breakdown
of disability payments by program is reported in table 5.4. More

Table 5.4
Disability Income in 1965 of Respondents out of the Labor Force, by
Source of Income and Race (percentage distributions)

Source of income	Whites	Blacks
Number of respondents	78	64
Total percentage	100	100
Social Security disability	55	60
Veteran's compensation	26	22
Workmen's compensation	2	1
Aid to blind and disabled	5	9
Other	14	8

than half the aid to the disabled comes from Social Security, 55 percent for whites and 60 percent for blacks. Veteran's compensation accounts for an additional 25 percent, which is larger than the combined total contributions of the remaining programs.

Since total family income is sharply lower for males out of the labor force than for those in, a larger share for a given earnings source for the former does not imply that absolute incomes from that source are higher. This point is particularly important for the proper appreciation of the earnings of other family members in total family income. Although such earnings are a larger percentage of total income for males out of the labor force, they are on average smaller in absolute terms than for workers who remain in the labor force. Indeed, other family earnings are 24 percent less for whites out of the labor force than for those in the labor force, while the corresponding ratio for blacks is 51 percent. A major reason for this is that there are relatively fewer married men out of the labor force. Only 75 percent of the white males out of the labor force and 60 percent of the black are married and living with their wives, in contrast to 91 percent and 82 percent of the white and black males, respectively, who are in the labor force.

An Empirical
Model

The preliminary evidence suggests that the downward trend in labor force participation is the result of greater withdrawal from the labor force by low-income individuals who may also be in poor health. In this section the analysis of the market and transfer incentives that affect the withdrawal decision are modeled and the resulting model is then estimated with data from our NLS sample. The more complete analysis requires careful specification of a model of the individual's decision process.[6]

The model for this decision can be treated as a dichotomous choice between participating in the market or not. The propensity for individuals to be permanently in or out of the market in this age-sex group was noted for the NLS sample. Census data suggest a similar process at work. In the 1970 census, for example, about two-thirds (67.1 percent) of those out of the labor force in the 50–54 age interval had no work experience in 1969, while 80.0 percent worked 13 weeks or less. Conversely, 79.6 percent of those in the labor force worked 50 to 52 weeks, and about 93 percent worked 40 or more weeks.

The dichotomous nature of the choice considerably simplifies the analysis. The decision to participate or not to participate in the labor force depends on the relative utilities derived from the two alternatives. Under the traditional consumption-leisure trade-off assumption, the utility from market work is related to labor market earnings, nonlabor income, and leisure, while the utility from nonparticipation depends on nonlabor income, transfer payments, and leisure. The individual then chooses to participate in the labor force only if the utility from working exceeds the utility from not working. This decision is affected by factors such as health, marital status, race, unemployment incidence, and potential Social Security benefits.

To summarize, the determinants of labor force participation include (1) health status, (2) demographic characteristics such as age, marital status, and, of particular interest in this study, race, and (3) economic variables such as market wages and unemployment incidence, potential Social Security disability benefits, and levels of welfare payments.

The model suggests, then, that the decision to withdraw from the labor force depends on a variety of forces, including age, health, transfer income possibilities, and market work opportunities. To assess the importance of these effects and to determine whether these forces explain racial differences in labor force participation requires a multivariate analysis of the decision. Estimates of the effects of health, economic, and other demographic variables on the participation decision of males 45 to 59 years of age in 1966 appear later in this chapter. In the following section the resulting behavioral model is used to project participation rates over the period 1966 to 1976. The projections are then compared with the actual participation behavior of blacks and whites over this period.

The panel aspect of the National Longitudinal Surveys is exploited in a crucial way in the 1966 analysis. In the NLS, as in most large-scale labor market surveys, the only direct health measures are self-reported. Such measures are not likely to be completely accurate in the best of circumstances. More damaging, the health estimates may be biased by economic incentives to misreport. Since the clinical determination of poor health is inexact and since disability benefits are paid only to those determined to be in poor health among those who claim to be in poor health, an otherwise healthy individual who decides to leave the labor force has an incentive to declare himself in poor health. The declaration of poor health may therefore be an economic phenomenon, one that confounds the analysis of the economic determinants of labor force participation. The longitudinal character of the NLS, however, provides an indirect measure of the respondent's health condition in 1966 that is completely objective, namely, the probability of his dying at some time between 1966 and 1976. The effect of subsequent death on 1966 labor force participation was estimated for deaths that were reported at each survey after 1966. These values were then combined into a single mortality index that is used to represent the respondent's 1966 health condition.[7]

The model is estimated in three forms of increasing complexity. At each stage an important issue is whether statistically significant racial differences in labor force participation remain after controlling for the added factors. The gross difference in participation in this sample is about 4 percent—94.5 percent for whites, 90.4 percent for blacks. The first model tests whether this difference is due simply to differences in the age and health structure of the two groups. The second model includes economic factors as well, in particular, the Social Security replacement ratio (the ratio of potential benefits to market wage rate) and the ratio of general welfare availability in the local area (states) to the individual's wage rate. A more complete model is estimated which includes, in addition, marital status, schooling of respondent and of his wife, if married, and a dummy if the individual's current or last job was manual (blue collar).

The models are estimated using probit analysis because that specification of the dichotomous labor market choice follows naturally from a labor force participation decision model.[8] Since individuals currently out of the market are more likely not to report a current or last wage rate, a wage function was estimated and a predicted wage was assigned the individual if a reported wage was not available. The precise form of the wage function is reported in the appendix to this chapter, but essentially the model involves substituting the mean wage of the appropriate age-race-schooling group for the unobserved wage. The potential Social Security benefit measure was constructed from the wage measure, using standard Social Security benefit tables. (See the appendix of this chapter for details.)

The coefficient estimates of the three models are reported in table 5.5. Looking first at the age-health model (column 1), one can see that both age and poor health (indexed by mortality) have powerful negative effects on labor force participation. Controlling for these factors does not eliminate the systematic

Table 5.5
Labor Force Participation of Males 45 to 59 in 1966, Probit Estimates[a]

Variable	(1)	(2)	(3)
CONSTANT	3.935	4.586	3.002
	(10.75)	(11.84)	(6.64)
BLACK[b]	−0.252	−0.0779	0.151
	(4.09)	(1.14)	(2.04)
Price variables			
SSB/W[c]		−0.0172	−0.00650
		(6.36)	˙(2.12)
WEL/W[d]		−0.0004	0.00275
		(0.14)	(0.78)
Demographic variables			
MORTALITY[e]	−1.253	−1.239	−1.138
	(12.01)	(11.77)	(10.48)
AGE[f]	−0.0417	−0.0393	−0.0348
	(6.02)	(5.56)	(4.77)
SCH[g]			0.0521
			(4.93)
MARRIED[h]			0.406
			(2.91)
MARRIED*SCHW[i]			0.0146
			(1.11)
BLUDUM[j]			−0.229
			(2.94)
Log of Likelihood	−1,062	−1,041	−994
Number of Respondents	4751	4751	4794

[a]Absolute values of asymptotic t-ratios in parentheses.
[b]Dummy equal to one if race black, zero otherwise.
[c]The ratio of potential social security benefits to the hourly wage rate (see appendix to this chapter).
[d]The ratio of local welfare to the hourly wage rate (see appendix to this chapter).
[e]An index of poor health; see text and note 7.
[f]Age in years.
[g]Years of schooling completed.
[h]Dummy equal to one if married, spouse present, zero otherwise.
[i]Years of schooling completed by wife times MARRIED.
[j]Dummy equal to one if occupation is blue collar.

racial difference in behavior, however. At the mean values of the independent variables, the black coefficient is still negative and strongly significant. At the mean values of the independent variables, the black rate of participation in the labor force is approximately 3 percent (2.77 percent) less than that for whites.

The second model (column 2) includes two economic variables, the ratio of potential Social Security benefits to wages and the ratio of general welfare to wages. The Social Security measure is powerfully and significantly negative. At the point of means of the independent variables, the elasticity of nonparticipation with respect to the Social Security replacement ratio is 1.6. A 10 percent increase in potential benefits relative to the wage rate will induce a 16 percent increase in nonparticipation.

The racial dummy is also dramatically reduced in magnitude and statistical significance. The black coefficient is reduced by two-thirds, reflecting less than a percentage point difference in participation rates after controlling for the difference in economic conditions of the two racial groups. This difference is not statistically significant. Apparently the differences in participation behavior between the two groups are due largely to differences in their economic position and not to any behavioral differences, given economic conditions.

Estimates of the model with additional economic and demographic variables are reported in column 3. Controlling for factors such as schooling, marital status, and occupation results in a positive estimate of the black coefficient. When these factors are controlled, black men in this age group are more likely than their white counterparts to be in the labor force. Higher participation rates are associated with more schooling, with being married with spouse present, and with being in a nonmanual occupation. Since older blacks are overrepresented in the low schooling, unmarried, and manual occupation groups, the reason for the reduced negative black effect when these variables are added is apparent.

Trends in Nonparticipation

Since the objective of this study is to explain recent increases in nonparticipation in the labor force among prime-age males, particularly black males, the question that naturally arises is how well the model predicts recent trends in nonparticipation. Expected nonparticipation rates for the NLS sample are projected over the period 1966 to 1976 using the 1966 estimated labor force participation model. Then these projections are compared with actual labor force behavior by this group. The extent of correspondence between the projections and actual behavior provides a powerful test of the validity of the underlying model.

Age is a powerful determinant of labor force behavior, yet it is incidental to the trend in nonparticipation of males of given age. Thus the following analysis focuses on a comparison of actual trends and projections for males 55 to 59 years old. This age

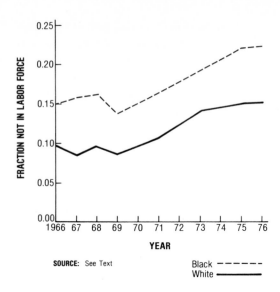

Figure 5.7
Rates of Nonparticipation in the Labor Force of Males 55 to 59 Years of
Age, by Race, 1966–1976

group allows construction of a consistent time series from the
NLS since a 55- to 59-year-old sample is available in every survey year. The nonparticipation rates of blacks and whites 55 to
59 from the NLS sample are reported in figure 5.7. Black nonparticipation rises from 15.0 percent to 22.5 percent, while
white nonparticipation rises from 9.6 percent to 15.2 percent
over the period 1966 to 1976.

The ability to explain time series trends is, of course, a difficult
test for any cross-sectional model. The effects of factors that
are constant at any point in time but vary over time cannot be
estimated in a cross-sectional analysis. In this case the relative
severity of the medical determination of disability under Social
Security is one potentially important factor that may be reasonably uniform at a point in time yet vary significantly over
time. Second, the cross-sectional analysis is assumed to be estimated on a sample in long-run equilibrium and therefore
provides no information on the adjustment lags of behavior (in
this case labor force participation) behind changes in market
conditions.

Time series projections were constructed over the period
1966 to 1976 in the following fashion. Individuals 55 to 59 in
1966 were assumed to have behavioral patterns specified by the

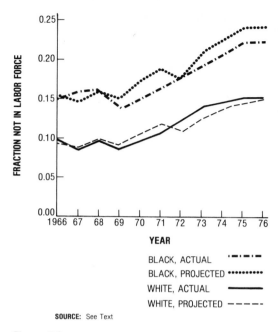

Figure 5.8
Actual and Projected Rate of Nonparticipation in the Labor Force of
Males 55 to 59 Years of Age, by Race, 1966–1976

simple price-health model of labor force participation reported in
table 5.5, column 2. Among the independent variables, age is
held constant in order to characterize the behavior of individuals
of given age. Trends in the remaining independent variables
were constructed in the following way. For mortality, welfare,
and wage rates, the base year (1966) values were adjusted for
each individual by trends in closely related, consistent series.
The wage rate for each year for a given individual, for example,
is his 1966 wage rate times the ratio of personal per capita income in the year in question to personal per capita income in
1966. Potential Social Security benefits were estimated using
the projected wage in the appropriate formula for Social Security
benefits in the year in question.

The projected nonparticipation rates for blacks and whites are
compared in figure 5.8 with the actual nonparticipation rates.
The correspondence is striking. For blacks the projected rate
rises from 15.3 percent in 1966 to 24.3 percent in 1976, and the
actual rate rises from 15.0 percent to 22.5 percent. For whites
the projected rate rises from 9.3 percent to 15.1 percent, the

actual from 9.6 percent to 15.2 percent. Even the most fundamental price-health model performs excellently over this sample
period.

To illustrate the insignificance of race in this process, the
black nonparticipation rate was also projected for the black sample using the "white" model. That is, the race dummy was not
included in the projections. The differences were modest. Even
if blacks behaved precisely as whites, their less favorable economic condition would lead us to predict that their nonparticipation would rise from 13.7 percent in 1966 to 22.1 percent in
1976.

Conclusion
Substantial evidence has been presented that the labor force
participation of males, particularly black males, has been declining because of the increasing generosity of social welfare
transfers, including Social Security disability payments. Census
data indicate that nonparticipation in 1970 and decreases in participation over the decade 1960 to 1970 are concentrated among
low-schooling (low-income potential) groups. An analysis of income sources from the NLS identifies Social Security and other
disability payments as the principal income offset to lost earnings among middle-aged males currently out of the labor force.

The fact that Social Security benefits have become increasingly generous and increasingly progressive (low-wage workers
have relatively high benefits) suggests two hypotheses: that this
program has induced ever-larger numbers of workers to leave
the labor force and that it has affected blacks differentially since
they are overrepresented among prime-age males with low
wage potential.

A multivariate analysis of labor force participation of males 45
to 59 in 1966 confirms these two hypotheses. The ratio of potential Social Security benefits to the market wage has a large
estimated effect on the participation decision. For the average
individual in the sample a 10 percent increase in benefits without a corresponding rise in wage rates will induce a 16 percent
rise in nonparticipation. Moreover, controlling for differences in
the generosity of transfer payments relative to market opportunity eliminates any statistically significant difference in the
participation rate of black and white males.

To test the validity of the model, nonparticipation rates of
males are projected over the period 1966 to 1976. These projections correspond closely with actual rates over this interval.

For the black males 55 to 59 actual nonparticipation in this sample rose from 15.0 percent to 22.5 percent over the period. With the white behavioral model the rate would have been expected to rise from 13.7 percent to 22.1 percent. For the white sample nonparticipation rose from 9.6 percent to 15.2 percent, while the estimated model predicted a rise from 9.3 percent to 15.1 percent.

The conclusion is that the decline in labor force participation for men of this age is due to increasingly attractive alternatives to work, even though the principal program (Social Security disability) appears to be rigidly conditioned by health restrictions. Similarly, the differentially large decline among blacks is due to their relatively poor market opportunities and the increasingly progressive structure of Social Security benefits. From a positive viewpoint, one would predict that if wage rates for blacks and whites do ultimately converge, their labor force participation behavior will converge as well.

The analysis clearly illustrates a general difficulty with social transfers to particular groups. The transfer program creates its own clients as individuals alter their behavior and perhaps even their perceptions of themselves to qualify for the program. The more attractive disability benefits are, the greater the number of individuals who claim to be disabled, and, given the imprecision of clinical health determination, the greater the number certified as disabled. If the social objective is only to provide income to those individuals who cannot provide for themselves under any circumstance, this positive response of "disabled" workers to more generous benefits simply increases the cost of achieving that objective. To the extent that a more prosperous society wishes to relieve less severely disabled workers from the need to work, the increase in claimants may be an additional objective of the program.

Appendix   Construction of Variables

Social Security benefits   This variable represents potential monthly Social Security benefits should the individual qualify as disabled. A recent measure of monthly wages (hourly wages times 168 hours) is used as a measure of the individual's average monthly earnings, and a 1966 benefits table is used to compute a potential Social Security benefits measure. Since wages have risen over the work lives of these individuals, this wage

151

was adjusted downward over the most likely calculation period for covered wages (1955 to 1966) by the growth in per capita personal income to determine an appropriate covered wage.

Welfare benefits   The welfare benefits for which a nonparticipant in the work force may be eligible vary widely from locality to locality and state to state. A state index constructed for 1966 reflects the generosity of the state's welfare programs. The measure is the number of dollars of public assistance (general assistance plus Aid to Families with Dependent Children) paid in each state per family below the poverty line of $3,000.

The wage rate   The wage estimates assigned to individuals for whom no wage rate was reported were derived from the following model, estimated on the 1966 sample. Experimentation with the censoring bias model suggested by Heckman (1977) suggests that the potential bias is not important in this application, perhaps because of the relatively small number out of the labor force (about 7 percent).

Table 5A.1
Log_e Hourly Wage Rate Regression, Males 45 to 59 in 1966

Variable	Coefficient	t-value
CONSTANT	0.709	7.52
AGE 66	−0.00286	−1.68
SCH	0.0580	23.22
BLACK	0.0107	0.27
BLACK*SCH	−0.0251	5.93
R^2	0.32	
SAMPLE SIZE	3,548	

Table 5A.2

Means and Standard Deviations of Variables in the Labor Force
Participation Model

Variable	Mean	Standard deviation
LFP1966	0.934	0.249
BLACK	0.277	0.448
SSB/W	45.54	12.42
WEL/W	10.68	8.45
MORTALITY	0.0868	0.213
AGE	51.51	4.27
SCH	9.34	3.92
MARRIED	0.872	0.334
MARRIED*SCHW	8.98	4.47
BLUDUM	0.632	0.482

Source: Table 5.5, column 3

153

Notes

1. See Masters (1975) and Marshall (1974) for a review of the literature in this area and further references.

2. See, for example, Parsons (1977) and the work cited therein.

3. See Cain and Watts (1973) and the summaries of the New Jersey experiments in Pechman and Timpane (1975).

4. Parsons (1977).

5. Parnes et al. (1974), p. 253.

6. A more detailed description of this model and an elaboration of the statistical methodology can be found in Parsons (1979).

7. Mortality dummies were introduced into a model of labor force participation with the dummy equal to one if the respondent is recorded as deceased during a particular interview interval, zero otherwise. A single mortality index was then constructed by using a weighted average of these dummies, where the weights are the coefficients of the model normalized by the coefficient on the labor force participation effect of death between 1966 and 1967, the first reinterview interval.

The mortality index (MORTALITY) is

$$
\begin{aligned}
\text{MORTALITY} = \text{MORTDUMMY } 66\text{--}67 &+ 0.0524 \text{ MORTDUMMY } 67\text{--}68 \\
&+ 0.747 \text{ MORTDUMMY } 68\text{--}69 \\
&+ 0.593 \text{ MORTDUMMY } 69\text{--}71 \\
&+ 0.560 \text{ MORTDUMMY } 71\text{--}73 \\
&+ 0.286 \text{ MORTDUMMY } 73\text{--}75 \\
&+ 0.270 \text{ MORTDUMMY } 75\text{--}76.
\end{aligned}
$$

8. See Parsons (1979).

References

Bowen, W. G., and Finegan, T. A. 1969. *The economics of labor force participation*. Princeton, N.J.: Princeton University Press.

Cain, G. G., and Watts, H. W., eds. 1973. *Income maintenance and labor supply*. Chicago: Markham Books.

Heckman, J. J. 1977. Sample selection bias as a specification error (with an application to the estimation of labor supply functions). University of Chicago Center for Mathematical Studies in Business and Economics, Report 7720.

Marshall, R. 1974. The economics of racial discrimination: a survey. *Journal of Economic Literature* 12: 849–871.

Masters, S. H. 1975. *Black-white income differentials*. New York: Academic Press.

Parnes, H. S., Adams, A. V., Andrisani, P., Kohen, A. I., and Nestel, G. 1974. *The pre-retirement years*, vol. 4. U.S. Department of Labor Manpower R&D Monograph 15. Washington, D.C.: U.S. Government Printing Office.

Parsons, D. O. 1977. Health, family structure, and labor supply. *American Economic Review* 67.

———. 1979. The male labor force participation decision: health, reported health, and economic incentives. Mimeographed. The Ohio State University.

Pechman, J. A., and Timpane, P. M., eds. 1975. *Work incentives and income guarantees: the New Jersey negative income tax experiment*. Washington, D.C.: The Brookings Institution.

Smith, J. P., and Welch, F. R. 1977. Black/white male wage ratios: 1960–1970. *American Economic Review* 67: 323–338.

Welch, F. R. 1973. Black-white returns to schooling. *American Economic Review* 63: 893–907.

Chapter 6

The Retirement Experience

Herbert S. Parnes
and
Gilbert Nestel

Retirement has become an important public policy issue in recent years and is likely to attract even more attention over the next several decades. The reasons are fairly clear. The labor force participation rate of males 65 years of age and over dropped by half in slightly over two decades, from 40 percent in 1955 to 20 percent in 1978. Among men 60 to 64 years of age the corresponding drop has been from 83 percent to 63 percent. For many years after the Social Security Act was passed, 65 years was regarded as the normal age of retirement. This is changing as more workers choose early retirement under liberalized provisions of the Social Security Act and private pension plans. By the late 1960s half of the newly entitled beneficiaries under the Social Security program were retiring before 65, and the proportion has since risen.[1]

This increase is exacerbated by the increasing proportion of the total population who are in their sixties. The ratio of persons 65 and older to the total population has increased from 8.1 percent in 1950 to 10.7 percent in 1976 and is projected to rise to a range of 12.7 percent to 17.8 percent by the year 2020, depending on the assumptions about the fertility rate. Expressed as a percentage of the population of working age (18 to 64) the projected increase is even more dramatic. According to the intermediate projection of the Census Bureau, the population 65 and over will increase from 18.2 percent of the working-age population in 1977 to 29.6 percent in 2025.[2] These trends have created doubts about society's willingness and ability to accept the implied growing burden of adult dependency.[3] Increasing the retirement age under the Social Security Act and reducing the replacement ratio of benefits to preretirement earnings as real earnings levels rise over time are among the proposals that have been made to reverse the trend toward earlier retirement. The 1978 amendments to the Age Discrimination in Employment Act that prohibit mandatory retirement below the age of 70 are also relevant.

Despite the importance of the problem and the increasing attention it has drawn, a great deal remains to be learned about retirement. The term itself is ambiguous. It is not clear whether retirement is most appropriately conceived as an event, a process, a social role, or a phase of life.[4] At one extreme, the term

We gratefully acknowledge the conscientious research assistance of Mary Gagen, Jacqueline Mercier, and Nan Maxwell.

retirement implies the permanent cessation at some reasonably advanced age of all labor market activity; at the other, it implies simply the termination of a job at a pensionable age even if the individual immediately takes another job involving as many hours of work.

Furthermore, it is hard to be satisfied with what is known about the reasons for retirement. The sharp differences of opinion about the likely impact of the 1978 amendments to the Age Discrimination in Employment Act are testimony to our ignorance about the numbers of individuals under mandatory retirement plans who are truly "involuntarily" retired.[5] As another illustration, the many studies that have cited poor health as the single most important reason for retirement have invariably been based on retrospective questions addressed to retirees, and it is not clear how much post hoc rationalization is involved in their responses.[6]

Finally, relatively little is yet known about postretirement experience and its relation to individual preretirement history.[7] To what extent and under what circumstances do retirees remain in the labor market? When they do, how do their jobs compare with those from which they retired in terms of occupational assignment, wage rate, and number of hours worked? Irrespective of their labor market status, what are the sources of income of retirees, and how does their financial condition compare with their preretirement condition?

Research Objectives

This chapter attempts to fill some of the gaps in our knowledge about the retirement process on the basis of the ten-year records of the NLS sample. Specifically, the research is directed at four major questions.

1. What is the relative importance of the following three routes to retirement: (a) unwilling separation from a job as the result of the application of mandatory retirement provisions; (b) retirement because of health problems; (c) "voluntary" retirement?
2. How do these proportions vary depending on whether one (a) exploits longitudinal data on the respondents' periodic reports on their health, their retirement expectations, and their work histories prior to their retirement or (b) uses retrospective explanations of the retirement decision that were offered by the respondents in the 1976 interview?
3. How does the route to retirement vary according to the

demographic and preretirement employment characteristics of retirees?

4. How is the route to retirement related to postretirement work experience, economic status, attitudes toward retirement, and satisfaction with various aspects of life?

Definition and Categories of Retirement

For this study the criterion of retirement is the individual's report that he had already stopped working at a regular job.[8] In the seven interviews conducted between 1966 and 1976, about 40 percent of the original sample of 5,000 men reported retirements. Of these only about 1,600 were alive and interviewed in the 1976 survey. The latter were representative of 4.7 million men between the ages of 55 and 69 in 1976 who regarded themselves as retired in the sense described here.[9] It is on this group, the 1976 retirees, that most of the analysis focuses.[10] This group cannot be construed to be a representative sample of all retirees as of 1976. Because no one in our sample can be over 69 years of age, individuals who have been retired for long periods of time are not represented. Thus early retirees constitute a larger proportion of this sample than of all retirees, and a smaller proportion of this sample than of all retired males should be expected to receive Social Security and private pension benefits.

Retirees are classified into three major categories: those who were involuntarily retired under a mandatory retirement plan (forced out); those whose retirement appears to have been dictated by poor health; and those who appear freely to have chosen to retire (voluntary retirement). This classification is based, not on respondents' retrospective explanations of their retirement, but on our longitudinal records for each individual up to the time of his reported retirement. The forced-out category is reserved for those who were separated from their jobs against their will by the operation of a mandatory retirement plan, that is, those who (1) were employed in the year prior to their retirement in an establishment with a mandatory plan, (2) retired at the mandatory age, and (3) indicated in the survey preceding retirement that they would have preferred to work beyond the retirement age.

Retirees who did not qualify for inclusion in the forced-out group are classified as having retired for health reasons if there was evidence of work-limiting health problems in the year pre-

157

Table 6.1
Retirees by Route to Retirement, Selected Universes (percentage distributions)

Route to retirement	Total re-tirements 1966–1976	1976 retirees[a]			
		Retired 1966–1976	Retired 1966–1975	Retired 1967–1975	Retired 1967–1976
Number of respondents	2,016	1,584	1,326	1,211	1,469
Total percent	100	100	100	100	100
Forced out[b]	3	3	3	3	3
Poor health[c]	51	46	47	45	44
Voluntary	46	51	50	52	53
Early[d]	32	35	35	36	36
Normal[e]	14	16	15	16	17

[a]Men who had reported themselves retired sometime between 1966 and 1976 (inclusive) and who were interviewed in 1976.
[b]Includes men who were covered by mandatory retirement plan, retired at mandatory age, and had previously indicated they would have preferred to work longer.
[c]Includes men who were not forced out and whose record prior to retirement indicates that the retirement was likely attributable to health problems. Almost 90 percent of the group retired prior to age 65. For a detailed description of the criteria for inclusion see note 9.
[d]Retired early means prior to mandatory retirement age for those covered by mandatory plans and prior to age 65 for all others.
[e]Normal age means the mandatory retirement age for those covered by mandatory plans and at age 65 or later for all others. To be included in the former category, respondents must have indicated no desire to work beyond the mandatory age.

ceding the year of retirement.[11] The remaining retirees are classified as voluntary. This group includes individuals retiring under a mandatory retirement plan at the specified age if they had in the preceding year indicated no desire to work beyond that age. It also includes those who retired under such a plan at an earlier age than was required by the plan.

The Route to Retirement

The distribution of retirees according to this classification system is shown in table 6.1 for each of several universes used in the subsequent analysis. Percentages are relatively insensitive to variations in the specification of the universe. In all cases only 3 percent of the retirees were the unwilling victims of mandatory retirement plans. When all retirements over the ten-year period are considered, including those of men not interviewed in 1976, about half were attributable to poor health. When the universe is confined to retirees interviewed in 1976, the proportion is several percentage points lower. This difference is due to the death of above-average proportions of the unhealthy retirees by 1976. About half of the retirees who were interviewed in 1976 had re-

Table 6.2
1976 Retirees 65 to 69 Years of Age, by Route to Retirement (percentage distributions)

Route to retirement	All retirees 65 to 69			Retirees 65 to 69 subject to mandatory retirement		
	Total	Whites	Blacks	Total	Whites	Blacks
Number of respondents	795	567	228	275	203	72
Total percentage	100	100	100	100	100	100
Forced out by mandatory plan	5	5	8	15	14	26
Poor health	39	38	47	21	21	24
Voluntary	56	57	45	64	65	51
Early	26	27	21	39	40	28
Normal	30	31	24	25	25	23

tired voluntarily, and seven of ten of these had retired before age 65.

For evaluating the relative impact of mandatory retirement it is clearly inappropriate to observe the proportion of all retirees accounted for by this route, since very few of the men who had retired before 65 could have been affected by mandatory retirement provisions.[12] Table 6.2 shows the distribution by route to retirement of retirees who were 65 to 69 at time of interview in 1976 as well as the subset who had been in jobs subject to mandatory retirement. Only 5 percent of the retirees who had attained age 65 had unwillingly left their jobs by virtue of mandatory retirement plans. However, among the minority of men whose preretirement jobs had been covered by mandatory retirement provisions, 15 percent had been forced out unwillingly. About one in five had left the job prior to the mandatory age for health reasons, and an additional two-fifths had done so completely voluntarily. One-fourth had retired at the mandatory age but with no desire to have continued longer.

The weight of this evidence, then, supports those who foresaw relatively little impact of the 1978 amendments that raised the minimum permissible mandatory retirement age from 65 to 70. It appears that very small proportions of retired men over 65 have been victims of mandatory retirement. Of the minority of all employed men subject to such plans, large proportions either retire before the mandatory retirement age because of health problems or by choice or are not inclined to work beyond that age. An important reason is the increasing lib-

159

erality of private pension plans, which are more likely to exist in conjunction with mandatory retirement than in its absence.[13]

This conclusion could have been anticipated on the basis of evidence produced by the first interview with the sample in 1966. At that time 36 percent of men employed in the survey week (including those in self-employment) were covered by mandatory retirement plans, of whom only about one-third professed to want to work beyond that age. Thus if we assume that those attitudes held over time, a maximum of 12 percent (one-third of 36 percent) would have faced involuntary retirement. When deterioratng health over a decade is taken into account, as well as the increasing liberalization of public and private retirement plans, that figure would be expected to become substantially smaller.[14]

Retrospective Reports

We have chosen to rely on our longitudinal records for determining the reason for retirement, for this avoids the danger of post hoc rationalization. Nevertheless, the men who in 1976 reported that they were retired were asked an open-ended question on the reason for their retirement ("Why did you decide to retire?"), and it is therefore possible to compare a classification of these retrospective responses with the classification based on the longitudinal data (table 6.3).

Men who reported that they retired because of a mandatory plan were asked whether they would have continued to work if their employer had permitted them to work longer. All other reported reasons for retirement were recorded verbatim on the schedules by the interviewers. While 15 percent of the respondents attributed their retirement to a mandatory plan, only half of these men said that they wanted to work longer. Thus the number who attribute their retirement to a mandatory retirement plan almost certainly overstates the number who are forced out by such plans.

However, even among those who would have liked to work longer there is not a close correspondence with those classified as forced out on the basis of the longitudinal records. The proportion based on the retrospective responses is twice as great (8 percent versus 4 percent), and the intersection of the two categories is small. Only one-fifth of the forced-out group on the ret-

Table 6.3
Reason for Retirement Based on Longitudinal Records Compared with Reason Reported Retrospectively by 1976 Retirees (percentage distribution)

Retrospective reported reason	Number of respondents	Total percentage	Forced out by mandatory plans	Health	Voluntary		
					Total	Early	Normal
Longitudinal record (vertical distributions)							
Number of respondents	1,296		47	622	625	432	193
Total percentage	100		100	100	100	100	100
Mandatory retirement	15		66	10	15	8	31
Wanted to work longer	8		38	5	8	5	14
Did not want to work longer	5		19	4	5	2	13
Not ascertained	2		8	1	2	1	4
Health	46		11	76	18	19	17
Voluntary	40		23	14	66	73	52
Longitudinal record (horizontal distributions)							
Number of respondents	1,296	100	4	48	48	33	15
Mandatory retirement	186	100	17	34	50	18	31
Wanted to work longer	98	100	19	32	50	23	27
Did not want to work longer	68	100	13	38	48	10	38
Not ascertained	20	100	20	25	55	15	40
Health	581	100	1	80	19	14	6
Voluntary	501	100	2	17	80	61	20

rospective question were so classified by the longitudinal criteria. Conversely, slightly under two-fifths of those placed in this category by the longitudinal records were similarly classified by the responses to the retrospective question.

A careful examination of the longitudinal records of the 98 individuals who reported retrospectively in 1976 that they had been forced out by a mandatory retirement plan leads us to place greater credence in the classification based on the longitudinal records. In 17 instances the retrospective responses appeared to be correct. Of the remaining 81 cases there were 25 in which the respondent had told us in the interview preceding his retirement that he was not covered by a mandatory plan, an additional 15 cases in which the respondent had retired early, and 16 cases in which the respondent had told us in the preretirement interview that he had no desire to work beyond the mandatory retirement age. These findings reinforce our a priori view that retrospectively reported reasons for retirement are suspect. In the remainder of the analysis, therefore, the classification based on the longitudinal records is used.

Variations in Route

Table 6.4 shows the age distribution of the categories of retirees both at the time of retirement and at the time of the 1976 interview. The overall age distributions vary only slightly between blacks and whites. As of 1976 about half of the sample were 65 or older, while 15 percent had not yet reached 60. At time of retirement only about one-fourth of the sample had reached 65, and as many as 43 percent of the whites and 50 percent of the blacks were under 62. Almost nine out of ten who retired for health reasons did so before 65. These age distributions remind us that this sample cannot be construed to be representative of all retired men in 1976.

The routes to retirement differ between whites and blacks (table 6.5). More black than white men had retired for health reasons (52 percent versus 43 percent), and a correspondingly larger proportion of the whites had retired voluntarily (54 percent versus 42 percent). While very small minorities of both groups were forced out by mandatory retirement plans, the proportion for blacks was somewhat higher than that for whites (6 percent versus 3 percent). Almost nine of ten of the white retirees and

Table 6.4
Age of 1976 Retirees at Time of Retirement and in 1976, by Route to Retirement and Race (percentage distributions)

Age	Whites						Blacks					
	Total	Forced out	Health	Voluntary			Total	Forced out	Health	Voluntary		
				Total	Early	Normal				Total	Early	Normal
At time of retirement												
Number of respondents	1,113	30	505	569	396	173	471	20	265	176	121	55
Total percentage	100	100	100	100	100	100	100	100	100	100	100	100
Under 62	43	3	60	30	43	0	50	16	67	29	43	0
62–64	31	6	28	36	51	1[a]	26	7	20	39	55	5[a]
65–69	26	91	12	34	6[a]	99	24	77	13	32	2[a]	95
In 1976												
Number of respondents	1,113	30	505	569	396	173	471	20	265	176	121	55
Total percentage	100	100	100	100	100	100	100	100	100	100	100	100
55–59	15	0	21	9	13	0	18	12	24	11	16	0
60–64	33	6	35	34	49	0	32	11	34	31	44	3[a]
65–69	52	94	44	57	38	100	50	77	42	58	40	97

[a]For an explanation of this apparent anomaly, see the definitions of early and normal in notes d and e of table 6.1.

Table 6.5
Route to Retirement, by Selected Preretirement Characteristics and Race: Men Retired between 1967 and 1976 (percentage distributions)

	Whites							Blacks						
		Total			Voluntary				Total			Voluntary		
Characteristic	Number of respondents	percentage (median)	Forced out	Health	Total	Early	Normal	Number of respondents	percentage (median)	Forced out	Health	Total	Early	Normal
Marital status	1,047ᵃ	100	3	43	54	37	17	422	100	6	52	42	28	14
Married, spouse present	907	100	3	41	56	38	18	327	100	6	53	41	28	13
Other	132	100	3	54	43	34	9	90	100	5	49	46	30	16
Number of years of school completed	1,047	100	3	43	54	37	17	422	100	6	52	42	28	14
Under 12	653	100	3	49	48	31	17	376	100	7	54	39	25	14
12	232	100	3	37	60	44	16	30	100	0	44	56	53	3
13 or more	158	100	4	27	69	52	17	12	—ᵇ	—ᵇ	—ᵇ	—ᵇ	—ᵇ	—ᵇ
Occupation of pre-retirement job	1,047	100	3	43	54	37	17	422	100	6	52	42	28	14
Professional and managerial	243	100	3	29	68	46	22	23	100	0	58	42	26	17
Clerical and sales	120	100	3	37	60	41	19	23	100	9	37	54	50	4
Craftsmen	257	100	3	40	57	41	16	51	100	0	61	39	25	14
Operatives	193	100	2	49	49	32	17	106	100	5	46	49	33	16
Laborers, nonfarm	51	100	4	54	42	32	10	102	100	13	51	36	25	11
Service	75	100	5	49	46	28	17	68	100	5	53	42	26	17
Farmworkers	96	100	0	71	29	21	8	40	100	3	71	27	16	11
Income per dependent in year preceding retirement	1,047	100	3	43	54	37	17	422	100	6	52	42	28	14
Less than $2,000	135	100	2	62	36	25	11	150	100	5	58	37	21	16
2,000–3,999	218	100	3	52	45	28	17	101	100	12	48	40	30	10

4,000–5,999	184	100	4	41	55	36	20	44	100	4	47	49	28	21
6,000 or more	336	100	4	29	67	47	20	45	100	4	33	63	44	19
Median	4,906		5,660	3,693	5,725	5,856	5,541		2,511	3,033	2,171	3,197	3,245	3,092
Industry of preretirement job	1,047	100	3	43	54	37	17	422	100	6	52	42	28	14
Agriculture	105	100	—b	69	31	22	9	49	100	2	72	26	17	9
Construction	130	100	2	52	46	29	18	52	100	8	63	29	21	8
Manufacturing	289	100	5	32	63	46	17	118	100	9	46	46	30	15
Public administration	82	100	4	42	55	47	8	26	100	9	33	58	51	7
Other	430	100	3	41	56	35	21	168	100	4	53	43	27	16
Class of worker, pre-retirement job	1,047	100	3	43	54	37	17	422	100	6	52	42	28	14
Wage or salary	847	100	4	40	56	39	17	364	100	7	50	44	30	14
Private	677	100	4	41	55	37	19	289	100	7	50	43	28	15
Government	170	100	4	37	59	48	11	75	100	8	48	45	36	9
Self-employed	188	100	0	54	46	29	17	48	100	0	76	24	10	14
Pension coverage, pre-retirement job	687c	100	4	37	59	40	19	286c	100	7	46	47	32	15
Covered	489	100	6	31	63	46	17	150	100	10	41	50	39	11
Not covered	118	100	0	59	41	24	17	84	100	4	56	40	22	18

aTotal number of sample cases in the relevant universe. For each variable, the difference between this figure and the sum of the number of respondents in each category represents the number of sample cases for which no information on the variables was obtained.

bStatistics are not shown where base is fewer than 20 sample cases.

cMen who responded "don't know" when asked about pension coverage were included with those for whom the information was not ascertained.

eight of ten of the blacks were married and living with their wives in the year preceding their retirement. Retirement because of poor health was more common among unmarried than among married white men, but no such relationship is discernible among the black men.

Within each racial group there are differences in the reasons for retirement according to several indicators of socioeconomic status (table 6.5). Retirement because of health is greatest among the poorly educated, those in the lower occupational strata, and those whose preretirement income per dependent was low. Except for the complete absence of involuntary mandatory retirement among farm workers, there is little variation by occupation in the relative importance of this route to retirement. In none of the occupational categories of white men did the proportion of retirees who were forced out of jobs exceed 5 percent. Among blacks the proportion exceeded 10 percent only among nonfarm laborers (13 percent).

Industrial differences in routes to retirement are less pronounced than those according to occupation, except for the disproportionately large numbers of retirees from the agricultural sector who had retired because of poor health (69 percent of the whites and 72 percent of the blacks). Men who had worked in the construction industry also had an above-average incidence of retirement attributable to poor health and a correspondingly lower proportion of voluntary retirements, while those in manufacturing had somewhat lower proportions of health-related retirements. The highest proportion of cases in which men were forced out of jobs by mandatory retirement occurred in manufacturing—5 percent among whites and 9 percent among blacks. The only noteworthy difference in route to retirement by class of worker is the higher-than-average incidence of early voluntary retirement among government workers and the above-average proportion of the self-employed who retire because of health problems.

The circumstances in which retirement occurred differed substantially between wage and salary workers who had been covered by private pension plans and those who had not. Unwilling separation from jobs under mandatory retirement plans was more frequent among men covered by pensions, reflecting the greater prevalence of mandatory retirement provisions in establishments with pension plans. As also might be expected, the probability of voluntary early retirement is almost twice as great for a man covered by a private pension plan as for one who is not. Retirement for health reasons, on the other hand, is considerably more common among men without pension coverage. This, of course, reflects in part the industrial differences in routes to retirement. For example, workers in agriculture, who are unlikely to be covered by pensions, have a high incidence of retirement for health reasons.

Postretirement Labor Market Activity

In examining the extent and character of the postretirement labor market activity of the categories of retirees, our original intention was to give special attention to a comparison of the forced-out group with those who retired voluntarily and those who retired for health reasons.[15] However, the small number of sample cases in the first category precludes such comparisons. For men with postretirement labor market activity the sample sizes—stratified by race—become too small for statistically reliable estimates. Accordingly the forced-out group is not shown separately in the tables in this and the next section, although they are included in the totals.

Nevertheless, the best available evidence suggests that the men who retired against their wishes as the result of mandatory retirement provisions did not differ substantially from men who retired voluntarily at 65 in either the extent of their postretirement labor market activity or their inclination to take postretirement jobs. In tabulations in which whites and blacks were combined (with appropriate weights) and in which the sample size of the forced-out group was therefore large enough for at least rough estimates, we found that the labor force participation rate of that group in the survey week of 1976 was identical to the participation rate of the normal retirees (79 percent). Equal proportions of both groups (92 percent) disclaimed any work-seeking intentions in the year ahead, and very similar proportions reported unconditionally that they would not take a job if one were offered (78 percent of those who had been forced out, 83 percent of the normal retirees). Only 2 percent of each group responded unconditionally in the affirmative to this hypothetical job offer. Thus, even though they had indicated a desire to remain in their preretirement jobs, once they had been forced out these men evidenced no greater disposition than the voluntary retirees to take other work.

167

Extent of Participation

A minority of the retirees—about one in every five—was in the labor force in the survey week of 1976 (table 6.6).[16] Within each racial group there is surprisingly little difference in the extent of labor force participation among the categories of retirees; the range is only six percentage points among the whites and nine points among the blacks. Looking at the number of weeks worked during the 12 months prior to the 1976 survey, one again finds relatively little labor market activity overall as well as little variation among the groups. The percentages of retirees who did not work during this period averaged 80 percent for whites and 82 percent for blacks. At the other end of the continuum, fewer than one in ten of the retirees worked on a full-year basis.

Among the minority of the sample of retirees who were employed, part-time jobs were considerably more common than full-time work, a finding that would be expected in view of the Social Security Act's constraints on the earnings of beneficiaries. Somewhat less than two-fifths of the men with some employment during the year (40 percent of the whites and 34 percent of the blacks) worked 35 or more hours per week. As a consequence both of part-year work and reduced weekly hours, only 17 percent of the employed whites and 9 percent of the employed blacks worked as many as 2,000 hours per year. Almost three-fifths of each racial group worked under 1,000 hours in the 12 months preceding the 1976 interview.

Relatively few of the retirees (3 percent of the whites and 10 percent of the blacks) experienced any overt unemployment in the 12-month period preceding the 1976 interview. Although small sample size makes generalization perilous, there appears to be a difference in this respect between men who were forced out of their preretirement jobs by a mandatory retirement plan and the other categories of retirees. Ten percent of the white mandatory retirees experienced unemployment, and all of these reported that they had been looking for work for at least half the year. The smallest amount of unemployment occurred among white men who retired voluntarily at the normal retirement age. Only about 2 percent of these men reported any unemployment.

Reasons for being out of labor force All men who spent any time out of the labor force during the year preceding the 1976

Table 6.6
Selected Measures of Postretirement Labor Market Activity, by Route to Retirement and Race: Men Retired between 1966 and 1975 (percentage distributions)

Measure	Whites Total or average	Forced out	Voluntary Total	Early	Normal	Health	Blacks Total or average	Forced out	Health	Voluntary Total	Early	Normal
Labor force and employment status survey week 1976												
Number of respondents[a]	921	24	460	323	137	430	405	16	234	145	103	42
Total percentage	100	100	100	100	100	100	100	100	100	100	100	100
Employed	17	12	18	18	20	15	15	—b	13	19	21	15
Unemployed	1	9	1	—c	2	1	3	—b	3	2	3	0
Out of the labor force	82	79	81	82	78	84	82	—b	84	79	76	85
Number of weeks worked 12 months prior to 1976 survey												
Number of respondents[a]	921	24	459	322	137	429	405	16	232	145	103	42
Total percentage	100	100	100	100	100	100	100	100	100	100	100	100
No weeks	80	84	78	78	76	82	82	—b	85	74	73	76
1–25 weeks	6	12	6	7	6	5	7	—b	8	7	9	2
26–49 weeks	5	0	6	6	8	5	5	—b	3	9	6	15
50–52 weeks	9	4	10	9	10	8	6	—b	4	10	12	7
Hours per week usually worked, 12-month period prior to 1976 survey: men who worked during the period												
Number of respondents[a]	183	4	103	71	32	74	77	1	35	39	28	11
Total percentage	100	100	100	100	100	100	100	100	100	100	100	100
Less than 15	21	—b	25	25	25	16	21	—b	23	22	30	—b
15–34	39	—b	41	40	45	36	45	—b	41	44	40	—b
35 or more	40	—b	34	35	30	48	34	—b	36	34	30	—b

Table 6.6 (continued)

Measure	Whites			Voluntary			Blacks			Voluntary		
	Total or average	Forced out	Health	Total	Early	Normal	Total or average	Forced out	Health	Total	Early	Normal
Total hours worked in 12-month period prior to 1976 survey: men who worked during the period												
Number of respondents[a]	183	4	74	103	71	32	77	1	35	39	28	11
Total percentage	100	100	100	100	100	100	100	100	100	100	100	100
1–499	29	—[b]	27	30	30	31	35	—[b]	45	26	33	—[b]
500–999	29	—[b]	27	31	29	36	23	—[b]	25	20	21	—[b]
1,000–1,499	19	—[b]	18	19	25	6	22	—[b]	10	34	27	—[b]
1,500–1,999	6	—[b]	8	6	4	9	11	—[b]	9	11	9	—[b]
2,000 or more	17	—[b]	20	14	12	18	9	—[b]	11	9	10	—[b]
Number of weeks unemployed, 12-month period prior to 1976 survey												
Number of respondents[a]	921	22	421	448	314	134	405	14	228	142	102	40
Total percentage	100	100	100	100	100	100	100	100	100	100	100	100
No weeks	97	90	97	96	96	98	90	—[b]	91	89	90	86
1–26 weeks	2	0	2	2	2	2	6	—[b]	5	6	7	6
More than 26 weeks	1	10	1	2	2	0	4	—[b]	4	5	3	8
Reason for periods out of labor force, 12-month period prior to the 1976 survey: men with some time out of labor force												
Number of respondents[a]	804	19	386	391	271	120	356	13	208	122	87	35
Total percentage	100	100	100	100	100	100	100	100	100	100	100	100
Health	39	—[b]	66	14	15	11	56	—[b]	77	27	28	25
"Retired" or "did not want to work"	54	—[b]	30	75	75	76	37	—[b]	18	62	63	60

No work available	—[c]	—[b]	0	1	1	0	3	—[b]	2	4	6	0
Other	7	—[b]	4	10	4	13	4	—[b]	3	7	3	15

Job-seeking intentions during ensuing 12-months: men out of the labor force at time of 1976 survey

Number of respondents[a]	754	19	358	367	261	106	334	14	197	113	79	34
Total percentage	100	100	100	100	100	100	100	100	100	100	100	100
Definitely or probably yes	2	—[b]	2	3	3	3	4	—[b]	2	6	5	10
Perhaps or don't know	4	—[b]	3	4	4	5	8	—[b]	8	8	8	9
No	94	—[b]	95	93	93	92	88	—[b]	90	86	87	81

Reaction to hypothetical job offer: men out of labor force at time of 1976 survey

Number of respondents[a]	754	19	361	366	261	105	334	14	19	113	79	34
Total percentage	100	100	100	100	100	100	100	100	100	100	100	100
Yes, unconditional	2	—[b]	1	3	4	1	5	—[b]	—[b]	7	6	9
Yes, conditional	12	—[b]	10	14	13	15	13	—[b]	—[b]	18	20	14
No, because of health	44	—[b]	70	21	23	18	61	—[b]	—[b]	34	32	37
No, other reason	42	—[b]	19	62	61	66	22	—[b]	—[b]	41	42	40

[a] Total number of cases in the relevant universe. For each variable, the difference between this figure and the sum of the number of respondents in each category represents the number of sample cases for which no information on the variable was obtained.
[b] Statistics are not shown where base is fewer than 20 sample cases.
[c] Less than 0.5 percent.

interview were asked the reason for their not having worked or looked for work. Over one-half of the white men and one-third of the blacks responded to this question by simply observing that they were "retired." However, about two-fifths of the white and about three-fifths of the black retirees cited poor health. These proportions vary among the groups of retirees. For example, among white men whose retirement we have explained in terms of poor health, almost two of three used that factor to explain their absence from the labor force; that response was given by only 14 percent of those who retired voluntarily. That none of the whites and only 3 percent of the blacks cited an inability to find a job suggests that the discouraged worker phenomenon is not common among men who acknowledge that they are retired.

Work-seeking intention Men who were not in the labor force at the time of the 1976 survey were asked whether they intended to look for work during the next 12 months. The overwhelming majority of these respondents, about nine out of ten, expressed no intention of seeking work. Only 2 percent of the whites and 4 percent of the blacks indicated that they definitely or probably would do so. There is little variation in this respect according to reason for retirement. Whether they had been compelled to retire by poor health or whether they had left their jobs voluntarily at normal retirement age or earlier, the proportion of men who indicated no intention of seeking work in the near future was generally not far from 90 percent.

Reaction to hypothetical job offer The most extreme measure of a retiree's interest in taking a job is his reaction to a hypothetical job offer. Men who were not in the labor force in 1976 were asked whether they would take a job if an employer offered them one. As can be seen in table 6.6, only 2 percent of the white men and 5 percent of the black responded affirmatively and unconditionally, while an additional 12 or 13 percent of each racial group said that they would accept under certain circumstances. This left over four-fifths of the retirees who indicated no desire for work. The white men in this category were approximately equally divided between those who attributed their lack of interest to poor health and those who gave other reasons. Among blacks almost three times as many mentioned health as mentioned other reasons.[17]

Character of Postretirement Work Experience

Although few men worked after retirement, it is useful to inquire how the postretirement jobs of those men who held them compared with their earlier jobs. We compare various aspects of the jobs held by the retirees in 1976 with the work they had been doing immediately prior to their reported retirement (table 6.7).[18]

Nature of job   About two-fifths of the white retirees and slightly over one-half of the blacks who were employed in the survey week of 1976 were in the same specific occupation in which they had served prior to retirement. Of those who had moved into a different occupational category, more had moved down the socioeconomic hierarchy of jobs than up.[19] There is not much difference in this respect among the retirement categories.

About one-half of the employed retirees worked in the same industry as that of their preretirement job. This proportion was slightly higher for blacks than for whites but within each racial group was virtually invariant among the route-to-retirement groups. Men who did not remain within the same narrow industrial category almost invariably made shifts across major industry divisions—from manufacturing to construction, trade to finance, insurance to real estate, agriculture to manufacturing. Not much more than 5 percent shifted industries within a major division, for example, from one manufacturing industry to another.

Somewhat over two-thirds of the white retirees were in wage and salary jobs both before and after retirement. This proportion was even higher—almost nine-tenths—among black men. About one-fifth of the whites and one-tenth of the blacks moved from self-employment to a wage or salary position. Movement into self-employment was considerably less frequent, occurring in only 6 percent of the cases among white retirees and not at all among the black. Here again there are no perceptible differences among the route-to-retirement groups.

Earnings and hours   Seventy-one percent of the whites and 66 percent of the blacks who took postretirement jobs experienced a reduction in average hourly earnings expressed in dollars of constant (1976) purchasing power. Overall, about one-third of the men experienced a decline of at least $2.00 per hour. Median real average hourly earnings shrank by 39 percent among white men and by 32 percent among blacks.

173

Table 6.7
Selected Characteristics of 1976 Job Compared with Those of Preretirement Job, by Route to Retirement and Race: Men Employed in 1976 Who Retired between 1967 and 1975 (percentage distributions)

	Whites					Blacks		
	Total or average	Health	Voluntary			Total or average	Health	Voluntary
Characteristic			Total	Early	Normal			
Occupation								
Number of respondents[a]	186	74	106	73	33	78	33	42
Total percent	100	100	100	100	100	100	100	100
Same 3-digit occupation	41	43	40	41	40	53	42	62
Different 3-digit occupation	59	57	60	59	60	47	58	38
Higher status level in 1976	17	16	17	16	18	9	16	4
Same status level in 1976	10	13	19	9	9	18	17	19
Lower status level in 1976	32	28	34	34	33	20	25	15
Industry								
Number of respondents[a]	186	74	107	74	33	78	34	42
Total percent	100	100	100	100	100	100	100	100
Same 3-digit industry	48	50	47	46	49	55	54	55
Different 3-digit industry	52	50	53	54	51	45	46	45
Same 1-digit	4	5	4	4	3	6	7	5
Different 1-digit	48	45	49	50	48	39	39	40
Class of worker								
Number of respondents[a]	186	72	104	72	32	78	34	41
Total percent	100	100	100	100	100	100	100	100
Wage or salary worker both jobs	68	67	67	64	73	87	85	88
Self-employed both jobs	4	5	4	4	6	2	4	0
From wage or salary worker to self-employed	6	4	7	9	3	0	0	0
From self-employed to wage or salary worker	22	24	22	23	18	11	11	12

Average hourly earnings (1976 $)

Number of respondents[a]	60	19	38	24	14	32	15	15
Total percent	100	100	100	100	100	100	100	100
Same or higher earnings in 1976	29	—[b]	27	26	—[b]	34	—[b]	—[b]
Lower earnings in 1976	71	—[b]	73	74	—[b]	66	—[b]	—[b]
by $1.00 per hour or less	15	—[b]	13	16	—[b]	27	—[b]	—[b]
by $2.00 per hour or more	34	—[b]	34	33	—[b]	31	—[b]	—[b]
Median hourly earnings, pre-retirement job	4.88	—[b]	5.15	4.95	—[b]	3.08	—[b]	—[b]
Median hourly earnings, 1976 job	2.98	—[b]	3.30	2.98	—[b]	2.08	—[b]	—[b]

Usual hours worked per week

Number of respondents[a]	186	49	64	45	19	78	20	28
Total percent	100	100	100	100	100	100	100	100
Same or more in 1976 job	34	44	26	28	—[b]	35	36	34
Fewer in 1976 job	66	56	74	72	—[b]	65	64	65
by 1–19 hours	19	18	18	16	—[b]	34	32	34
by 20–24 hours	11	9	12	15	—[b]	8	9	7
by 25 or more hours	36	29	44	41	—[b]	24	24	24

Median annual earnings[c] (1976 $)

Number of respondents[a]	72	27	42	29	13	38	17	19
Year prior to retirement	10,998	10,029	14,110	14,874	—[b]	6,472	—[b]	—[b]
Calendar year 1975	2,219	2,105	2,538	2,124	—[b]	1,268	—[b]	—[b]
Percentage decrease	80	79	82	86	—[b]	80	—[b]	—[b]

Table 6.7 (continued)

Characteristic	Whites		Voluntary			Blacks		
	Total or average	Health	Total	Early	Normal	Total or average	Health	Voluntary
Attitude toward job								
Number of respondents[a]	151	51	74	49	25	58	20	26
Total percent	100	100	100	100	100	100	100	100
Like both "very much"	42	37	44	39	54	27	24	27
Liked 1976 job "very much," not preretirement job	20	18	22	25	18	10	8	12
Liked preretirement job "very much," not 1976 job	19	23	18	18	16	30	32	30
Did not like either job "very much"	19	22	16	18	12	33	36	31

[a]Total number of sample cases in the relevant universe. For each variable, the difference between this figure and the sum of the number of respondents in each category represents the number of sample cases for which no information on the variable was obtained.

[b]Statistics are not shown where base is fewer than 20 sample cases.

[c]Excludes men who retired after 1974.

There was also a substantial reduction in weekly hours of work. About one-third of the employed retirees were working as many hours as they had in their preretirement days, but another one-third of the whites and one-fourth of the blacks had cut their hours by as many as 25 or more per week. Given the lower average hourly earnings and the curtailed work activity, it follows that annual wage and salary income (in real terms) of men who continued to work was only a fraction of what it had been prior to retirement. Overall, median annual earnings of white men (expressed in 1976 dollars) dropped from $10,998 in the preretirement job to $2,219 in calendar year 1975, a reduction of four-fifths. For blacks the levels were lower, but the percentage decrease was identical.

Degree of satisfaction   About two-fifths of the white men reported liking very much both their preretirement job and their 1976 job. The remaining white retirees were almost equally divided, about one-fifth in each category, between those who were less than completely enthusiastic about both jobs, those who liked their preretirement job very much but felt otherwise about the 1976 job, and those who liked their 1976 jobs very much but had reported less satisfaction with their preretirement jobs. There was not much variation in these proportions among the categories of white retirees, although those who retired for health reasons had above-average proportions of individuals who were less than completely happy with both jobs and who were less satisfied with the postretirement than with the preretirement job. There is also a rather substantial difference between blacks and whites in this regard. A much smaller proportion of blacks than of whites expressed high satisfaction both with their preretirement and their 1976 jobs.

Adjustment to Retirement

In assessing the quality of the adjustments that retirees appear to have made to their new status, we look first at objective measures of financial well-being in relation to preretirement economic circumstances, then at the retirees' retrospective evaluation of their retirement decision, and finally at their satisfaction with various aspects of their lives. In all these aspects we continue to be interested in the variation among the categories of retirees. However, only in the case of satisfaction with life, which was measured among all 1976 retirees, are there

177

sufficient sample cases of individuals who were forced out to warrant showing them separately.

Financial Condition

One way of assessing the financial impact of retirement is to examine the change in real family income. Table 6.8 compares total family income in the year prior to retirement with that for 1975, expressed in 1976 dollars.[20] The decrease was substantial, about two-fifths in the case of whites and one-third among the blacks.[21] Among the white men those who had retired for health reasons had the lowest preretirement income and also the largest drop accompanying retirement, so that their postretirement real income was only 79 percent of the overall average. The early voluntary retirees, on the other hand, had the highest 1975 income, 27 percent above the average for all white retirees.

Although the percentage reduction in family income was smaller among blacks than among whites, the absolute level of black postretirement income was only 64 percent of that of whites. Among blacks the percentage reduction was somewhat greater for the voluntary retirees than for those who retired for health reasons. But the latter nevertheless had the lowest level of postretirement family income, 81 percent of the average for the total group of blacks.

Sources of family income, 1975 Figure 6.1 shows the proportion of average family income that derives from each of the designated sources, while figure 6.2 indicates the proportion of retirees who receive each type of income.

As might be expected, the most ubiquitous source of income is Social Security retirement (OASI) benefits, which go to about three-fifths of the white and black retirees.[22] Pension and disability benefits are the next most prevalent forms of income among the retirees, but the relative frequency of their receipt differs substantially between the two racial groups. Almost one-half of white retirees receive pensions, and over one-quarter have disability benefits. For blacks the two sources are roughly equal in relative frequency; about three men in ten receive each. Larger proportions of the retirees' families enjoy income derived from the employment of the wives than of the retirees themselves—about 21 percent versus 12 percent.

Turning now to the amounts of income generated by each

Table 6.8
Median Family Income (1976 Dollars) in Year Preceding Retirement and in 1975, by Route to Retirement and Race: 1976 Retirees Who Retired between 1967 and 1974

Route to retirement	Whites				Blacks			
	Number of respondents	Year before retirement	1975	Percentage decrease	Number of respondents	Year before retirement	1975	Percentage decrease
Total[a]	422	$14,753	$ 8,521	42	194	$ 8,183	$5,493	33
Health	211	11,552	6,760	41	115	6,745	4,474	34
Voluntary	201	16,510	10,547	36	67	10,527	6,619	37
Early	144	17,139	10,857	37	44	12,426	6,947	44
Normal	57	14,809	9,301	37	23	10,114	5,521	45

[a]Includes seven white and six black men who were forced out of their jobs.

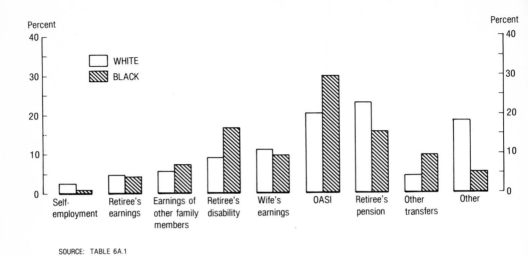

SOURCE: TABLE 6A.1

Figure 6.1
Distribution of Family Income of Retirees, by Source and Race, 1975 (percentage distribution)

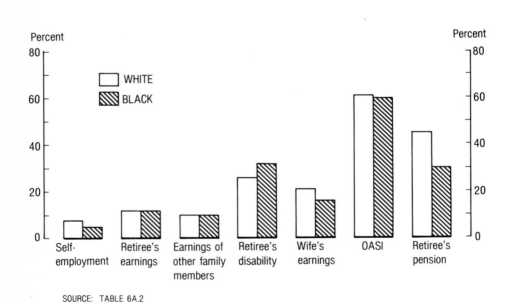

SOURCE: TABLE 6A.2

Figure 6.2
Percentage of Retirees Receiving Selected Forms of Family Income, by Race, 1975

source, one notes that the combination of OASI,[23] pensions, and disability payments accounts for 53 percent of the average family income of white retirees and 62 percent of the much lower level of black family income. OASI and disability benefits are relatively more important and pension income relatively less important among blacks than among whites.

There is substantial variation in the prevalence of some of the income sources of retirees depending on the circumstances of their retirement (table 6.9). About nine-tenths of white retirees who retired voluntarily at or beyond age 65 were receiving OASI benefits in contrast with only three-fifths of the early voluntary retirees and one-half of those who retired for health reasons. The receipt of private pensions, on the other hand, was most prevalent among the early voluntary retirees. These benefits were paid to two-thirds of that group but to only slightly over one-half of the normal age voluntary retirees and one-fourth of those retiring because of poor health. Disability benefits were received by almost half of the men who retired for health reasons, a proportion three or four times as great as that prevailing in any other group. In contrast to these types of income, the other major sources shown in table 6.9 do not vary much in frequency across the categories of retirees. Especially noteworthy is that the retiree's self-employment income and the wage and salary income of both the retiree and his wife are almost invariant among the categories.

In table 6.9 several important relationships are discernible among the average amounts of income of the white retirees. Median pension income is substantially higher among the early voluntary retirees than among any other group, exceeding that for the normal-age voluntary retirees by $2,000, or 62 percent. This difference is much larger than the difference in the opposite direction in OASI benefits, where the normal voluntary group received only 29 percent, or about $950, more than the early retirees. Disability benefits, although much less frequent among the early voluntary retirees than among those who retired with health problems, are equally high. The receipt of these benefits by the early voluntary retirees signifies either the onset of disability subsequent to retirement or the unreported presence of infirmities prior to retirement.

Replacement ratios The proportion of preretirement wage and salary income that the retirees received in 1975 in the form

Table 6.9
Proportion of Retirees Receiving Selected Forms of Income and Average Amount per Recipient, by Route to Retirement and Race, 1975: 1976 Retirees Who Retired 1966–1974

	Whites										Blacks					
	Total[a]		Health		Voluntary						Total[a]		Health		Voluntary	
					Total		Early		Normal							
Source of income	%	Median	%	Median	%	Median	%	Median	%	Median	%	Median	%	Median	%	Median
Number of respondents		804		396		385		271		114		357		220		115
OASI benefits ($)	61	3,473	52	2,836	68	3,809	58	3,314	90	4,266	60	2,697	52	2,197	70	3,429
Retiree's pension ($)	45	3,811	28	2,985	62	4,656	65	5,143	54	3,177	30	3,306	20	3,047	49	4,059
Retiree's disability benefits ($)	26	3,301	44	3,387	10	2,998	13	3,048	4	—[b]	32	2,650	44	2,540	16	—[b]
Wife's earnings ($)	21	4,233	22	4,444	19	4,235	20	4,237	18	—[b]	16	3,553	16	3,735	14	—[b]
Retiree's earnings ($)	12	2,118	10	2,108	13	2,535	12	2,123	13	—[b]	12	1,269	10	959	17	1,269
Earnings of other family members ($)	10	3,305	10	3,173	10	3,794	11	3,273	7	—[b]	10	3,180	13	4,233	6	—[b]
Retiree's self-employment ($)	8	1,957	8	2,114	7	1,937	8	1,577	6	—[b]	5	—[b]	4	—[b]	7	—[b]

[a]Totals include 8 whites and 11 blacks who were forced out of jobs by mandatory retirement plans.
[b]Includes OASI benefits to wife and other family members.
[c]Statistics are not shown where base is fewer than 20 sample cases.

of OASI benefits and/or private pensions is shown in table 6.10. To adjust for changes in the price level over time, all calculations are in 1976 dollars. Almost one in five of the white and one in four of the black retirees receive no OASI or pension income, while at least one-fourth of each racial group recovers at least 60 percent of preretirement earnings in these forms. As might be expected, the high proportion of retirees with no OASI pension income is accounted for largely by those who retired for health reasons, among whom this proportion is one-third. Among the remaining groups it varies from 2 percent among white men who retired voluntarily at age 65 or later to 15 percent among the black early voluntary retirees.

The median replacement rate is about 43 percent for all white retirees, the rate ranging from 55 percent for those who chose normal retirement to 29 percent for men who retired for health reasons. Except for this latter group, the median rate is in no case lower than 47 percent.[24] When men with no OASI or private pension benefits are excluded from the calculations, the median replacement rates become 50 percent for the white retirees and 53 percent for the blacks.

Retrospective Evaluation of Retirement Decision

One way of evaluating the psychological adjustment to retirement is to inquire to what extent preretirement expectations have been fulfilled, although there is some ambiguity in this approach stemming from our ignorance of what those expectations were. In the 1976 interview respondents were asked, "All in all, how does your life in retirement compare with what you expected it to be?" A forced-choice response ranged from "much better" to "much worse." Three-fifths of the white retirees reported that their preretirement expectations were fulfilled, while the remainder were almost equally divided between those who were disappointed and those who found their experience better than they had anticipated (table 6.11). The picture is less sanguine among blacks. A considerably larger proportion (31 percent) were disappointed with their retirement experience. Men who had been forced into retirement by health problems were most likely to have found retirement worse than their expectations. One-third of the whites and over two-fifths of the blacks reported this response. At the other extreme, less than 10 percent of the white voluntary retirees expressed disap-

Table 6.10
Wage and Salary Income in Year Preceding Retirement Replaced in 1975 by OASI and Pension Benefits (1976 Dollars), by Route to Retirement and Race[a] (percentage distributions)

| | Whites | | | | | Blacks | | | | |
| | | | Voluntary | | | | | Voluntary | | |
Replacement rate (%)	Total[b]	Health	Total	Early	Normal	Total[b]	Health	Total	Early	Normal
Number of respondents	537	245	275	192	83	250	134	96	70	26
Total	100	100	100	100	100	100	100	100	100	100
0	18	33	7	9	2	23	33	12	15	6
1–29	16	18	15	14	17	12	15	8	7	11
30–39	11	12	10	11	8	11	9	15	15	16
40–49	14	10	17	19	14	9	7	13	16	6
50–59	13	8	18	17	20	16	13	20	20	19
60–69	11	6	10	13	15	11	6	14	13	15
70 or more	17	13	19	17	24	18	17	18	14	27
Median replacement rate	43	29	50	47	55	44	31	51	47	54
Median replacement rate[c]	50	43	52	50	55	53	52	52	51	56

[a]Universe confined to men who were wage and salary workers in year preceding retirement.
[b]Totals include 13 whites and 12 blacks who were forced out.
[c]Universe further restricted to respondents who received OASI or pension benefits in 1975.

Table 6.11
Selected Attitudes toward Retirement in 1976, by Route to Retirement and Race (percentage distributions)

Measure	Whites						Blacks					
	Total	Forced out	Health	Voluntary Total	Voluntary Early	Voluntary Normal	Total	Forced out	Health	Voluntary Total	Voluntary Early	Voluntary Normal
Evaluation of actual retirement as compared with expectations												
Number of respondents	1,113	28	395	471	327	144	471	19	206	145	99	46
Total percentage	100	100	100	100	100	100	100	—[a]	100	100	100	100
Much better	12	18	7	16	15	19	14	—[a]	6	23	27	14
Some better	9	15	8	10	11	10	10	—[a]	9	13	13	14
About the same	60	52	53	65	66	63	45	—[a]	44	49	44	59
Some worse	13	15	21	7	6	7	19	—[a]	26	10	11	9
Much worse	6	0	11	2	2	1	12	—[a]	16	5	6	4
Would respondent retire at same age if he were deciding now?[b]												
Number of respondents	985	9	362	408	311	97	410	7	191	118	84	34
Total percentage	100	—[a]	100	100	100	100	100	—[a]	100	100	100	100
Yes	72	—[a]	64	80	80	80	66	—[a]	62	72	75	68
No, earlier	4	—[a]	3	5	4	7	2	—[a]	1	4	6	0
No, later	19	—[a]	25	13	14	12	26	—[a]	30	18	17	20
Don't know	5	—[a]	8	2	2	1	6	—[a]	6	6	2	13

[a] Statistics are not shown where base is fewer than 20 sample cases.
[b] Respondents who indicated compulsory retirement were not asked this question.

pointment, and even among black retirees in this category the proportion was only 15 percent.

Another way to assess the degree of satisfaction with retirement is to inquire whether the retirees would have retired at the same age if they had it to do over again. About three-fourths of the white retirees responded affirmatively to this question, one-fifth indicated that they would have retired later, and approximately 5 percent said that they would have retired earlier (table 6.11). Among blacks the proportion who would have chosen a later retirement was somewhat higher, about one-fourth. The voluntary group contains the largest proportion who say they would have chosen to retire at the same age.

Satisfaction with Life

Most retirees who were between 55 and 69 in 1976 reported being reasonably happy with their lives and with the five specific aspects that they were asked to comment on: their housing and the area in which they lived,[25] their health, their standard of living, and their leisure activity (table 6.12). Indeed, except for their health, a majority of the white retirees reported that they were very happy with each of these dimensions; in the case of health the corresponding proportion was two-fifths. Satisfaction was most pronounced with housing and area of residence; more than two-thirds of the white retirees professed to be very happy with these, and less than one in ten expressed some degree of unhappiness. About one-half of the white group reported themselves to be very happy with their standard of living, leisure time activity, and life overall, and no more than 15 percent registered any degree of unhappiness with these.

Among black retirees the pattern is pretty much the same, but levels of satisfaction are perceptibly lower than among whites, especially concerning their standard of living. Only 35 percent of black retirees were very happy with their standard of living while 23 percent expressed some degree of unhappiness. Curiously, when questioned about their satisfaction "all things considered," the black men do not respond very differently from the white.

As a means of assessing the impact of retirement on the quality of life, it would be helpful to be able to compare the responses shown in table 6.12 with responses to the same set of questions prior to the men's retirement, but these questions

Table 6.12
Degree of Satisfaction with Selected Aspects of Life in 1976, by Race (percentage distributions)

Measure	Whites					Blacks				
	Number of respondents	Total percent	Very happy	Somewhat happy	Unhappy	Number of respondents	Total percent	Very happy	Somewhat happy	Unhappy
Housing	1,113	100	68	24	8	471	100	58	31	12
Local area	1,113	100	69	23	8	471	100	59	26	14
Health	1,113	100	40	26	34	471	100	31	29	40
Standard of living	1,113	100	50	37	13	471	100	35	42	23
Leisure activity	1,113	100	53	32	15	471	100	47	36	17
All things considered	1,113	100	51	38	11	471	100	47	39	14

Table 6.13
Degree of Satisfaction with Various Aspects of Life, Retirees versus Nonretirees with 12 Years of Education, 1976 (percentages)

Measure	Very happy			Somewhat or very unhappy		
	Non-retirees	Retirees	Healthy retirees[a]	Non-retirees	Retirees	Healthy retirees[a]
Number of respondents	503	299	185	503	299	185
How happy are you with						
Housing	70	67	72	5	8	6
Local area	68	64	66	7	10	8
Health condition	59	47	62	10	29	11
Standard of living	62	54	59	5	11	8
Leisure time activities	54	57	65	10	13	8
Things overall	59	51	60	4	10	6

[a]Includes all retirees except those classified as having retired for health reasons.

were not asked prior to 1976. It is possible, however, to compare the responses of the retirees with those of comparable men who had not retired as of 1976. In table 6.13 responses to the life-satisfaction questions are tabulated for three categories of individuals, all of whom have completed exactly 12 years of education: (1) nonretirees, (2) retirees, and (3) healthy retirees, that is, those who retired for reasons other than poor health. The nonretirees are more likely than the total group of retirees to register high satisfaction with regard to each item except leisure activity, in which case the retirees enjoy an advantage of only three percentage points. At the other end of the continuum, a higher proportion of retirees report some unhappiness on every item including leisure time activity. The differences in satisfaction are most pronounced in the case of health, standard of living, and "things overall."

Eliminating the men who retired because of poor health dramatically alters the comparison between the retirees and nonretirees. Differences between the two groups either shrink substantially or change directions. In their evaluation of things overall the two groups are virtually indistinguishable, and in the evaluation of leisure time activities the healthy retirees include a substantially higher proportion of very happy individuals than the men who have continued to work.[26]

Table 6.14
Retirees Very Happy with Selected Aspects of Life in 1976, by Route to Retirement (percentages)

Measure	Total	Forced out	Health	Voluntary Total	Early	Normal
Number of respondents	1,584	50	777	754	526	228
Housing	67	66	61	73	71	78
Local area	68	58	65	72	70	77
Health	39	59	18	57	55	61
Standard of living	49	55	35	61	61	62
Leisure activities	52	59	38	66	65	66
All things considered	51	51	40	61	59	67

Finally, one may ask about variations in contentment among the categories of retirees. Table 6.14 indicates that, by and large, happiness tends to be greatest among the voluntary retirees, particularly those who retired at 65 or later, and lowest among those who retired as the result of poor health. Men forced out of jobs by mandatory retirement plans are also perceptibly less content with life than the voluntary retirees. The early voluntary retirees generally fall between the normal-age retirees and those who have been forced out of jobs by mandatory retirement plans. More noteworthy than these differences, perhaps, is that in all categories of retirees except the unhealthy, a majority of the men report the highest degree of happiness on each of the six items covered by the questions.

Summary and Conclusions

Several myths relating to retirement are in the process of dying, and much of the evidence produced by this study should hasten their demise.[27] Perhaps the most influential myth has been the notion that large proportions of elderly male workers are unwillingly removed from jobs by mandatory retirement plans. The evidence demonstrates that this proportion is actually exceedingly small. Only 3 percent of the more than 2,000 retirements that occurred among our sample of men over the decade 1966 to 1976 could realistically be classified as involuntary in this sense, and even when the analysis is confined to those who had reached age 65 by 1976 the percentage was only 5. The reason is not that mandatory retirement plans are uncommon; it is that large majorities of workers covered by them either retire earlier or retire at the mandatory age with no desire to remain in their jobs.

189

Far greater numbers of men are driven into retirement by poor health than by mandatory retirement plans. Somewhat over two-fifths of the total number of retirements over the ten-year period covered by our data were presaged by reports of health problems by the men in the year preceding retirement. Nevertheless, slightly over one-half of the retirements appear to be truly voluntary in every sense; about twice as many of these occur prior to age 65 as at 65 or later.

A second and somewhat related myth about retirement is that substantial numbers of retirees are involuntarily idle and would be eager to work if only they had the opportunity to do so. About one-fifth of retirees do choose to continue to work, and this proportion is roughly the same whether retirement was completely voluntary or due to a mandatory retirement plan or poor health. Since most of these men are on curtailed work schedules compared with their preretirement jobs, and since their average hourly earnings are substantially lower, their wage and salary income in 1975 was, on average, only one-third of what it had been in real terms prior to their retirement.

Among the large majority of retirees who are not in the labor force, relatively few manifest a substantial interest in work. Only 3 percent of this group respond unconditionally in the affirmative to a hypothetical job offer, while 84 percent respond unconditionally in the negative. Here again there is little variation in these proportions among the categories of retirees, although those whose retirement was associated with health problems are more likely than the voluntary retirees to attribute their disinterest in a job to poor health. Of all retirees who spent any time out of the labor force in the year preceding the 1976 survey, only 1 percent (3 percent among the blacks) attributed this to the unavailability of work.

Finally, there appears to be a general belief that large proportions of retirees are disenchanted with the retired status. While our evidence on this point is less complete than on the other issues, it is inconsistent with the belief that retirement typically inflicts psychological pain. Three-fifths of the retirees reported that their preretirement expectations were fulfilled, and an additional one-fifth found that their retirement experience exceeded their expectations. If they had it to do over again, at least three-fourths would have retired at the same or an earlier age. Finally, a majority of the retirees report themselves to be very happy with their lives, and only one-tenth admit to being some-what or very unhappy.

There are differences in those respects among the several categories of retirees and, to a lesser extent, between blacks and whites. Those who retired for health reasons tend to be less satisfied than other retirees with virtually every aspect of life that we measured. This is hardly surprising, for this group differs substantially from the voluntary retirees in many important re-spects in addition to health. They are considerably more likely to come from lower occupational and educational strata, and both their preretirement and postretirement financial circumstances are substantially less favorable than those of the voluntary retirees.

When the men who retired for health reasons are removed from the total, the remaining retirees express the same degree of satisfaction with the various facets of their lives as is reported by men with comparable educations who are still at work. In-deed the retirees are perceptibly more satisfied with their lei-sure activities than their nonretired counterparts. When one keeps in mind that even voluntary retirement brought a decline of over one-third, on average, in total family income, it is re-markable that approximately equal proportions of healthy re-tirees and nonretirees with 12 years of education are very happy with their standard of living.

From a policy perspective, perhaps the most significant con-clusion that can be drawn from our findings is that labor force participation rates of the elderly are not likely to be affected to any significant degree by alterations in mandatory retirement provisions. This does not necessarily mean that discouraging mandatory retirement is poor public policy, for it may be de-fended on grounds of equity even if large numbers of persons are not affected. It does mean, however, that if the objective is to keep older workers in the work force, other policy instru-ments must be used.

Table 6A.1
Distribution of Family Income of Retirees, by Source and Race, 1975

Source of income	Whites		Blacks	
	Mean[a]	Percentage distribution[d]	Mean[a]	Percentage distribution[d]
Number of respondents		540		278
Total income	$10,715	100	$6,244	100
Earnings of retiree	516	5	267	4
Earnings of retiree's wife	1,211	11	612	10
Earnings of other family members	612	6	470	8
Self-employment (family)	294	3	65	1
Retiree's disability benefits	984	9	1,044	17
OASI (family)	2,181	20	1,863	30
Retiree's pension	2,465	23	981	16
Other transfers[b]	491	5	598	10
Other[c]	1,961	18	344	6

[a]In 1976 dollars.
[b]Includes public assistance and pension or disability paid to other family members.
[c]Includes property income and food stamps.
[d]Percentage distributions may not add to 100 due to rounding.

Table 6A.2
Percentage of Retirees Receiving Selected Forms of Family Income, by Race, 1975

Source	Whites	Blacks
Earnings of retiree	12	12
Earnings of retiree's wife	21	16
Earnings of other family members	10	10
Self-employment	8	5
Retiree's disability benefits	26	32
OASI	61	60
Retiree's pension	45	30

1. U.S. Department of Health, Education, and Welfare (1976a), p. 11; (1976b), p. 71.

2. U.S. Senate (1979), pp. xxv, 4.

3. Sheppard and Rix (1977); *Business Week* (1978), pp. 72–89.

4. See Atchley (1976), p. 1.

5. See *U.S. News and World Report* (1977), p. 71.

6. See, for example, Reno (1976), p. 43; Bond (1976), p. 5.

7. For an early longitudinal study, see Streib and Schneider (1971). The Social Security Administration's Retirement History Study is providing valuable information on these topics See Irelan (1972).

8. Respondents were asked in each survey at what age they expected to stop working at a regular job. Those who indicated that they had already done so were classified as retired. In the 1973 and 1975 telephone surveys individuals who responded "retired" to the initial question on their principal activity during the survey week were not asked the question on expected age of retirement. In these two surveys, therefore, such individuals were also included among the retirees. Our concern is with the individual's first reported retirement; hence the date of retirement is fixed at some time between the survey date on which the respondent first reported the retired status and the preceding survey.

9. Some men may leave an employer at a pensionable age and embark on another job without thinking of or reporting themselves as having retired. To explore the prevalence of such a pattern, we examined in detail the work histories of all respondents who had never reported themselves retired but who at some time received either Social Security benefits or pension income. Within this group we identified individuals whose records during the ten-year period showed the receipt of such income on a more or less regular basis following a change of employer. Of the 42 such cases, all but two were early retirements. The two exceptions were individuals who retired under a mandatory retirement plan at the mandatory age (55 years in one case and 65 in the other), and neither had previously expressed a desire to work longer for that employer. If these 42 individuals had been included in our analysis, the principal effects on our findings would be to increase by about 3 percentage points the proportion of men with postretirement work activity and to increase the measure of the intensity of such employment (hours per week) on the part of those who engaged in it.

10. For certain purposes the sample will be further restricted. For example, when preretirement characteristics are being examined, men who reported themselves retired in the initial survey (1966) are excluded since we cannot pinpoint the date of their retirement and are therefore unable to know about certain aspects of their status immediately prior to retirement. Similarly, when we wish to characterize the experience of the retirees in the year following their retirement, it is necessary to exclude those who first reported themselves retired in 1976, for the required postretirement data are not available for that group. It follows that in comparisons between preretirement and postretirement status, only those who reported their retirements between the 1967 and 1975 surveys can be included in the analysis.

11. Specifically, this category includes men who (a) reported poor health as the reason for having left their preretirement job; (b) reported poor health as the reason for absence from the labor force in the 12-month period prior to the report of retirement; (c) revised their expected age of retirement downward for health reasons in the survey preceding retirement; (d) specified poor health as the reason for not seeking work either

in the year of retirement or in the preceding year; (e) reported an inability to work in the year of retirement or the preceding year; or (f) reported a work-limiting health problem in each of the two years preceding retirement. Very few of the respondents fell into the retired-by-health category by virtue of this last criterion alone.

12. Of all employed wage and salary earners 45 to 59 years of age in 1966, 45 percent reported that they were covered by mandatory retirement plans. Fewer than 5 percent of these reported a mandatory retirement age under 65. About seven of ten faced mandatory retirement at age 65, 7 percent between 66 and 69, and 20 percent at age 70 or over. See Parnes et al. (1970), pp. 175–176. For the results of a 1974 survey of firms with pension plans, see Kittner (1977).

13. For evidence on the important role of anticipated pension income in the retirement decision, see Parnes and Nestel (1975), pp. 153–196, Barfield and Morgan (1969).

14. For an earlier presentation of this line of reasoning, see Parnes (1976), pp. 52–53. Even earlier, Schulz used data from a survey of newly entitled Social Security beneficiaries to show that the proportion of men who would be retired against their will solely by virtue of a mandatory retirement plan would probably be only about 7 percent (Schulz, 1974).

15. We have explored the question in two ways: first, by examining the status of the men in the year immediately following their reported retirement and, second, on the basis of their activity as reported in the 1976 interview. Careful scrutiny of the two sets of results showed very little difference in either the levels or patterns of activity between these two points in time. Hence we report the results only for 1976. To illustrate, in the survey year following retirement 17 percent of the respondents were employed, 2 percent were unemployed, and 81 percent were out of the labor force. In 1976 the corresponding percentages were 18, 2, and 80. In the former case the labor force participation rate varied among the categories of retirees over the narrow range of four percentage points; it was highest for those forced out and lowest for those who retired for health reasons. In 1976 the range was two percentage points and the pattern was the same.

16. Although a number of factors make the results noncomparable, this proportion is lower than the proportion of newly entitled male beneficiaries under OASI who were employed in 1968. That percentage was 40 for those eligible for reduced benefits and 36 for those eligible for nonreduced benefits (U.S. Department of Health, Education, and Welfare, 1976a, p. 15).

17. For an analysis based on very different types of data that also concludes that there is only limited "availability" for work among retirees, see Motley (1978), p. 27.

18. Preretirement jobs were also compared with the jobs held in the year immediately following retirement. As in the case of patterns of work activity, these comparisons were so similar to those involving the 1976 job that only the latter are reported here.

19. The socioeconomic status of occupational assignment is measured in terms of the Duncan Index of Socioeconomic Status. Occupations within four points of each other on this scale are considered here to be of equal status. See *occupational status* in appendix B.

20. For this purpose, we have confined the analysis to men who retired before January 1975 in order to be certain to exclude preretirement earnings from the incomes for calendar year 1975 that were reported in the 1976 interviews. In another tabulation, not shown here, we restricted the analysis to men who were married and living with their

wives both in the year preceding retirement and in 1975. This restriction raises all the income figures and causes the percentage decrease in family income to be somewhat smaller for whites (38 percent) and somewhat larger for blacks (38 percent).

21. A study based on the Social Security Administration's Retirement History Survey calculated that the average (median) decrease in real family income of married men who retired between 1968 and 1972 was 41 percent. The age range of the sample in 1972 was 61 to 66. See Fox (1976), p. 22.

22. Our sample is representative only of retirees under age 70. As a consequence, the relative importance of different income sources should not be expected to be the same as for the full age range of retirees. Because younger retirees are overrepresented in our sample (many retired because of poor health), the proportion receiving disability benefits is higher and the proportions receiving Social Security and private retirement benefits are lower than would prevail in the total universe of retired men. The distinction between Social Security retirement benefits and Social Security disability benefits cannot be accepted with complete confidence because there is evidence from the Retirement History Survey that respondents tend to misreport type of Social Security benefit. On this point, see Fox (1976), p. 16.

23. Actually, the figures on OASI payments do not differentiate between payments to the retiree and those to other members of his family.

24. For data from the Social Security Administration's Retirement History Survey on replacement rates for married men age 63 to 69 who had begun receiving Social Security retirement benefits by 1974, see Fox (1979). Differences in the universes covered and in the method of calculating replacement ratios make Fox's data noncomparable with those presented here.

25. A large majority of men (84 percent) were living in the same local area in which they had lived before retirement. The proportion of migrants was lowest among those who had been forced out of jobs by a mandatory retirement plan, only 3 percent overall. There was little variation in the migration rate among the remaining categories of retirees. A substantial majority of the men who did migrate remained within the same region of the country. However, 4 percent had moved to a different region, most frequently to the South.

26. For a somewhat similar finding, see the study by Thompson (1973), which concluded that among men 65 and older "the retired exhibit lower morale than the employed principally because they are older, functionally more disabled, more likely to view their health in negative terms, and less well off financially and not because of any negative reaction to the loss of the worker role" (p. 344).

27. See, for example, Ossofsky (1977); Sheppard (1979), p. 9. For evidence based on the Panel Survey of Income Dynamics and an interpretation similar to that presented here, see Morgan (1980).

References

Atchley, R. 1976. *The sociology of retirement.* Cambridge, Mass.: Schenkman Publishing Company.

Barfield, R., and Morgan J. 1969. *Early retirement: the decision and the experience.* Ann Arbor, Mich.: Institute for Social Research.

Bond, K. 1976. Retirement history study's first four years: work, health, and living arrangements. *Social Security Bulletin* 39 (December): 3–14.

Business Week. 1978. When retirement doesn't happen (June 19), pp. 72–75.

Fox, A. 1976. Work status and income change, 1968–1972: retirement history study preview. *Social Security Bulletin* 39 (December): 15–31.

———. 1979. Earnings replacement rates of retired couples: findings from the retirement history study. *Social Security Bulletin* 42 (January): 17–39.

Irelan, L. M. 1972. Retirement history study: introduction. *Social Security Bulletin* 35 (November): 3–8.

Kittner, D. R. 1977. Forced retirement: how common is it? *Monthly Labor Review* 100 (December): 60–61.

Morgan, J. 1980. Retirement in prospect and retrospect. In *Five thousand American families: patterns of economic progress*, vol. 8, chap. 3. Ann Arbor, Mich.: Survey Research Center, Institute for Social Research. 1980.

Motley, D. K. 1978. Availability of retired persons for work: findings from the retirement history study. *Social Security Bulletin* 41 (April): 18–27.

Ossofsky, J. 1977. Statement before Subcommittee on Equal Opportunities of House Committee on Education and Labor on September 14, 1976. Excerpted in *Congressional Digest* 56 (October): 274–278.

Parnes, H. S. 1976. The National Longitudinal Surveys: lessons for human resource policy. In *Current issues in the relationship between manpower research and policy.* National Commission for Manpower Policy. Special Report No. 7 (March).

Parnes, H. S., Fleischer, B. M., Miljus, R. C., and Spitz, R. S. 1970. *The pre-retirement years*, vol. 1. U.S. Department of Labor, Manpower Administration, Manpower Research Monograph 15. Washington, D.C.: U.S. Government Printing Office.

Parnes, H. S., and Nestel, G. 1975. Early retirement. In H. S. Parnes et al., *The pre-retirement years,* vol. 4. U.S. Department of Labor, Manpower Administration, Manpower Research Monograph 15. Washington, D.C.: U.S. Government Printing Office.

Reno, V. 1976. Why men stop working before age 65. In U.S. Department of Health, Education and Welfare, Social Security Administration. *Reaching retirement age.* Washington, D.C.: U.S. Government Printing Office.

Schulz, J. H. 1974. The economics of mandatory retirement. *Industrial Gerontology* 1 (Winter): 1–10.

Sheppard, H. L. 1979. Employment-related problems of older workers: a research strategy. U.S. Department of Labor, Employment and Training Administration. R&D Monograph 73.

Sheppard, H. L., and Rix, S. E. 1977. *The graying of working America: the coming crisis in retirement-age policy.* New York: Free Press.

Streib, G. R., and Schneider, D. J. 1971. *Retirement in American society.* Ithaca, N.Y.: Cornell University Press.

Thompson, G. B. 1973. Work versus leisure roles: an investigation of morale among employed and retired men. *Journal of Gerontology* 28: 339–344.

U.S. Department of Health, Education, and Welfare, Social Security Administration. 1976a. *Reaching retirement age.* Washington, D.C.: U.S. Government Printing Office.

———. 1976b. *Social Security Bulletin* 39 (June).

U.S. News and World Report. 1977. New retirement rules: their impact on business, workers. (November 7), pp. 71–73.

U.S. Senate, Special Committee on Aging. 1979. Developments in aging: 1978. 96th Congress, 1st sess. Report No. 96-55. Washington, D.C.: U.S. Government Printing Office.

Chapter 7

The Impact
of Health
Problems and
Mortality
on Family
Well-Being

Frank L. Mott
and
R. Jean Haurin

Because most deaths in the United States occur after age 65, there is a tendency to neglect the social and economic problems associated with mortality during the prime working years. In particular, family income inadequacy related to the deaths of males between 45 and 64, most of whom have spouses and many of whom have minor children, constitutes a socioeconomic problem of major proportions.

In 1976 the U.S. civilian male population between 45 and 64 numbered over 20 million. Most of these men were in the labor force serving as primary breadwinners of their family units. More than 17 million were living with their wives, and large proportions had at least one child under 18 living at home. Of those in husband-wife families an estimated 3.6 million, or 21 percent, will die before they reach the usual retirement age of 65, and over nine out every ten of these will be survived by a widow.[1]

Little literature focuses specifically on the characteristics and special needs of these disrupted families. Several questions warrant investigation: How does the family respond to the loss of the male breadwinner? What are the principal economic effects of a woman's transition into widowhood? What was the husband's health status in the years before death? Because the duration of illness preceding death affects the labor market behavior patterns and the well-being of the family unit, analysis of family income dynamics during this phase of the life cycle must give attention to this important dimension. Although an extensive literature about older workers with health problems is available,[2] little is known about the work activity and earnings ability of men of working age in the years just before death.

This chapter identifies members of the sample who had died by 1976 before reaching 65, and compares their records prior to death with those of a reference group of nondecedents. The data include detailed income and employment information and permit us to distinguish the needs of families whose primary breadwinners have lingering health problems from those in which the husbands are presumably healthy until shortly before death.

The Data Base
and Plan of
Analysis

The data base described in chapter 1 provides longitudinal records that permit examination of family and individual circumstances of men who are still below retirement age when they die. In addition, information about the labor force and income situation of wives before and after the husband's death is available from the NLS mature women's cohort—women 30 to 44 years of age in 1967 for whom we have information covering the period 1967 to 1976. The longitudinal nature of the data makes it possible to follow both men and their wives for a number of years and to compare the resources and family status of men who die with comparable individuals whose families remain intact. This opportunity to examine dynamic aspects of family change in the immediate premortality years is a substantial improvement over the traditional cross-sectional view obtained from one-point-in-time data sets.

Our principal focus is on the subset of the original sample of men who were under 65 when they died between 1966 and 1976. More specifically, the decedent sample includes the 468 white and 269 black men who were between 45 and 64 at the last survey before death. A reference group of 1,385 white and 444 black men 45 to 64 years of age during the same decade was constructed by randomly selecting survivors (as of 1976) across all the survey years. The reference sample matched the decedent sample in age distribution and in distribution among the survey years in which the deaths of the latter were reported.[3]

The data for these groups are used in several ways. Cross-sectional analysis permits us to compare the socioeconomic characteristics of the decedents and the reference group at the last survey before death. A trend analysis, which is limited to subsets of the samples who were interviewed at least three times at intervals of two years, allows an examination of the impact of declining health in the years before death. Finally, the data for the women permit a comparison of their circumstances and behavior before and after the death of their husbands.[4]

Antecedents of Mortality: A Multivariate Perspective

Before focusing specifically on the income and employment circumstances of families in the years immediately preceding the death of the primary breadwinner, we examine the extent to which background environmental and demographic variables are significantly associated with the mortality of prime-age men. This is an appropriate introduction to the subsequent analysis, because many of the differences in income and employment patterns between the men who die before 1976 (hereafter

199

termed decedents) and those who survive (reference group) may be as much reflections of differences in background as of differences directly related to death.

Appendix table 7A.1 uses an ordinary least-squares multivariate framework to predict, on the basis of a number of socioeconomic, demographic, and environmental characteristics, whether a mature man will die. The dependent variable in these models is coded one if the respondent died between 1966 and 1976 (before reaching 65) and zero if he is a member of the reference group.[5] Included as explanatory variables are the educational attainment of the respondents, their marital status (married—wife present, other), joint health-employment variables, and variables indicating whether the respondent lived in a central city or the suburb of a Standard Metropolitan Statistical Area (SMSA).[6]

Somewhat surprisingly, there is no significant inverse association between probability of death and educational attainment for either white or black men, as had been expected on the basis of other research.[7] This is doubtless attributable, at least in part, to the correlation of variables such as health status and employment status with education.[8]

Consistent with other research, our analysis shows that both black and white men who are not living with a spouse have decidedly higher probabilities of dying in this age range.[9] Several reasons have been advanced for this fact. Men without wives, on average, may have physical or other social characteristics that are associated with a lower probability of marriage and a higher probability of death. Also, single men may receive less attention when they become ill than men with wives.[10]

By far the dominant variables in the model are the employment and health factors, which will be at the core of this analysis.[11] Having a health problem, not surprisingly, was the most significant predictor of death. Yet when health was controlled, respondents who were not employed had much higher probabilities of dying. In interpreting this finding, as well as those described later, we must recognize that a reported health problem accompanied by nonemployment is probably more severe than a health problem reported by an employed individual.[12]

The importance of the joint health-employment variables in predicting mortality is shown in table 7.1, which is based on the regression results presented earlier. The table shows how the probability of death varies according to health and employment

Table 7.1

Index of Mortality Probability Relative to that of Healthy, Nonemployed Men, by Health and Employment Status and Race[a]

Health and employment status	Whites	Blacks
Healthy, employed	1.0	1.1
Not healthy, employed	2.2	1.6
Not healthy, not employed	3.6	2.8

[a]Figures represent the probability of death for each group expressed as a ratio to the probability for men who were healthy and not employed. Probabilities were calculated from the regression results shown in appendix table 7A.1, based on a hypothetical cross section of respondents with 12 years of schooling, who were married, wife present, and lived in the suburb of a metropolitan area.

status. With all other factors controlled, it uses as a point of reference men who were healthy and not employed, among whom the probability of death is lowest.[13] To illustrate, the table shows that among white men, the probability of death is 3.6 times higher for men who were not healthy and not employed than among the reference group. Black and white respondents in the healthy and employed category have mortality probabilities that hardly differ from those of the reference group (retirees). However, the black and white respondents who are employed but not healthy were significantly more likely to die before 1976 than the two categories of healthy respondents. Finally, respondents who had a health problem and, in addition, were not employed, were most likely to die, suggesting that, on average, their health problems were more severe.[14]

Thus it is clear that health conditions interact in a complex manner with various dimensions of employment and employability. Some health conditions are more limiting than others as a constraint to gainful employment. One way of gauging a posteriori the seriousness of a condition is by noting whether death followed. By then moving backward in time, one can compare the income and employment records of unhealthy individuals who died with those of their more fortunate counterparts who had health problems but survived (at least until 1976).

We can also compare the socioeconomic experiences of families whose breadwinner died suddenly (with no previously reported health problem) to the experiences of those in which decedents reported a health problem in the last interview before death. The predeath experiences of the family may be quite different for these two groups. Relatively sudden death of the principal breadwinner leaves little time for other family members to prepare by making such adjustments as entering the work force or gaining necessary work skills. On the other hand, it also involves only minimal predeath expenses, since there is no lengthy illness with its often debilitating medical expenses.[15] In addition, the husband probably loses little time from work and is thus earning a salary until shortly before he dies. Conversely, a death preceded by a chronic illness may have quite different economic implications for the family unit; other family members have more time to acquire job skills, partly in anticipation of a death and partly to help meet the family's expenses.

Income and Employment in the Years before Death: The Cross-Section Sample

Personal and Employment Characteristics

In this section we examine the degree to which men within a year or two of dying are systematically disadvantaged in terms of income and employment and to what extent any such disadvantage may be a reflection of poor health. Table 7.2 highlights a number of sociodemographic characteristics of white and black reference group members and decedents. White respondents who died by 1976 had a slightly lower level of educational attainment than their surviving counterparts, were more likely to have lived in a central city, were less likely to be married and living with their wives, and, most important, were twice as likely to have reported a health problem.[16] For black respondents the only differences between the decedents and the reference group are that a much lower percentage of decedents lived with a spouse and, as with the whites, there was a much higher likelihood that the decedents would report a health problem.

In general, there are more differences between men with and without health problems (in each of the major categories) than there are between the reference group and decedents (within each health status category). In other words, it seems likely that health status, regardless of prospective mortality status, is a better predictor of income or employment problems than prospective mortality status per se. The cross-sectional employment characteristics in table 7.3 support this view. Men without health problems have strikingly similar employment characteristics, regardless of prospective mortality status. The labor force participation rates for all the healthy subsets—reference group as well as decedents—are over 90 percent. In contrast, about 72 percent of the white reference group members with a health problem and 54 percent of their decedent counterparts were

Table 7.2

Selected Personal Characteristics of Decedents and Reference Group, by Health Status and Race: The Cross Section[a]

Personal characteristic	Decedents			Reference group		
	Total	Health problem	No health problem	Total	Health problem	No health problem
	Whites					
Number of respondents[b]	426	249	177	1,350	381	969
Less than 12 years of school (%)	64	68	58	55	62	52
Living in central city of SMSA (%)	32	34	30	26	23	27
Living in suburb of SMSA (%)	37	33	42	43	39	44
Health problem (%)	58	—	—	28	—	—
Mean duration of health problem (years)	—	8	—	—	9	—
Married, wife present (%)	81	78	86	90	87	92
Separated, divorced, widowed (%)	12	16	8	6	9	4
Mean age	57.1	57.6	56.4	57.2	57.9	56.9
	Blacks					
Number of respondents[b]	250	151	99	427	137	290
Less than 12 years of school (%)	84	90	76	82	92	78
Living in central city of SMSA (%)	58	53	65	57	48	61
Living in suburb of SMSA (%)	13	16	9	12	16	11
Health problem (%)	59	—	—	30	—	—
Mean duration of health problem (years)	—	8	—	—	8	—
Married, wife present (%)	64	62	69	79	78	79
Separated, divorced, widowed (%)	28	28	27	16	13	17
Mean age	56.5	56.6	56.5	56.5	57.8	55.9

[a]Characteristics are measured as of the last survey before death for the deceased respondents and at a comparable survey point randomly assigned for the reference group. See the appendix to this chapter for further details on the sample.
[b]Nonresponse rates may vary slightly from item to item.

working or looking for work, and a similar pattern prevailed among blacks.

The substantial differential in participation rates between the reference group and the decedents with health problems is further evidence that the health problems reported by men who subsequently died were, on average, more serious than those reported by members of the reference group.[17] This greater severity of health problems in the decedent group has several implications. It suggests that at least some families have some

Table 7.3
Selected Employment-Related Characteristics of Decedents and Reference Group, by Health Status and Race: The Cross Section[a]

Employment-related characteristic	Decedents			Reference group		
	Total	Health problem	No health problem	Total	Health problem	No health problem
Whites						
Number of respondents[b]	426	249	177	1,350	381	969
Employed, at work (%)	60	42	86	79	62	86
Employed, not at work (%)	9	11	7	8	7	8
Retired (%)	8	11	4	6	14	4
Unable to work (%)	18	30	1	3	10	0
Labor force participation rate (%)	71	54	95	88	72	95
Unemployment rate (%)	2.4	2.3	2.4	1.9	3.0	1.5
Mean hourly rate of pay at current job[c] ($)	5.96	5.77	6.08	6.68	5.49	6.96
Mean weeks worked in past year	37	29	47	45	38	48
Mean hours worked per week in past year	34	27	43	41	35	44
White-collar occupation[d] (%)	35	33	37	39	33	41
Blue-collar occupation[d] (%)	52	55	48	46	45	47
Farm occupation[d] (%)	6	6	5	10	17	8
Mean Duncan Index score[d,e]	36	35	37	38	32	40
Blacks						
Number of respondents[b]	250	151	99	427	137	290
Employed, at work (%)	50	28	82	73	57	80
Employed, not at work (%)	6	5	9	10	8	12
Retired (%)	7	8	6	4	9	2
Unable to work (%)	31	53	0	5	16	1
Labor force participation rate (%)	58	35	92	88	69	96
Unemployment rate (%)	3.3	7.3	2.0	5.0	7.1	4.4
Mean hourly rate of pay at current job[c] ($)	3.91	3.80	3.96	4.32	4.01	4.39
Mean weeks worked in past year	30	18	47	44	34	48
Mean hours worked per week in past year	26	18	38	38	29	41
White-collar occupation[d] (%)	10	10	9	14	11	15
Blue-collar occupation[d] (%)	54	48	60	55	48	58
Farm occupation[d] (%)	10	14	4	8	11	7
Mean Duncan Index score[d,e]	17	16	18	20	18	21

[a]Characteristics are measured as of the last survey before death for the deceased respondents and at a comparable survey point randomly assigned for the reference group. See the appendix to this chapter for further details on the sample.
[b]Nonresponse rates may vary slightly from item to item.
[c]All income and earnings are adjusted to 1976 dollars.
[d]Current or last job.
[e]See Glossary for definition of Duncan Index.

forewarning of the death, with perhaps concomitant changes in the work behavior of other family members. This severity is probably associated with higher average medical expenditures for the unhealthy decedents than for unhealthy reference group members. Thus the families with the heaviest burdens of medical expenses are the ones in which the erstwhile breadwinner is least likely to be bringing home regular earnings. Finally, the greater severity of the illness may make it more difficult for the respondent's wife or other family members to accept employment outside the home. Undoubtedly, there are many families in which the wife or other adult family members face a difficult conflict between needing to work to supplement the family's income and needing to stay home to assist an increasingly disabled husband or father.[18] The income and earnings data presented in a later section clarify how this conflict is often resolved.[19]

Unhealthy white men who were later to die worked an average of 29 weeks during the year preceding the interview, fewer than the 38 weeks for the unhealthy reference group members and far fewer than the 47 weeks for the decedents with no history of a health problem. There was no basis, in terms of either weeks worked per year or hours worked per week, for predicting the deaths of men who had not reported a health problem before the survey in which their demise was reported. Thus in many respects they may serve as a useful reference group for interpreting the predeath income experiences of those decedents who had suffered deteriorating health.

The evidence in table 7.4, which presents data for husbands and wives, indicates that the labor supply behavior of wives in this age group is moderately sensitive to the husband's labor force commitment. For example, within the reference group, white men with health problems worked on average about 10 weeks less during the year than their healthy counterparts, whereas the compensating difference among their wives was only one week. Within the decedent group the men with health problems worked 19 fewer weeks than those who died without any reported history of health problems, and their wives worked an average of 7 weeks more during the year than the wives of men who died suddenly.[20] For both blacks and whites the mean number of weeks worked by the wives of men with health problems was virtually invariant between the decedent and reference groups, despite substantial differentials among the hus-

Table 7.4
Selected Employment-Related Characteristics of Husbands and Wives: Decedents and Reference Group, by Health Status and Race: The Cross Section[a]

Employment-related characteristic	Decedents			Reference group		
	Total	Health problem	No health problem	Total	Health problem	No health problem
Whites						
Number of respondents[b]	349	194	155	1,224	331	893
Mean weeks worked by husband in past year	38	29	48	46	38	48
Mean annual hours worked by husband	1,330	812	2,112	1,932	1,330	2,112
Mean weeks worked by wife in past year	22	25	18	22	23	22
Mean annual hours worked by wife	718	821	590	729	809	700
Mean hourly rate of pay of wife at current job ($)	4.53	4.67	4.34	4.45	3.94	4.64
Percentage of past year worked by wife[c]	35	39	28	35	39	34
Blacks						
Number of respondents[b]	166	95	71	333	105	228
Mean weeks worked by husband in past year	32	20	47	45	36	49
Mean annual hours worked by husband	928	420	1833	1,710	1,116	2,009
Mean weeks worked by wife in past year	24	24	23	26	24	27
Mean annual hours worked by wife	675	625	739	790	700	826
Mean hourly rate of pay of wife at current job ($)	2.68	2.77	2.56	2.68	2.10	2.89
Percentage of past year worked by wife[c]	32	30	36	38	34	40

[a]Characteristics are measured as of the last survey before death for the deceased respondents and their wives and at a comparable survey point randomly assigned for the reference group. See the appendix to this chapter for further details.
[b]Nonresponse rates may vary across characteristics.
[c]Percentage of 2,080 hours (40 hours × 52 weeks).

bands in favor of the reference group. On an annual basis, however, the mean hours worked during the year by white wives whose husbands had health problems was somewhat above the corresponding value in cases where the husband was healthy, regardless of whether the husband died. The extent to which the relationship between the husband's and wife's work activity varied over the several years preceding a death is examined later.[21]

Occupational Differentials

Respondents in both the white and black decedent groups had jobs of slightly lower status than the reference groups, whether gauged from the perspective of their Duncan Index or Census one-digit occupation group (table 7.3).[22] In both the decedent and the reference group, respondents with health problems were generally more likely than their healthy counterparts to be in lower-status, more physically demanding, blue-collar or farm occupations. The lower socioeconomic status of respondents in these categories may be partly responsible for a higher incidence of health problems, since there is evidence that individuals from lower-status backgrounds are less attentive to their physical well-being and, when ill, less likely to seek necessary medical assistance.[23]

On the other hand, the data may simply reflect a greater likelihood of respondents in blue-collar and other physically demanding occupations to have difficulty maintaining their employment when they have physical disabilities. It is often possible to continue working at many white-collar or other sedentary jobs with a physical disability that would constrain a worker in a more physically demanding occupation.[24] Table 7.5 shows employment rates by occupational level for the four groups of whites and blacks on which the analysis has been based. The data offer dramatic confirmation of the effect of health condition on the likelihood of employment. More particularly, however, they also show that this effect is greater for men in lower-status than in higher-status jobs. For example, employment rates for all white healthy reference group members or decedents were over 90 percent, regardless of occupational level. In contrast, only about 70 percent of the white reference group with health problems were currently employed, regardless of their occupational level. However, among decedents with health problems, about 69 percent of those in higher-status occupations were employed compared with only 49 percent of their lower-status counterparts. The data not only reinforce the view that the prospective decedents probably have more serious health problems but also indicate that the joint impact of a

Table 7.5
Employment Rates of Decedents and Reference Group, by Occupational Status, Health Status, and Race: The Cross Section[a]

Occupational status[b]	Decedents		Reference group	
	Health problem	No health problem	Health problem	No health problem
Whites				
Duncan Index score less than 30				
Number of respondents	119	85	211	432
Employment rate	.49	.94	.72	.93
Duncan Index score 30 or more				
Number of respondents	106	92	157	532
Employment rate	.69	.92	.71	.94
Blacks				
Duncan Index score less than 30				
Number of respondents	116	88	110	230
Employment rate	.35	.90	.66	.93
Duncan Index score 30 or more				
Number of respondents	14	11	20	59
Employment rate	—[c]	—[c]	—[c]	.89

[a]The employment rates were constructed by dividing the number of employed respondents reporting a given occupation by the number of employed and unemployed respondents reporting that occupation as their current or last occupation. Characteristics are measured as of the last survey before death for the deceased respondents and at a comparable survey point randomly assigned for the reference group. See the appendix to this chapter for further details on the sample.
[b]Socioeconomic status is measured by the Duncan Socioeconomic Index of occupations. See Duncan (1961). The index assigns a two-digit status score to each three-digit occupational category in the Census classification scheme. The Duncan scores range from 0 to 96 and reflect for each occupation (1) the proportion of male workers in 1950 with educational attainment of four years of high school or more and (2) the proportion of males with incomes of $3,500 or more in 1949.
[c]Statistics are not shown where the base is fewer than 25 sample cases.

health problem and a lower-status job result in a higher rate of withdrawal from work, either voluntarily or involuntarily.[25]

Income and Earnings Differentials

The employment differentials are predictive of parallel differentials in income and earnings between families in the different prospective mortality and health categories. Family income

Table 7.6
Mean Components of Family Income for Decedents and Reference Group, by Health Status and Race: The Cross Section[a]

Component[b]	Decedents			Reference group		
	Total	Health problem	No health problem	Total	Health problem	No health problem
	Whites					
Number of respondents	294	165	129	906	256	650
Total family income ($)	14,553	12,364	17,345	17,910	13,744	19,556
Earnings of respondent ($)	8,199	5,483	11,662	10,961	6,579	12,685
Earnings of wife ($)	1,741	1,687	1,811	2,079	1,826	2,179
Other income ($)	4,613	5,194	3,872	4,870	5,339	4,692
	Blacks					
Number of respondents	179	116	63	293	87	206
Total family income ($)	7,471	7,276	7,825	10,129	7,577	11,142
Earnings of respondent ($)	3,841	2,570	6,144	6,733	3,705	7,935
Earnings of wife ($)	1,142	1,284	886	1,271	912	1,414
Other income ($)	2,488	3,422	795	2,125	2,960	1,793

Note: Limited to families with data on family income, respondent's earnings and wife's earnings (if married and spouse present). Families where no wife is present are assigned a zero for wife's earnings. Information from the 1973 survey is excluded since data on wife's earnings were not available for that year.
[a]Characteristics are measured as of the last survey before death for the deceased respondents and at a comparable survey point randomly assigned for the reference group. See the appendix to this chapter for further details on the sample.
[b]All income and earnings are adjusted to 1976 dollars.

levels are much more sensitive to the health status of the primary male breadwinner than to prospective mortality (table 7.6). For example, white reference group families where the respondent is healthy have a mean family income in 1976 dollars of about $19,500 compared with about $13,700 for reference group families where the respondent has a health problem. Virtually all this difference of about $5,800 is accounted for by the lower annual earnings of the respondent who has a health problem. There is no apparent substitution of other income sources for the lost earnings of the respondent.

Among families of white decedents the situation is essentially the same. Families where the respondent has an illness have a family income about $5,000 below that for the decedent families where the respondent has no apparent illness. A loss of over $6,000 in respondent's earnings was only slightly compensated for by an increase in other earnings, which include all forms of pensions, Social Security, and other transfer payments as well as earnings of family members other than the respondent's wife.[26]

For black families the pattern of income deterioration was somewhat different for the decedent group. Where the respondent had a health problem, families were able to compensate for the loss of his earnings by a substantial increase in other income sources. About 10 percent of the unhealthy decedent group received a pension, 33 percent received Social Security, and 44 percent had access to other income.

Overall, however, the black decedent group had by far the lowest family income—only $7,471 compared with about $10,000 for the black reference group, $14,500 for the white decedents, and almost $18,000 for the white reference group. In all instances a health problem approximately halved the respondent's earnings, but in no instance did the wife's earnings substantially increase as the respondent's earnings declined.[27] Thus it appears that in most instances the need for the wife to provide assistance in the home overrides the need and ability to seek and find remunerative employment outside the home. This decision must often be painful, for in each of the two racial groups the decedent families where the respondent has a health problem also have the lowest family incomes. These are presumably also the families most in need of special financial assistance because of above-average medical and nursing care expenses. Finally, as we know, the financial situation of these families can only deteriorate further with the impending death of the breadwinner.

Income and Employment Adequacy before Death

Employment Trends

The longitudinal framework of the NLS permits one to follow the decedents backward from death, noting whether the income and employment problems associated with impending mortality are short-term or whether they constrain the well-being of a family over a long period.

The characteristics of an eligible subset of all the reference group and decedents for periods of up to six years before death were examined to clarify the extent to which income and employment deterioration associated with a decline in health are of a long-term nature. The last predeath point in this trend analysis (referred to as the T-2 survey point) may be as long as two years or as little as one day before a death (thus averaging about one year before the death event). T-4 represents a survey point approximately two years preceding T-2, and T-6 precedes T-4 by two years. Thus T-4 is in actuality between two and four years (averaging three years) before a death, and T-6 is between four and six years (averaging five years) before a death.[28]

The data in table 7.7 suggest that the health problems of decedents and reference group members, where they existed, were of relatively long duration. Over 70 percent of the white decedents who had a health problem at T-2 were reporting health problems at T-4, and over 60 percent at T-6. A comparable pattern prevailed among the black decedents. How these long-standing disabilities are reflected in labor force disadvantage may be noted in figure 7.1. Only 69 percent of white decedents who were not healthy at T-2 were in the labor force at T-4, and only about 75 percent were working or seeking work at T-6, an average time interval of five years before death. Unhealthy reference group members displayed a trend line that was higher than that of the decedents with health problems but substantially below the trend lines of the two groups without health problems.[29]

The labor force trend line for unhealthy black decedents shows a level of participation similar to that of their white counterparts at the T-6 and T-4 points but a much more precipitous decline in work attachment between T-4 and T-2. It is apparent that the more severely handicapped black respondents are much less able than their white counterparts to maintain employment ties in the period shortly before death. This may reflect a number of factors, including the lower occupational status of blacks,[30] and perhaps the more serious physical manifestations of illness in the period immediately preceding death. Supporting evidence for this latter point is that similar proportions of unhealthy black and white decedents reported being unable to work at T-6 and T-4; but at T-2 almost 55 percent of the blacks reported that they were unable to work, compared with 30 percent for the whites (table 7.7).

Both white and black decedents with health problems show fairly substantial declines in mean weeks worked over the period from T-6 to T-2, a decline of 10 weeks (from 40 to 30) for whites and 17 weeks (from 37 to 20) for blacks.[31] Thus even the substantial decline in labor force participation over the four-year period understates the full impact of the respondents' declining health on their attachment to the labor force.

211

Table 7.7
Selected Employment-Related and Income Characteristics of Decedents and Reference Group, by Health Status at T-2 and Race: Trend Results[a]

| | Whites | | | | | | Blacks | | | | | |
| | Decedents | | | Reference group | | | Decedents | | | Reference group | | |
Selected characteristic	Total	Health problem	No health problem	Total	Health problem	No health problem	Total	Health problem	No health problem	Total	Health problem	No health problem
Number of respondents[b]	247	159	88	836	232	604	147	84	63	262	85	177
Labor force participation rate												
T-2	69	55	96	88	67	96	62	36	95	89	72	96
T-4	80	69	99	94	83	98	79	65	97	93	77	99
T-6	84	76	99	96	90	99	83	74	94	96	85	100
Percentage employed and not at work												
T-2	11	14	6	9	8	10	9	7	13	12	6	14
T-4	6	4	10	9	8	9	11	9	13	8	5	8
T-6	6	6	8	6	7	5	3	2	5	4	6	4
Percentage unable to work												
T-2	19	30	0	3	10	0	29	53	0	4	14	0
T-4	16	25	0	3	11	0	14	23	2	5	18	0
T-6	12	19	0	2	6	0	11	19	2	4	12	0
Mean usual hours worked per week in past year												
T-2	31	26	45	40	31	44	26	15	39	36	29	41
T-4	34	29	47	43	37	46	30	20	42	37	31	41
T-6	36	31	47	42	38	44	32	23	42	36	32	39
Mean weeks worked in past year												
T-2	37	30	48	46	37	49	32	20	49	46	37	49
T-4	41	35	50	48	43	50	40	34	49	47	39	50
T-6	43	40	49	49	45	50	42	37	49	47	42	49

Mean Duncan Index[c] score of current job (employed workers)											
T-2	37	39	35	39	34	40	20	21	19	21	21
T-4	36	36	36	39	34	41	18	18	19	20	21
T-6	35	34	36	39	33	41	20	19	20	19	19
Mean hourly rate of pay at current job (employed workers)[d] ($)											
T-2	5.76	5.44	6.01	6.91	6.13	7.08	4.05	—[e]	4.14	4.56	4.70
T-4	5.51	5.24	5.76	6.58	5.86	6.75	3.98	4.04	3.93	4.47	4.57
T-6	5.40	5.16	5.64	6.37	5.78	6.51	4.08	4.45	3.81	4.11	4.15
Mean family income[d] ($)											
T-2	12,873	10,434	17,178	18,903	14,831	20,474	6,659	6,249	7,462	10,462	11,618
T-4	14,617	13,070	17,469	19,596	15,009	21,357	8,691	7,883	9,698	10,939	12,010
T-6	14,525	13,747	15,982	18,854	15,617	20,084	8,207	6,824	9,976	10,366	11,005
Mean earnings of respondent[d] ($)											
T-2	7,438	4,714	12,428	11,648	7,494	13,119	4,091	2,353	7,123	7,282	8,383
T-4	8,391	6,804	11,298	11,686	7,859	13,158	6,009	4,864	7,565	7,567	8,448
T-6	8,967	7,714	11,186	11,721	8,734	12,860	5,971	4,781	7,539	7,086	7,751

Table 7.7 (continued)

| | Whites | | | | | | Blacks | | | | | |
| | Decedents | | | Reference group | | | Decedents | | | Reference group | | |
Selected characteristic	Total	Health problem	No health problem	Total	Health problem	No health problem	Total	Health problem	No health problem	Total	Health problem	No health problem
Percentage with health problem												
T-2	64	100	0	27	100	0	56	100	0	29	100	0
T-4	51	71	14	25	60	12	44	65	16	30	57	19
T-6	45	63	12	24	54	12	40	56	18	26	57	13
Mean poverty ratio												
T-2	3.08	2.76	3.63	4.38	3.43	4.76	1.90	1.44	2.48	2.35	1.76	2.63
T-4	3.28	2.93	3.86	4.19	3.52	4.45	1.93	1.76	2.14	2.26	1.86	2.45
T-6	3.09	2.85	3.50	4.01	3.57	4.18	1.74	1.45	2.12	3.12	1.86	3.71

[a]Only respondents whose last survey occurred at least two years before they were first reported as deceased (or a randomly assigned survey for the reference group) are included in the trend sample. Therefore only respondents for whom T-2 was the 1969, 1971, or 1973 survey are included here. See the appendix to this chapter for further details on the sample.
[b]Nonresponse rates may vary from item to item.
[c]See Glossary for definition of Duncan Index of Socioeconomic Status.
[d]All income and earnings are adjusted to 1976 dollars.
[e]Statistics are not shown where base is fewer than 25 sample cases.

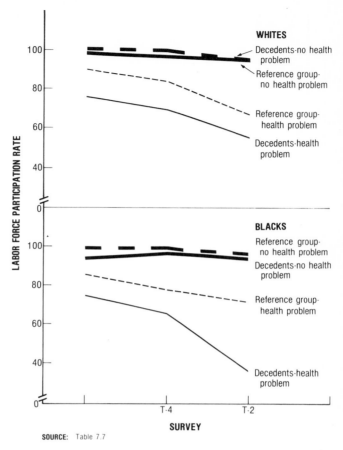

SOURCE: Table 7.7

Figure 7.1
Labor Force Participation Rates, by Health Status (at T-2) and Race: Decedents and Reference Group, Selected Time Periods

Family Income and Employment Dynamics

Because most of the reference group and decedents lived with their wives, the income analysis in this section is confined to husband-wife households. As may be noted in table 7.8, there was generally little income or earnings variation during the period T-6 to T-2 for the healthy subsets (except for white decedents), but the subsets of respondents with health problems showed substantial declines in husband's earnings. However, the full economic impact of this decline is assuaged somewhat by increases in the family's access to other income sources such as Social Security, welfare, or perhaps the income of other

215

Table 7.8
Mean Family Income and Mean Earnings of Respondent and Wife for Married, Spouse-Present Families of Decedents and Reference Group, by Health Status at T-2 and Race: Trend Results[a]

| | Whites | | | | | | Blacks | | | | | |
| | Decedents | | | Reference group | | | Decedents | | | Reference group | | |
Mean income or earnings[b]	Total	Health problem	No health problem	Total	Health problem	No health problem	Total	Health problem	No health problem	Total	Health problem	No health problem
Number of respondents	93	56	37	315	86	229	48	27	21	85	25	60
T-2												
Family income ($)	12,846	10,510	16,447	19,637	14,969	21,387	8,276	7,871	8,818	10,940	8,668	11,841
Earnings of respondent ($)	6,878	3,514	12,064	12,820	7,464	14,828	4,861	3,158	7,146	7,708	5,023	8,771
Earnings of wife ($)	1,522	1,126	2,134	2,561	2,292	2,662	1,729	2,119	1,205	1,885	1,660	1,974
T-4												
Family income ($)	13,212	10,475	17,432	19,033	14,173	20,855	9,127	8,992	9,308	11,262	8,281	12,443
Earnings of respondent ($)	7,920	5,238	12,054	12,440	8,194	14,032	6,082	4,869	7,677	8,367	5,946	9,327
Earnings of wife ($)	1,614	1,504	1,784	2,417	2,167	2,511	1,732	2,009	1,360	1,560	954	1,800
T-6												
Family income ($)	12,921	11,477	15,148	18,735	14,618	20,279	8,206	7,389	9,302	11,001	8,481	12,000
Earnings of respondent ($)	8,393	6,737	10,946	12,475	8,553	13,945	5,780	4,524	7,464	7,599	5,446	8,452
Earnings of wife ($)	1,306	1,387	1,183	2,071	1,742	2,194	1,521	1,476	1,580	1,928	1,757	1,996

[a] Only respondents whose last survey occurred at least two years before they were first reported as deceased (or a comparable, randomly assigned survey for the reference group) are included in the trend sample. See the appendix to this chapter for further details on the sample. In this table respondents have data on family income, respondent's earnings, and wife's earnings at each point in time. Since data on wife's earnings were not obtained in the 1973 survey, only respondents whose T-2 point was 1969 or 1971 are included here.
[b] Income and earnings are adjusted to 1976 dollars.

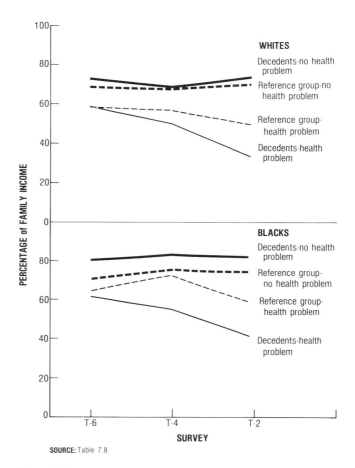

SOURCE: Table 7.8

Figure 7.2
Percentage of Family Income Contributed by Husband's Earnings, by
Health Status (at T-2) and Race: Decedents and Reference Group,
Selected Time Periods

family members (appendix table 7A.5). Between T-4 and T-2 the
percentage of black decedent families with health problems
who received Social Security increased from 2 to 18, and welfare recipients increased from 8 percent at T-6 to 19 percent at
T-4 and to 27 percent at T-2. The increases in these payments
are probably related to the higher incidence of serious (defined
by being unable to work) illness among the black decedents.

Figure 7.2 shows that the proportion of the family income
contributed by the respondents with health problems (particularly prospective decedents) declines steadily over the period included in the analysis. While the proportion of the family income

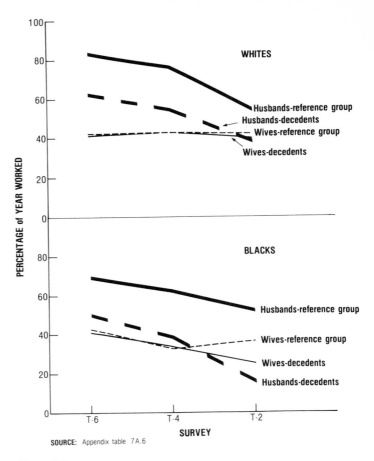

Figure 7.3
Percentage of Year Worked by Husbands and Wives, by Race: Decedents and Reference Group Members with Health Problems (at T-2), Selected Time Periods

contributed by the black respondents is somewhat higher than that of white men, the absolute levels of black income and earnings are well below those of their white counterparts.

The ability and willingness of the wives of respondents with health problems to compensate for the lost earnings of their husbands by entering the work force or increasing their annual hours of work is a question of some interest. The working wife at this critical point in the life cycle can help replace the lost earnings of the ill husband, help in the payment of often catastrophic medical bills, and acquire work experience that will stand her in good stead if her husband dies. Figure 7.3 clarifies the extent to which a work role substitution occurs between husbands with health problems and their wives. The figure includes estimates of the percentage of the year preceding the survey date that husbands and their wives were employed.[32] White decedents with health problems at T-2 showed a gradual decline in the percentage of the year worked between T-6 and T-2. During the same period there was no change in the percentage of the year worked by the white wives. Black decedents with health problems showed a modest decline in the percentage of the year worked between T-6 and T-4 and a precipitous decline (from about 40 percent of the year to less than 20 percent of the year) between T-4 and T-2. During the same interval their wives showed a fairly substantial decline in their work involvement. Thus it is readily apparent that there is no net movement into the labor force by wives of decedents with health problems. Perhaps the family demands placed on the woman (particularly the black woman) in addition to outdated work skills (reflecting an often lengthy exile from gainful employment for white women) keep her from seeking and finding steady employment at a reasonable wage. Even though the average work contribution of the black wife declined over the interval, the level of her activity was above that of her husband at the end of the interval. Furthermore, our data suggest that it was the lowest-wage black women who were withdrawing from the labor force, for average earnings of black women increased during the period even though the amount of work activity decreased (table 7.8).

The Short-Run Economic Impact of Widowhood

Over one million widowed women 30 to 54 years of age are in the United States today, and their social, economic, and psychological problems are of increasing importance, especially as the changing age structure will produce proportionately greater numbers in the not too distant future.[33] To examine how the widows of middle-aged men adjust economically to their husbands' final illness and death, we use data from the NLS sample of mature women. Women who first became widowed between the 1967 and 1976 surveys constitute the sample of widows, and a reference group of married women was drawn in a manner analogous to that used for the reference group of men used in the preceding sections (see the appendix to this chapter). Most of the analysis involves comparisons between the status or activity reported by the women in the last survey before the death of the husband and in the first survey after his

219

death. For a subset of women widowed before 1972, trends are observed over the period of three surveys after the husband's death.[34] The women under consideration are somewhat younger than the widows of the deceased men who have been the subjects of investigation so far, since the oldest could not be over 53.[35]

The onset of widowhood represents the most traumatic period of the life cycle for a large proportion of married persons. Grief over the loss of a spouse appears to transcend differences in social and economic status. Moreover, whether death occurs after a lingering and burdensome illness or is due to a sudden accident, a period of disrupted daily activity for the widow is likely.[36]

In addition to this psychological trauma, death of a husband also imposes on the survivors the problem of coping economically. This section focuses on changes in the widow's work behavior and in family economic and social characteristics during this transition period. Most previous research reviewing the economic aspects of widowhood has been based on cross-sectional data for widows and nonwidows or on retrospective data from samples of widows who rely on their recall for information about the period prior to the husband's death.[37] Our longitudinal data offer a unique opportunity to examine the actual behavior of the same women before and shortly after the death of their husbands. Moverover, comparisons over the same period of time can be made with a sample of women whose husbands remain alive.

Characteristics before the Death of the Spouse

A woman's ability to cope with dramatic changes in economic circumstances is frequently conditioned by her personal and family characteristics prior to the change. It is therefore of interest to inquire how married women who are shortly to become widows compare in terms of socioeconomic characteristics, even before their husbands die, with women of similar ages whose husbands will survive. Data presented in tables 7.9, 7.10, and 7.11 provide answers to these questions and are consistent with what we have learned from our previous comparison of the sample of decedent males and their reference group.

The prospective widows are by a variety of criteria more heavily concentrated than the reference group in the lower so-

Table 7.9
Sociodemographic Characteristics of Widows before and after Death of Husband Compared with Reference Group of Married Women, by Race: Mature Women's Cohort

Sociodemographic characteristic	Before[a]			After[a]		
	Total	Whites	Blacks	Total	Whites	Blacks
Widows						
Number of respondents[c]	200	124	76	200	124	76
Mean age	44.6	44.9	42.7	—[c]	—[c]	—[c]
Mean number of dependents	2.0	1.7	3.3	2.0	1.8	2.8
Percentage with less than 12 years education[d]	44	37	82	—[c]	—[c]	—[c]
Mean years of education[d]	10.6	10.8	8.9	—[c]	—[c]	—[c]
Percentage with health limitation	19	17	29	23	20	40
Mean number of children	1.5	1.3	2.7	1.2	1.1	2.2
Percentage with children under 18 living in household	63	62	71	53	51	70
Percentage residing in rural area	33	33	35	31	31	33
Reference group						
Number of respondents[b]	3,150	2,500	650	3,150	2,500	650
Mean age	42.0	42.0	41.6	—[c]	—[c]	—[c]
Mean number of dependents	2.5	2.5	2.7	2.3	2.3	2.7
Percentage with less than 12 years education[d]	31	29	55	—[c]	—[c]	—[c]
Mean years of education[d]	11.5	11.6	10.5	—[c]	—[c]	—[c]
Percentage with health limitation	16	16	20	18	17	20
Mean number of children	2.0	2.0	2.3	1.7	1.7	2.0
Percentage with children under 18 living in household	79	80	76	72	72	71
Percentage residing in rural area	34	35	21	34	35	21

[a]Before and after refer, respectively, to the time of the last survey before the death (or randomly assigned survey for the reference group) and the first survey thereafter.
[b]These sample sizes may vary somewhat according to the time period being referenced as well as by characteristic due to missing data. Therefore sample sizes represent maximum numbers of respondents possible for each category.
[c]Statistics are not shown where base represents less than 25 sample cases.
[d]Number of years of schooling was obtained only in the initial (1967) survey.

cioeconomic strata, and the differences are most pronounced among blacks. For example, the prospective widows have significantly lower levels of education than other married women. If employed, they are more likely than other women to be in lower-status occupations and to be earning lower wages. Moreover, there is no compensating tendency for them to be more likely to be upgrading their skills through occupational training. Their husbands, also, are in lower-status occupations than are the husbands of other married women, and these men tend to work fewer weeks per year and fewer hours per week,

Table 7.10
Employment and Income Characteristics of Widows before and after Death of Husband Compared with Reference Group of Married Women, by Race: Mature Women's Cohort

Characteristic[a]	Before[b]			After[b]		
	Total	Whites	Blacks	Total	Whites	Blacks
	Widows					
Number of respondents[c] employment	200	124	76	200	124	76
Occupation of current or last job (percentage distribution)						
Total	100	100	100	100	100	100
White collar	52	58	12	50	56	11
Blue collar	36	35	42	38	37	43
Farm	5	5	6	4	4	8
Other	7	2	40	8	3	38
Duncan Index of current or last job[d]						
Mean score	34	37	18	34	36	18
Percentage with low score (less than 30)	46	39	84	48	42	83
Mean hours usually worked at current or last job	36	36	37	35	36	32
Percentage receiving training in past year[e]	15	17	6	11	13	0
Labor force participation rate	52	50	66	56	58	44
Percentage employed	50	48	61	54	56	39
Income						
Mean annual earnings[f] ($)	2,681	2,813	1,861	2,760	2,918	1,779
Mean family income ($)	15,056	16,033	8,939	9,200	10,010	5,385
Mean welfare income[g] ($)	67	36	256	154	94	506
Mean pension income[h] ($)	493	522	292	1,750	1,832	1,300
Mean poverty ratio	2.83	3.07	1.35	2.12	2.35	1.02
Percentage below poverty line	24	19	47	36	29	67
Percentage receiving welfare income[g]	5	4	12	11	8	26
Percentage receiving pension income[h]	14	13	17	73	73	72

probably reflecting a greater incidence of health problems among them.[38] As a consequence, the annual earnings of these husbands are significantly lower than those enjoyed by husbands in the reference group; total family income, of course, is substantially lower, despite the greater likelihood of the receipt of Social Security and other transfer payments.

Table 7.10 (continued)

Characteristic[a]	Before[b]			After[b]		
	Total	Whites	Blacks	Total	Whites	Blacks
	Reference group					
Number of respondents[c]	3,150	2,500	650	3,150	2,500	650
Employment						
Occupation of current or last job (percentage distribution)						
Total	100	100	100	100	100	100
White collar	63	66	30	62	65	31
Blue collar	31	30	46	31	30	48
Farm	3	3	3	3	3	3
Other	4	2	20	4	3	19
Duncan Index of current or last job[d]						
Mean score	39	40	25	39	40	26
Percentage with low score (less than 30)	36	33	67	36	33	66
Mean hours usually worked at current or last job	34	34	36	34	34	36
Percentage receiving training in past year[e]	13	13	15	12	12	11
Labor force participation rate	52	47	66	53	52	66
Percentage employed	50	48	64	51	50	64
Income						
Mean annual earnings[f] ($)	2,779	2,693	3,816	2,915	2,826	3,985
Mean family income ($)	19,867	20,361	14,556	19,984	20,471	14,800
Mean welfare income[g] ($)	22	16	95	46	35	172
Mean pension income[h] ($)	203	205	179	303	307	256
Mean poverty ratio	3.35	3.44	2.42	3.43	3.52	2.47
Percentage below poverty line	5	3	18	4	3	14
Percentage receiving welfare income[g]	2	2	6	3	2	11
Percentage receiving pension income[h]	8	8	8	3	2	11

[a] Income and earnings are adjusted to 1976 dollars.
[b] Before and after refer, respectively, to the time of the last survey prior to the death (or randomly assigned survey for the reference group) and the first one thereafter.
[c] These sample sizes may vary somewhat by the time period being referenced as well as by characteristic due to missing data. Therefore sample sizes represent maximum numbers of respondents possible for each category.
[d] See Glossary for a description of the Duncan Index of Socioeconomic Status.
[e] The question on receipt of training was asked only for survey years 1969, 1971, and 1972.
[f] All women.
[g] Welfare income is composed of AFDC or public assistance payments as well as food stamp income in years where data were collected.
[h] Pension income includes income from private or government pension programs and Social Security, old age or survivors insurance.

Table 7.11
Employment Characteristics of Widows' Husbands prior to Death Compared with Husbands of Reference Group of Married Women, by Race: Mature Women's Cohort

Employment characteristic[a]	Widows			Reference group		
	Total	Whites	Blacks	Total	Whites	Blacks
Number of respondents[b]	200	124	76	3,150	2,500	650
Occupation of current or last job (percentage distribution)						
Total	100	100	100	100	100	100
White collar	36	39	8	44	46	20
Blue collar	48	45	67	45	44	58
Farm	7	6	13	5	5	3
Other	10	10	12	6	5	19
Mean usual hours worked per week in past year	34	35	32	44	44	38
Mean weeks worked in past year	40	39	40	49	49	46
Mean annual earnings ($)	8,649	9,168	5,118	2,980	13,319	8,832
Mean Duncan Index score of current or last job[c]	37	39	21	42	44	24
Percentage with health limitation[d]	44	45	42	12	12	16

[a]All income and earnings are adjusted to 1976 dollars.
[b]These sample sizes may vary somewhat by characteristic due to missing data. Therefore, sample sizes represent maximum numbers of respondents possible for each category.
[c]See glossary for a description of the Duncan Index of Socioeconomic Status.
[d]Health status of husband was asked only in survey years 1967, 1969, and 1971.

Other differences between the two groups are either smaller or nonexistent or are discernible only in one or the other racial group. Health status, for example, is not perceptibly different between prospective widows and the reference group except among blacks, where the prospective widows are more likely to have health problems. Residence in a rural area is also more frequent among blacks who are to become widows than among other black married women. Further, the number of dependents is somewhat lower among the white prospective widows than among their black counterparts. There are relatively few consistent differences between prospective widows and the reference group in measures of the extent of work activity.

In sum, the data show that women who are destined to become widows have already been at an economic disadvantage relative to other married women even before their husbands' death. Moreover, there is the ironic paradox that those who are to lose their husbands are, in terms of education and skills, less able to compensate economically for the loss than those women who will not need to do so.

The Transition to Widowhood

We now examine, by means of longitudinal analysis, the extent to which a widow can maintain or improve her economic status after the death of her husband. The most obvious way to improve her position is to increase the amount or quality of her employment. She may also make increased use of other income sources such as Social Security or private pension benefits, insurance, and welfare or public assistance payments. Finally, she may remarry.

The likelihood of each of these methods of adjustment is to some degree related to age at widowhood. For example, among those not regularly employed, the older the woman, the more likely are her work skills to be outdated and the less likely she is to find employment. Chances for remarriage also decrease with age.[39] On the other hand, older widows are less likely to have dependent children. Although, other things being equal, the chances of remarriage are greater for younger widows, they are more likely to have children at home, and the presence of children may tend to discourage prospective suitors. In addition, the presence of children may impede the ability of the widow to seek and find employment outside the home. Considerations of this kind remind us that it may be dangerous to generalize from the present data to the widows of the older men who are the major focus of this volume.

Tables 7.9 and 7.10 point up sociodemographic and economic changes that occurred among the widows between the survey before and the survey after the husband's death. Perhaps the most significant sociodemographic change is the 11 percent drop in the proportion of white women with children under age 18 living in the household. That the corresponding decrease among the somewhat younger reference group of white women was almost as large indicates that this phenomenon is attributable not to the death of the husband but to normal life cycle changes. Nevertheless, it does suggest some amelioration of financial burden among whites. Among blacks there is no comparable reduction in the number of children under age 18 living at home. Another noteworthy change is the increase in the proportion of black women with health problems (11 percentage

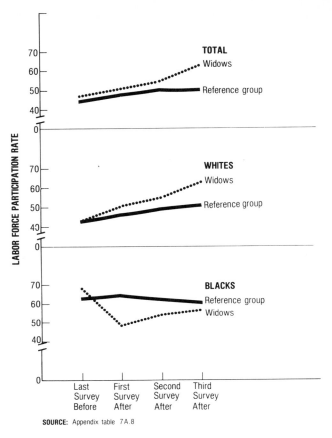

Figure 7.4
Labor Force Participation Rates of Widows before and after Death of
Husband Compared with Reference Group of Married Women, by Race:
Selected Time Periods

SOURCE: Appendix table 7A.8

points). Since no corresponding increase is evident in the black
reference group, the change may reflect the emotional stress
attributable to the death of the husband, although this is admit-
tedly merely an inference.

The moderate increase in labor force participation (table 7.10)
among white widows is only slightly greater than among the
reference group, while among blacks there is a precipitous drop
that does not occur among members of the reference group.[40]
Figures 7.4 and 7.5 show the trend in labor market activity for
the restricted group of widows whose husbands died before
1972. Although the very small sample sizes preclude confident
generalizations, figure 7.4 shows a dramatic difference in pat-

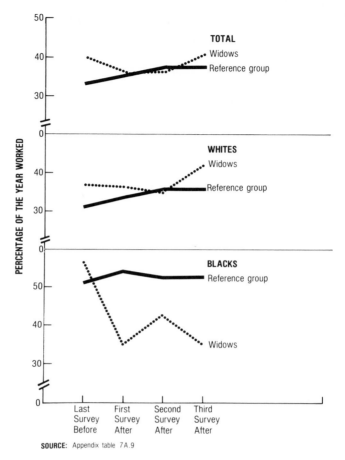

PERCENTAGE OF THE YEAR WORKED

TOTAL
Widows
Reference group

WHITES
Widows
Reference group

BLACKS
Reference group
Widows

Last Survey Before / First Survey After / Second Survey After / Third Survey After

SOURCE: Appendix table 7A.9

Figure 7.5
Percentage of Year Worked by Widows before and after Death of Husband Compared with Reference Group of Married Women, by Race: Selected Time Periods

terns of labor force participation rates between black and white widows. The latter increased their participation monotonically. By the third survey after the death of their husbands their rate, which had been about equal to that of the reference group prior to their husbands' death, was 14 percentage points higher. Among black widows, on the other hand, the participation rate—originally slightly higher than that of the reference group—dropped sharply immediately following the death of the husband, to approximately 20 percentage points below that of the reference group. Thereafter there was a gradual increase, but by the third survey following the death of the husband the

227

rate was still below its original level and slightly below that of the white widows and the black reference group as well. Where annual hours (expressed as a percentage of 2,080 hours) are the criterion (figure 7.5), the pattern is somewhat different for whites, but it shows an even more precipitous drop for black widows relative to their reference group and no clear recovery by the third survey after the death.

There is also little evidence of net changes in occupational distribution before and after widowhood. In the brief period under scrutiny here, there appears to be no perceptible qualitative improvement in employment among the widows, only a moderate quantitative increase for whites, and a fairly substantial quantitative decline for blacks. As a consequence, the real annual earnings reported by white widows in the survey following the death of their husbands is only 4 percent higher than those reported in the preceding survey, an increase comparable to that of the reference group. Among black widows, real annual earnings actually decrease by 4 percent, in contrast to a 4 percent increase among the black reference group.

The most dramatic changes occur in total real family income. There is a decrease of 38 percent (about $6,000) for white widows and 40 percent (approximately $3,500) for black widows, while the real incomes of the reference groups show very small increases. The very substantial increases in pension and Social Security income for the widows and the more modest increase in welfare income, along with changes in their own earnings, replace approximately 16 percent of the husband's earnings for whites and 23 percent for blacks. However, the proportion of white widows living below the poverty line is 29 percent, compared with 19 percent before the death of the husband. Among blacks the corresponding percentages are 47 before the death of the husband and 67 after. In the reference group there was no increase between the two survey dates in the much smaller proportion of families below the poverty line.

In summary, it appears that the means of income maintenance after the death of the spouse are severely limited and differ to some extent by the race of the widow.[41] For example, the difference between whites and blacks in the extent of labor market activity after the death of the husband may be attributable in part to racial differences in the number of children remaining in the home and the lower potential earnings of black women. Taken together, relatively low salaries and larger families may influence some black widows to rely more on Social Security and public assistance payments for primary income maintenance shortly after the death of their husbands. In addition, lesser occupational skills and educational qualifications may impede many of the black widows who seek to enter the labor market following the husband's death.

Summary and Conclusions

Two of every ten men between the ages of 45 and 64 will not survive to age 65. The large majority of these men who die during the prime adult years leave widows. The inability of many families to cope economically with the health deterioration and death of the person who was (in most cases) the primary breadwinner represents a major social problem.

Even before the husband's death, families of men with health problems are concentrated in lower socioeconomic strata than families of men who die with no evidence of illness. Husbands and wives in these families are more likely to have lower levels of education, lower-paying and less-skilled jobs, and lower income; the men are also more likely to be entirely without a job. Therefore these family units enter the crisis phase already economically disadvantaged and thus potentially less able to cope with future medical expenses.

This chapter has highlighted the gradual pattern of income deterioration for families where the head has a health problem in the years preceding his death. The gradual decline in his earnings is not replaced to any appreciable extent by increased earnings of the wife, although other income and earnings compensate to some extent. The pattern is the same but considerably more severe following the husband's death, particularly for the average black widow. These problems are especially pronounced in families where the man has been in a lower-status occupation. Such men are more likely to withdraw from the labor market when disability strikes (see chapter 5). In addition, families in this category have been plagued by low income even before the onset of the health problem. Moreover, the wife in these families probably has few job skills and little education to fall back on if she seeks employment as her husband's physical condition deteriorates. Finally, low potential earnings, coupled with family demands associated with an ailing husband may induce many women in this situation to remain at home rather than work.

In contrast, the prime-age man who dies without an extensive health disability history in most instances continues working until shortly before his death, and his family's income is thus maintained at a higher level. In addition, his medical expenses are undoubtedly lower.

While there is modest evidence that wives of unhealthy white men are more likely than wives of healthy men to work in the years preceding their husbands' death, some data from the sample of mature women suggest that an appreciable number of white women enter the labor force after their husbands die. Labor force participation rates for these women show some increase between the last survey before the husband's death and the several surveys thereafter. This delayed reaction probably reflects a number of circumstances, including the realization by the widow that her huband's earnings are permanently gone as well as a lesser need for her to be at home. However, the data do not reveal any substanial numbers of widows who choose to prepare for a more productive life of work by entering job-related training programs. In contrast to the white women, black women whose husbands have died decrease their labor force participation immediately after the death, possibly indicating a withdrawal of marginal workers whose increased child care responsibilities and low potential earnings induce them to rely on other means of replacing the lost earnings of their husbands.

It is clear that women encountering widowhood during their prime adult years are often severely disadvantaged economically. In addition, only a small proportion are in a position to reduce their economic disadvantage by entering the labor market or by increasing their earnings if they are already employed. In some instances a woman's relatively lengthy absence from the labor market and advancing age minimize the efficacy of training for gainful employment. In these situations income maintenance is often urgently needed. In other instances, however, job counseling and training in conjunction with temporary financial assistance can help a displaced homemaker enter or reenter the world of work with economic and psychological benefits accruing to both herself and her family.

Construction of Older Men's Mortality Sample

Deceased group Men who died between the 1966 and 1976
survey dates are included in the deceased group. When restricted to men aged 45 to 64, the decedents number 468
whites and 269 blacks. Information about the decedents is taken
from the last survey date at which they were interviewed; however, an individual whose last interview occurred more than two
years before the survey in which his death was first reported is
not included in the sample. Respondents who were institutionalized at the last survey prior to death represent a small exception to the preceding rule. For the 13 individuals who were institutionalized, the following characteristics used in this study
were imputed:

Age = Age at survey institutionalized. If gap between survey
institutionalized and survey deceased is two years, age
at midpoint year is taken.

Health status = Health limitation present.

Employment status = Out of labor force (unable to work).

All other characteristics for the institutionalized subgroup have
missing values.

Reference group Because blacks and whites experience different mortality patterns, every procedure used in the construction of the reference group was performed separately by race. In
addition, the selection procedure also utilized unweighted data
since differential assignment across survey years would have
meant that respondents represented different numbers of individuals at any point in time.

We began the selection of the reference group by obtaining a
distribution of the deceased men across the NLS survey years
from 1966 to 1976. This distribution established the proportions
of the deceased group who died between any two surveys.
Next, all men who were interviewed in 1976 and interviewed at
each of the earlier survey years were randomly assigned to a
survey year in direct proportion to the distribution of the deceased among the same survey years. This step resulted in the
retention of 2,369 whites and 893 blacks.

To account for the possible effects of differential age distributions between the decedents and the reference group on
other variables in the analyses, we used age as an additional
factor in the construction of the reference group. Accordingly,
the next step was to derive a distribution of decedents by age

and survey date. An arbitrary number of reference group members (1,500 whites and 500 blacks) was then selected as a base from which to determine how many reference group members in each age category were needed if we applied the age distribution of the deceased men to these arbitrary base numbers. If we had applied the age distribution of the deceased to the total reference group (2,369 whites and 893 blacks) rather than a smaller, abitrary base (1,500 whites and 500 blacks), we would have exhausted our universe and run out of cases needed for each age and survey year category.

Having determined the ideal number of reference group members needed for each age category, we made a second allocation by survey year in close approximation to the distribution of the deceased men across survey years. Where exact draws from specified age-survey groupings could not be made for the reference group, as many individuals as possible were randomly selected from other surveys (but of the same age) until the number in each age group reached, as nearly as possible, the ideal number. The result of these procedures yielded a reference group of 1,496 whites and 486 blacks matched as closely as possible to the decedents in terms of age and survey year distributions. Restricting the reference group to men aged 45 to 64 yielded 1,385 whites and 444 blacks.

The cross-sectional sample at last survey before death   This sample is composed of both deceased and reference group respondents whose last interview occurred between the 1966 and 1975 surveys, inclusive. The last interview is the last survey before death for the deceased respondents and a randomly assigned survey for the reference group.

The trend sample   The deceased respondents in the trend sample are confined to those whose last interview occurred at least two years before they were reported deceased (T-2), and reference group members have an analogous survey point that was randomly assigned. Therefore only decedents and reference group members for whom T-2 was the 1969, 1971, or 1973 survey are included in this sample. Points T-4 and T-6 represent surveys four years and six years, respectively, before the reported death. The T-2, T-4, and T-6 surveys represent points that average one, three, and five years before a respondent's death. These survey points were chosen in an effort to

Survey Points Available

1966	1967	1969	1971	1973	1975	1976
T-10	T-9	T-7	T-5	T-3	T-1	Died
T-9	T-8	T-6	T-4	T-2	Died	
T-7	T-6	T-4	T-2	Died		
T-5[a]	T-4	T-2	Died			
T-4	T-2	Died				
T-1	Died					
Died						

[a]Some license was taken to define T-5 (1966) as a T-6 point.

obtain sufficiently large sample sizes for comparative analysis across time. The table "Survey Points Available" depicts which time sequences were potentially available to us and outlines the actual time sequence chosen.

The following procedures were followed for both the deceased and reference groups:

1. Age = Age one year prior to survey in which death is reported.

2. Because of the paucity of data in the 1968 telephone survey, if the last interview happens to be in that year, as much information as possible is extracted from the interview, and the remaining information is obtained from the 1967 interview.

3. When analyses utilize weighted data, the weight variable for each decedent is taken from the last survey before death, and for each respondent in the reference group, it is taken from the survey year selected. For the trend analyses the weight variable is measured as of T-2.

Construction of the Mature Women's Widows' Sample

Basically, the widows' sample was developed in the same way as the men's mortality sample except that the NLS mature women's surveys were utilized. Women widowed between 1967 and 1976 numbered 124 whites and 76 blacks. First, it was necessary to determine between which two surveys from 1967 to 1976 the husband died. The earlier of these two surveys was termed the survey before widowhood, and the survey at which she first reported herself as widowed was defined as the survey after. Since we identify the first widowhood between 1967 and 1976, the survey before widowhood may be any of the surveys between 1967 and 1974 and the survey after may be any of the surveys between 1969 and 1976 (a change in marital status was not recorded in the 1968 survey). Full-length interviews were conducted with the mature women in 1967, 1969, 1971, and 1972. The 1968 interview was a mailed questionnaire and the 1974 and 1976 interviews were telephone surveys.

The next step was to derive a reference group based on the nonwidowed women's eligibility for widowhood at each survey interval. To be eligible the women must have been married with spouse present at both points of the interval. Having obtained a distribution of widows across the surveys, we randomly allocated the reference group members to a particular survey year in direct proportion to the widows' distribution through the process of sampling without replacement (a married, nonwidowed woman appears only once in the reference group).

As a result of this process, 2,887 white and 799 black reference group members were selected. An arbitrary base was then chosen (2,500 whites and 650 blacks) and the age distribution of the widows was applied to this base in order to ascertain the appropriate numbers of cases for each age. Although a single-year-of-age distribution was obtained for the widows, in selecting the reference group, we simply required that half be above and half below the median age of the widows. A more refined matching would have resulted in inadequate sample cases for the upper age ranges. The final selection of the reference group was thus based on the distribution of the widows by survey year of widowhood and by age. This draw resulted in a final count of reference group members matching the number desired (2,500 whites and 650 blacks).

A smaller sample was used for trend analyses over a period of three surveys after the husband's death (see figures 7.4 and 7.5). This sample contained a subgroup of women widowed before 1972. For these women the survey prior to the husband's death is either the 1967, 1969, or 1971 interview. The surveys after the death are represented by any of the interviews between 1969 and 1976, according to when the death occurred. For example, if the husband's death occurred between the 1967 and 1969 interviews, the 1967 survey is the survey before the death and the 1969, 1971, and 1972 surveys are the first, second, and third interviews after the death, respectively.

Table 7A.1
Predictors of Mortality between 1966 and 1976 for All Men Aged 45 to 64: Regression Results[a]
(*t*-values in parentheses)

Independent variables	Whites		Blacks	
	(1)	(2)	(1)	(2)
Educational attainment	−0.0019	−0.002	0.0075	0.0053
	(−0.67)	(−0.70)	(1.56)	(1.16)
Marital status	−0.107	−0.117	−0.130	−0.139
	(−3.49)***	(−3.81)***	(−3.24)***	(−3.44)***
Health and employment status[b]				
No health problem, employed	0.0052	—	0.026	—
	(0.15)		(0.44)	
Health problem, employed	0.146	—	0.150	—
	(3.76)***		(2.20)**	
Health problem, not employed	0.329	—	0.426	—
	(8.16)***		(6.58)***	
Residence[c]				
Central city of SMSA	0.054	—	0.0034	—
	(2.12)**		(0.08)	
Suburb of SMSA	0.0029	—	−0.018	—
	(0.13)		(−0.29)	
Employment status	—	−0.098	—	−0.130
		(−4.10)***		(−3.19)***
Health status	—	0.196	—	0.236
		(8.93)***		(5.88)***
Constant	0.253	0.367	0.294	0.442
	(4.78)***	(8.13)***	(3.88)***	(7.36)***
Mean of dependent variable	0.239	0.240	0.390	0.390
R^2 (adj)	0.095	0.087	0.126	0.111
F-ratio	27.37***	42.89***	14.78***	22.04***
Number of respondents	1,767	1,769	673	673

[a]Characteristics for decedents are for the last survey preceding death. Characteristics for survivors are for survey year randomly selected for reference group. The dependent variable is dichotomous; a code one if the respondent died between 1966 and 1976 and a code zero if he was alive in 1976. See Glossary for definition of variables.
[b]The reference group for this set of variables is "no health problem, not employed."
[c]The reference group for this set of variables is "rural."
**Significant at the 5 percent level.
***Significant at the 1 percent level.

Table 7A.2
Labor Supply of Wife Prior to Husband's Death, by Race: Mature Men's Cohort[a] Regression Results (t-values in parentheses)[b]

Independent variables	Dependent variables					
	Total		Whites		Blacks	
	Annual hours of work	Weeks worked in past year	Annual hours of work	Weeks worked in past year	Annual hours of work	Weeks worked in past year
Race	-84.92 (-0.77)	-5.73 (-1.89)**				
Husband's health-mortality status[c]						
No health problem, died	-121.78 (-1.40)	-4.31 (-1.80)*	-112.85 (-1.12)	-4.32 (-1.57)	-231.24 (-1.49)	-3.44 (-0.77)
Health problem, died	61.75 (0.76)	1.86 (0.84)	62.50 (0.66)	1.52 (0.59)	12.35 (0.09)	4.76 (1.21)
Health problem, alive	129.19 (1.84)*	2.29 (1.21)	122.09 (1.52)	2.07 (0.96)	162.84 (1.07)	4.75 (1.06)
Residence						
Central city of SMSA	-119.24 (-1.79)*	-1.41 (-0.78)	-117.77 (-1.52)	-1.77 (-0.85)	-41.06 (-0.33)	3.63 (1.01)
Suburb of SMSA	-144.81 (-2.26)**	-3.40 (-1.96)**	-146.42 (-2.02)**	-3.60 (-1.84)*	-53.00 (-0.27)	0.92 (0.16)
South	6.01 (0.10)	-1.18 (-0.73)	-5.56 (-0.08)	-1.25 (-0.68)	172.67 (1.42)	1.36 (0.37)
Educational attainment	43.16 (4.52)***	0.82 (3.14)***	44.24 (4.00)***	0.83 (2.74)***	30.32 (1.76)**	0.70 (1.46)*
Age	-21.22 (-4.38)***	-0.41 (-3.09)***	-23.40 (-4.13)***	-0.46 (-2.97)***	-2.92 (-0.37)	0.067 (0.29)
Health status of wife	-346.68 (-5.54)***	-10.51 (-6.17)***	-322.28 (-4.44)***	-10.28 (-5.24)***	-606.85 (-5.64)***	-13.25 (-4.10)***
Number of children under 18	-98.23	-2.25	-112.96	-2.49	-5.03	-0.69

in household	(−3.83)***	(−3.23)***	(−3.67)***	(−2.98)***	(−0.15)	(−0.69)
Family income less wife's earnings	−0.012	−0.00034	−0.012	−0.00034	−0.0046	−0.00014
	(−5.14)***	(−5.31)***	(−4.62)***	(−4.80)***	(−0.65)	(−0.73)
Constant	1,829.2	51.25	1,854.6	48.51	822.70	20.20
	(6.23)***	(6.40)***	(5.63)***	(5.44)***	(1.73)*	(1.47)
Mean of dependent variable	702.82	22.37	699.80	22.04	745.76	27.14
R^2 (adj)	0.076	0.080	0.074	0.077	0.115	0.061
F-ratio	9.15***	8.39***	7.61***	6.90***	4.29***	2.40*
Number of respondents	1,187	1,021	907	782	280	239

[a]Sample includes wives of decedents, and reference group and is limited to survey years 1966–1971 due to lack of data on wife's health status for 1973 and 1975. Regressions are based on weighted data. Number of respondents is unweighted. For a description of all variables see Glossary. Models presented here differ from those shown in table 7A.4 due to the inclusion of the independent variable "Family income less wife's earnings."

[b]Significance levels for the health-mortality variables and the SMSA residence variables are based on two-tailed tests of significance while all other in-dependent variables in the models are based on a one-tailed test.

[c]Reference group for this set of variables is "no health problem, alive."

* Significant at the 10 percent level.
** Significant at the 5 percent level.
*** Significant at the 1 percent level.

Table 7A.3
Labor Supply of Wife Prior to Husband's Death, by Race: Mature Men's Cohort[a] Regression Results (t-values in parentheses)[b]

Independent variables	Dependent variables					
	Total		Whites		Blacks	
	Annual hours of work	Weeks worked in past year	Annual hours of work	Weeks worked in past year	Annual hours of work	Weeks worked in past year
Race	−130.85 (−1.17)	−6.82 (−2.22)				
Husband's health-mortality status[c]						
No health problem, died	−101.10 (−1.15)	−3.65 (−1.51)	−91.48 (−0.90)	−3.65 (−1.31)	−224.28 (−1.45)	−3.21 (−0.72)
Health problem, died	109.25 (1.33)	3.07 (1.38)	113.53 (1.19)	2.83 (1.10)	18.15 (0.14)	4.84 (1.23)
Health problem, alive	171.91 (2.44)**	3.54 (1.85)*	166.52 (2.07)**	3.38 (1.56)	167.85 (1.10)	4.85 (1.09)
Residence						
Central city of SMSA	−127.22 (−1.89)*	−1.54 (−0.84)	−126.33 (−1.61)	−1.93 (−0.91)	−47.10 (−0.38)	3.48 (0.97)
Suburb of SMSA	−173.05 (−2.68)***	−4.28 (−2.45)**	−175.51 (−2.40)**	−4.52 (−2.29)**	−55.59 (−0.28)	1.04 (0.18)
South	23.18 (0.39)	−0.42 (−0.26)	12.93 (0.19)	−0.43 (−0.23)	174.70 (1.44)	1.45 (0.40)
Educational attainment	30.29 (3.25)***	0.46 (1.79)**	30.75 (2.85)**	0.44 (1.50)*	27.59 (1.65)**	0.62 (1.32)*
Age	−20.32 (−4.15)***	−0.38 (−2.80)***	−22.53 (−3.94)***	−0.43 (−2.71)***	−2.15 (−0.27)	0.095 (0.42)
Health status of wife	−330.81 (−5.24)***	−10.12 (−5.87)***	−305.30 (−4.17)***	−9.87 (−4.96)***	−604.60 (−5.63)***	−13.18 (−4.08)***
Number of children under 18	−101.56	−2.35	−116.63	−2.60	−4.96	−0.68

in household	(-3.92)***	(-3.33)***	(-3.75)***	(-3.07)***	(-0.15)	(-0.69)
Constant	1,764.4	48.77	1,748.7	45.05	766.37	18.21
	(5.95)***	(6.02)***	(5.26)***	(5.00)***	(1.64)*	(1.36)
Mean of dependent variable	702.82	22.37	699.80	22.04	745.76	27.14
R^2 (adj)	0.056	0.055	0.053	0.050	0.117	0.062
F-ratio	7.42***	6.42***	6.10***	5.13***	4.69***	2.59**
Number of respondents	1,187	1,021	907	782	280	239

[a] Sample includes wives of decedents, and reference group and is limited to survey years 1966–1971 due to lack of data on wife's health status for 1973 and 1975. Regressions are based on weighted data. Number of respondents is unweighted. For a description of all variables see Glossary. Models presented here differ from those shown in table 7A.3 due to the exclusion of the independent variable "Family income less wife's earnings."

[b] Significance levels for the health-mortality variables and the SMSA residence variables are based on two-tailed tests of significance while all other independent variables in the models are based on a one-tailed test.

[c] Reference group for this set of variables is "no health problem, alive." Models were also rerun with the reference group changed to "health problem, died." When this occurred, the total race and white models showed a negative and significant (at least at the 10 percent level) coefficient for the "no health problem, died" group.

* Significant at the 10 percent level.
** Significant at the 5 percent level.
*** Significant at the 1 percent level.

Table 7A.4
Predictors of Mortality between 1966 and 1976 for Married, Wife Present, Men Aged 45 to 64: Regression Results[a] (*t*-values in parentheses)

Independent variables	Whites		Blacks	
	Total	Health problem	Total	Health problem
Educational attainment	−0.0039	−0.0043	0.0040	0.0012
	(−1.21)	(−0.64)	(0.69)	(0.13)
Health and employment status[b]				
No health problem, employed	0.134	—	−0.011	—
	(0.37)		(−0.16)	
Health problem, employed	0.133	—	0.074	—
	(3.21)***		(0.90)	
Health problem, not employed	0.342	—	0.390	—
	(7.81)***		(4.85)***	
Residence[c]				
Central city of SMSA	0.071	0.142	0.041	0.060
	(2.51)***	(2.57)***	(0.79)	(0.69)
Suburb of SMSA	−0.00005	−0.0022	0.048	0.056
	(−0.00)	(−0.04)	(0.66)	(0.53)
Wife worked 1–26 weeks	0.0058	−0.021	−0.029	0.082
	(0.14)	(−0.27)	(−0.37)	(0.69)
Wife worked 27–52 weeks	−0.0013	0.054	−0.023	0.019
	(−0.06)	(1.18)	(−0.49)	(0.23)
Employment status	—	−0.206	—	−0.318
		(−4.65)***		(−4.08)***
Constant	0.159	0.461	0.216	0.579
	(3.09)***	(6.08)***	(2.56)**	(5.87)***
Mean of dependent variable	0.219	0.363	0.341	0.496
R^2 (adj)	0.085	0.059	0.092	0.075
F-ratio	17.25***	5.93***	6.49***	3.26**
Number of respondents	1,404	469	437	168

[a]Characteristics for decedents are for the last survey preceding death. Characteristics for survivors are for survey year randomly selected for reference group. The dependent variable is dichotomous; a code one if the respondent died between 1966 and 1976 and a code zero if he was alive in 1976. See Glossary for definition of variables.
[b]The reference group for this set of variables is "no health problem, not employed."
[c]The reference group for this set of variables is "rural."
**Significant at the 5 percent level.
***Significant at the 1 percent level.

240 Health Problems and Mortality

Table 7A.5
Selected Employment-Related and Income Characteristics of Married–Wife Present Decedents and Reference Group by Health Status at T-2 and Race: Trend Results[a]

Selected characteristic	Whites						Blacks					
	Decedents			Reference group			Decedents			Reference group		
	Total	Health problem	No health problem	Total	Health problem	No health problem	Total	Health problem	No health problem	Total	Health problem	No health problem
Number of respondents[b]	203	124	79	759	201	558	97	52	45	198	64	134
Labor force participation rate												
T-2	70		95	88	69	95	66	43	94	90	76	96
T-4	82	72	99	94	84	98	83	68	100	94	81	99
T-6	85	77	99	97	91	99	90	82	100	97	90	100
Percentage employed and not at work												
T-2	11	13	6	9	7	10	14	9	20	13	7	16
T-4	7	4	11	9	9	9	13	7	21	9	7	9
T-6	7	6	9	6	8	5	3	1	4	5	4	5
Percentage unable to work												
T-2	17	28	0	3	10	0	27	50	0	3	11	0
T-4	15	25	0	3	11	0	12	22	0	4	15	0
T-6	12	19	0	2	5	0	8	14	0	2	7	0

Table 7A.5 (continued)

Selected characteristic	Whites						Blacks					
	Decedents			Reference group			Decedents			Reference group		
	Total	Health problem	No health problem	Total	Health problem	No health problem	Total	Health problem	No health problem	Total	Health problem	No health problem
Mean usual hours worked per week												
T-2	33	27	45	40	31	44	25	15	40	36	30	40
T-4	37	32	47	44	37	46	31	22	43	39	33	42
T-6	37	32	48	43	38	44	33	26	44	37	34	39
Mean weeks worked per year												
T-2	38	30	48	46	37	49	35	24	48	46	37	50
T-4	42	36	50	49	43	50	43	37	50	47	40	50
T-6	44	41	49	49	46	50	45	41	49	48	43	50
Mean Duncan Index score[d] of current job (employed workers)												
T-2	39	42	36	40	35	41	21	—[c]	21	21	23	20
T-4	37	37	38	41	36	42	20	—[c]	21	21	20	21
T-6	37	37	38	40	34	42	21	—[c]	22	19	20	19
Mean hourly rate of pay at current job[e] (employed workers) ($)												
T-2	6.09	6.09	6.10	7.10	6.24	7.28	4.48	—[c]	4.63	4.73	4.25	4.87
T-4	5.72	5.60	5.83	6.77	6.07	6.94	4.29	—[c]	4.42	4.58	4.08	4.72
T-6	5.59	5.45	5.73	6.56	6.02	6.69	4.23	—[c]	4.28	4.19	3.98	4.25

Mean poverty ratio

T-2	3.17	2.89	3.61	4.50	3.51	4.86	2.00	1.58	2.48	2.38	1.91	2.58
T-4	3.33	3.02	3.82	4.25	3.55	4.51	2.12	1.92	2.35	2.28	1.91	2.45
T-6	3.16	2.94	3.51	4.06	3.60	4.24	1.90	1.48	2.38	2.26	1.91	2.42

Percentage receiving Social Security income

T-2	11	16	5	8	11	6	12	18	3	10	24	5
T-4	10	11	8	6	7	6	1	2	0	3	4	3
T-6	10	11	8	5	6	5	4	4	3	3	4	3

Percentage receiving pension income

T-2	11	15	7	8	12	7	1	2	0	8	18	4
T-4	4	4	3	6	8	5	1	0	3	2	6	0
T-6	4	5	3	5	6	4	2	0	4	3	6	1

Percentage receiving welfare income

T-2	2	4	0	1	1	0	16	27	2	8	14	6
T-4	2	4	0	1	2	1	11	19	2	8	13	6
T-6	1	2	0	1	2	1	7	8	4	7	11	5

Percentage with health problem

T-2	61	100	0	26	100	0	54	100	0	28	100	0
T-4	49	71	14	25	59	13	37	60	10	30	52	22
T-6	43	62	13	23	53	12	34	51	14	26	59	13

a The sample includes decedents whose last interview occurred at least two years before they are reported as deceased; for the reference group a comparable time frame is used with reference to a randomly assigned survey. Therefore only respondents whose T-2 point was the 1969, 1971, or 1973 survey are included in this sample. For further details, see the appendix to this chapter.

b Nonresponse rates may vary by characteristic.

c Statistics are not shown where base represents less than 25 sample cases.

d See Glossary for definition of Duncan Index of Socioeconomic Status.

e All income and earnings are adjusted to 1976 dollars.

Table 7A.6
Percentage of Year Worked by Husbands and Wives, by Race: Decedents and Reference Group Members with Health Problems (at T-2), Selected Time Periods[a]

| | Husband | | | | Wife | | | |
| | Whites | | Blacks | | Whites | | Blacks | |
Survey	Decedents	Reference group	Decedents	Reference group	Decedents	Reference group	Decedents	Reference group
Number of respondents	110	187	47	61	110	187	47	61
T-2	38.9	55.1	17.3	53.4	39.7	42.0	24.9	36.2
T-4	55.4	76.5	39.1	63.5	43.2	42.4	33.7	33.0
T-6	63.1	84.0	51.2	70.3	41.9	42.6	41.9	42.3

[a]Universe consists of married, spouse-present decedents and reference group members who provided information on hours of work at each survey point. Percentage of the year worked is derived by dividing mean annual hours of work by 2,080 hours (40 hours per week × 52 weeks). See the appendix to this chapter for further details on the trend sample.

Table 7A.7
Labor Supply of Wife at Survey after Husband's Death: Mature
Women's Cohort[a] Regression Results

Independent variables	Work status of wife at survey after husband's death	
	Coefficient	t-value[b]
Race	−0.14	−3.73***
Husband's health-mortality status[c]		
No health problem, died	−0.20	−2.08**
Health problem, died	0.05	0.55
Health problem, alive	0.04	0.95
Health status unknown—died	−0.06	−0.89
Health status unknown—alive	0.09	3.52***
Residence		
Central city of SMSA	−0.05	−1.82*
Suburb of SMSA	0.03	1.19
South	0.02	0.77
Education	0.03	7.45***
Age	0.001	0.49
Health status of wife	−0.19	−7.15***
Children in household		
Number under 18	−0.02	−1.76**
0–5 years	−0.24	−4.82***
6–13 years	−0.53	−1.44*
14–17 years	−0.02	−0.59
Family income less wife's earnings	−0.000009	−8.93***
Constant	0.47	3.39***
Mean of dependent variable	0.52	
R^2 (adj)	0.12	
F-ratio	18.11***	
Number of respondents	2,128	

[a]Universe includes white and black widows and reference group members and is limited to survey years 1969 through 1976. The dependent variable is dichotomous (1 = employed on survey date, 0 = not employed). For a description of all variables see Glossary. Regression is based on weighted data. Number of respondents is unweighted.
[b]Significance levels are based on two-tailed test for the health-mortality status and SMSA residence variables. All other t-tests are based on a one-tailed test.
[c]Reference group for this set of variables is "no health problem, alive."
  *Significant at the 10 percent level.
 **Significant at the 5 percent level.
***Significant at the 1 percent level.

Table 7A.8
Labor Force Participation Rates of Widows before and after Death of Husband Compared with Reference Group of Married Women, by Race: Selected Time Periods[a]

Survey	Total		Whites		Blacks	
	Widows	Reference group	Widows	Reference group	Widows	Reference group
Number of respondents	94	1,455	53	1,093	41	362
Last survey before	46.7	45.0	42.4	42.9	68.2	63.6
First survey after	50.1	48.5	50.6	46.6	47.9	65.1
Second survey after	55.5	51.1	55.8	49.8	53.8	62.7
Third survey after	62.7	51.3	63.8	50.2	57.4	61.3

[a]Universe consists of widows and reference group members whose last survey point before the death of the husband (or randomly assigned survey for reference group members) occurred prior to 1972 and who were interviewed at each of the four selected survey points.

Table 7A.9
Percentage of Year Worked by Widows before and after Death of Husband Compared with Reference Group of Married Women, by Race: Selected Time Periods[a]

Survey	Total		Whites		Blacks	
	Widows	Reference group	Widows	Reference group	Widows	Reference group
Number of respondents	75	1,210	44	905	31	305
Last survey before	40.1	33.5	36.9	31.5	56.8	51.4
First survey after	36.2	36.1	36.5	34.0	35.0	54.4
Second survey after	36.6	38.0	35.4	36.3	43.0	52.9
Third survey after	41.2	38.0	42.3	36.2	35.2	53.2

[a]Universe consists of widows and reference group members whose last survey point before the death of the husband (or randomly assigned survey for reference group members) occurred prior to 1972 and who provided data on annual hours of work at each of the four selected survey points. Percentage of the year worked is derived by dividing mean annual hours of work by 2,080 hours (40 hours per week × 52 weeks).

Notes

1. Survival rates for men and women by race were estimated from the L values in the life tables in U.S. Department of Health, Education and Welfare (1978). The relevant population estimates by age were from U.S. Bureau of the Census (1978).

2. See, for example, Motley (1972, 1975), and Schwab (1974).

3. A nondecedent could appear as a reference group member only once, and the survey year in which he appeared, as well as his age, were determined randomly. A more detailed explanation of the reference and decedent samples is included in the appendix to this chapter.

4. For this purpose we use a special subset of respondents from the NLS sample of mature women who were widowed between 30 and 53. Although most of the widows clustered near the upper end of this age range, they are somewhat younger than the widows of the deceased respondents in our sample of men. Nevertheless, since they represent women who were widowed during their husbands' prime working years, their characteristics and problems probably parallel the experiences of the widows of the deceased mature men.

5. The death rate implied by the dependent variable in these models does not represent a "real" decade death rate, since the reference group does not include all survivors. It includes a matched sample of 1,385 white and 444 black respondents who had an age distribution similar to that of the decedents and who have been assigned survey years in proportion to the across-year distribution of the decedents. See the appendix to this chapter for a complete description. Even though the models do not estimate accurate death rates from a population perspective, they are useful for estimating the relative importance of various factors as independent predictors of death.

6. The explanatory variables were measured as of the survey before the reported death of the respondent. We experimented with five- and ten-year death probability models, but these were less satisfactory than the one reported here. Earlier models included dummy variables that distinguished shorter-term illnesses (less than five years) from longer-term illnesses. However, none of the preliminary analyses revealed evidence of any significant association between the duration of an illness and probability of death.

7. Kitagawa and Hauser (1966, 1973).

8. All the other multivariate models mentioned in note 6 produced similar results; no inverse association between death probabilities and educational level was noted. However, this is not to suggest that education for this age group is not associated with health problems. Education as it affects occupational status is an extremely important determinant of the likelihood that an individual will report a work-limiting disability. It is also associated with labor force withdrawal probabilities.

9. See, for example, Tuckman, Youngman, and Kreizman (1965); Ortmeyer (1974); and Kobrin and Hendershot (1977).

10. The residence variables are generally insignificant with the exception of the central city dummy variable, which was significant for white men.

11. We acknowledge the limitations inherent in self-reporting health measures. The likelihood of reporting a health problem is certainly related to a person's job and life-style requirements. However, many people who report a work-limiting disability also consider their general health excellent (Parsons, 1977, p. 709). On the other hand, self-reported measures can be preferable to those based on objective, third-person reporting. Physical constraints inherent in specific occupations, differences in pain tolerances, or differences in cultural perceptions regarding ill health are not imaginary differences.

12. While there is an extensive literature focusing on socioeconomic (primarily educational and occupational) differentials in mortality, the literature focusing specifically on work status and mortality is extremely limited. Indeed, we have not been able to find any literature that controls specifically for both health and current employment status as predictors of imminent mortality. Our data point out the usefulness of employment status in such models as a way to further gauge the severity of an illness.

13. The reference group obviously includes a heavy representation of men without health problems who have voluntarily retired from the labor force and who, therefore, probably have above-average life expectancy.

14. Because the death rates reflected by these models are somewhat artificial, they are not cited in this research and only indexes are presented. The probability of death for the composite hypothetical respondent in this discussion based on the coefficients of the regressions in appendix table 7A.1 was about 0.46 for a white who was not employed and had a health problem and 0.66 for his black counterpart.

To examine whether the preceding explanatory variables predicted the death of married men to the same extent as all men, separate models limited to married respondents are presented in appendix table 7A.2. In general, the coefficients are similar. Of primary interest in these models is that the wife's work activity appears to show no association with her husband's impending death. There is no apparent anticipatory work on the part of the wife. This is true even when the models are limited to respondents who are known to have a health problem.

15. Unfortunately, the NLS does not include information about health care expenses associated with health deterioration. Motley (1972) and Carpenter, McArthur, and Higgins (1974) provide useful discussions concerning the extent to which aging, health status, and socioeconomic circumstances are associated with medical and other health care costs.

16. We are using the term *decedent*, which implies that an individual has died, in an anticipatory context for those respondents who are known to have died during the following year or two. In addition, in a multivariate analysis education was found not to be a significant independent predictor of mortality, and central city residence made a difference only for white respondents.

17. While there is no literature that considers the relationship of poor health and subsequent mortality to employment status, an extensive bibliography documents the association between health on the one hand and labor force participation and annual work experience on the other. For example, Davis (1972) notes how declining labor force activity of older men is closely correlated with health problems; Scheffler and Iden (1974) reported that weeks worked during the year are highly sensitive to the presence of health problems. Parsons (1977), using data from the NLS, measured the decline in annual hours worked due to health problems, focusing on differentials by marital status.

18. Parsons (1977) summarizes the push and pull forces that would tend to encourage and discourage a wife's work activity from an economic perspective. His paper also includes a useful discussion of how the presence or absence of a wife can be associated with the ability of the husband to work.

19. In addition to the self-report on health, the survey item that asks whether a respondent is able to work is a rather sensitive indicator of the seriousness of a health problem and can be used to compare the severity of health problems reported by decedents and reference group members. About one of every ten white reference group members with

a health problem reported that he was unable to work, compared with three of ten unhealthy decedents. Among the blacks the comparable statistics were 16 and 53 percent.

20. Multivariate analyses were also run examining the labor supply behavior of wives prior to their husbands' death. The results are presented in appendix tables 7A.3 and 7A.4. Annual hours and weeks of work were the dependent measures used, and a set of dummy variables interacting the husband's health and prospective mortality status were included to assess their independent effects on the woman's work behavior. Additional control variables included measures of the woman's residence, education, age, health status, and number of children. Models were run separately by race, and one model was run for the combined racial groups. Each model was run both with and without a variable representing family income less wife's earnings (see appendix tables 7A.3 and 7A.4, respectively). This variable is closely related to the health and mortality status of the husband. When it is incorporated into the model, the results reveal that the woman's work behavior shows little sensitivity to the husband's subsequent mortality status. However, when this variable is omitted, wives of white reference group members with health problems work significantly more hours per year than the wives of their healthy counterparts. The same relationship prevails among the white decedent categories, particularly when weeks worked during the year is the dependent variable.

21. Parsons (1977), using a cross-sectional approach with the NLS data, found that other income (of which wife's earnings was one component) increased as the husband's work declined. He found the most substantial increase in families where the wife has higher education. However, the loss of husband's earnings is not fully compensated for by increases in other earnings, a finding consistent with the results of this study. In separate analyses limited to married men and focusing on increases in other earnings, Parsons found little increase in other earnings paralleling the decline in husband's hours worked. Thus his empirical results are consistent with the idea that the increased need for the wife to work is essentially counterbalanced by the increased need for the wife to provide home services.

22. There is an extensive literature on the inverse association between occupational status and mortality. See, for example, Tuckman, Youngman, and Kreizman (1965), Moriyama and Guralnick (1956), and, more recently, Kitagawa and Hauser (1973) for extensive discussions of the direct and indirect effects of occupational status on longevity and, presumably, health status.

The occupational distribution of the respondents was examined both including and excluding self-employed respondents. Minor differences between the two distributions were noted; the self-employed included a larger proportion of respondents reporting a farm occupation. The greatest occupational differences between self-employed and other respondents were for the groups with health problems, since it was apparently easier for a respondent in a farm occupation to maintain at least loose ties with the labor force even when he had a health problem, and particularly if he was self-employed.

23. Carpenter, McArthur, and Higgins (1974).

24. Irelan (1972), Lando (1975) and others have noted this pattern. See additional discussion in chapter 4 of this volume.

25. At the census one-digit occupational level, employment rates ranged from 25 percent for unhealthy black decedents who were laborers to between 95 percent and 100 percent for many of the white-collar cate-

gories of healthy respondents. Employment rates were uniformly low in all blue-collar categories of unhealthy black men and almost as low for several blue-collar categories of unhealthy whites.

Larson and Spreitzer (1971) and Nagi (1969) have also noted that people less satisfied with the intrinsic characteristics of their job are more likely to leave it when they have a health-related excuse. To the extent that workers with marginal or in low-paying blue-collar or service jobs fall in this category, they would be the most likely to use a health problem to rationalize leaving a job. Unfortunately, Heidbreder (1972) also notes that these same people also tend to be the least satisfied with retirement. Thus a substantial minority of labor force exits may be in a no-win situation.

26. Thirty-three percent of white not-healthy decedent families received Social Security compared with 17 percent of their healthy counterparts. Eighteen percent received pension income and 40 percent received other income compared with 6 percent and 16 percent, respectively, of the healthy decedent group.

27. When this analysis was limited to husband-wife family units, the wife's earnings contribution to the family was similar, accounting for about 15 percent of the family's income in most of the race—mortality status—health status subcategories, with the exception of the black decedent with health problems category where her contribution neared 24 percent. However, the basic conclusion still holds: only for black decedents is there any evidence of higher earnings of wives in cases where the husband has had a health problem.

28. The three-year sequence for both decedents and the reference group was either 1973, 1971, and 1969; 1971, 1969, and 1967; or 1969, 1967, and 1966. In the last sequence the earliest year is, of course, not so far removed from time of death as the other sequences. A T-2, T-4, T-6 sequence was chosen because it provided a significantly larger sample than a T-1, T-3, T-5 sequence or any other sequence. While the T-2 to T-4 and T-4 to T-6 periods were in all cases approximately two years, the interval between a death and T-2 may have been much shorter. We know the decedent is dead as of the interview following T-2, but we do not know when he died in that interval since the precise dates of death of the respondents are unknown.

29. The associations between employment, health problems, and mortality may be complex. As Bixby (1976) notes, while many men who have a health problem retire, many may be unable to retire because of inadequate finances, and this may actually increase the likelihood of mortality. Thus some employed men with health problems may have poorer life prospects than their counterparts who are able to quit work.

30. At all points in time, the black respondents had jobs with substantially lower mean Duncan Index scores than their white counterparts.

31. Our data show declines in weeks worked during the year as well as in hours worked per week (although not as great) over the T-6 to T-2 time period. Both Davis (1972) and Scheffler and Iden (1974) found that weeks worked during the year is a more sensitive indicator of poor health than hours worked.

32. Percentage of year worked is defined as the mean usual hours worked per week times the mean weeks worked per year divided by 2,080 hours (52 weeks worked at 40 hours per week).

33. U.S. Bureau of the Census (1977), table 6, p. 33.

34. For this subset of women, the survey prior to the husband's death is either the 1967, 1969, or 1971 interview. The surveys after the death

are represented by any of the interviews between 1969 and 1976, according to when the death occurred. (See the appendix to this chapter for details.)

35. Several additional peculiarities and limitations of the data should also be noted. The period between the survey before and the survey after the death of the husband can be either one or two years, depending on when the death occurred, and these cases are lumped together. Moreover, the precise timing of the death of the husband is unknown. Hence, it is theoretically possible for the woman to have become widowed the day after the first of the two surveys in question or the day before the second. One implication of this is that information on the past 12 months collected in the first survey after the death of the husband will in many cases include periods antedating the husband's death.

36. For a discussion of the psychological impact of the spouse's death see Glick, Weiss, and Parkes (1974).

37. Examples of such studies include Mallan (1975); Glasser, Loren, and Solenberger (1970); and Lopata (1973).

38. Husbands in this analysis are, on average, several years younger than the men in the earlier cross-sectional analysis (for example, tables 7.2 and 7.6). Thus their characteristics and those of their families will differ somewhat from the families in the preceding sections, reflecting their differing placement in the adult life cycle. In addition, while we recognize that the health status of the husband is important to the family's economic well-being, small sample sizes precluded stratifying our analysis by his health status. Moreover, information on health status of the husband was obtained only in the 1967, 1969, and 1971 surveys.

39. According to a study by Cleveland and Gianturco (1976), approximately 40 percent of white women and 20 percent of black women widowed between the ages of 35 and 44 eventually remarry. The median interval to remarriage for these women is 4.2 years for whites and 6.4 years for blacks. Blacks generally experience longer intervals to remarriage and lower probabilities than whites, most likely because of their lower economic status and larger numbers of children. In our sample 8 percent of the white widows and 3 percent of the black widows remarried by the second interview after the death of the spouse, which represented an average interval of about two years.

40. Multivariate regressions for whites and blacks combined were run on the survey week work status (1 = employed, 0 = not employed) of women at the first survey after the husband's death to determine the effect of the husband's health and mortality status on their work behavior at this point. The results indicate that among women who lose their husbands after an illness, no difference in employment behavior after the death is evident compared with women married to healthy men who survive. In contrast, wives whose husbands die with no previous illness have a significantly lower probability of being employed after the death than wives of healthy men who survive, which may reflect the more traumatic nature of the death in these cases. Also, these wives tend to come from somewhat higher-status families and probably have greater access to pensions and other unearned income when their husband dies. See appendix table 7A.7 for complete regression results.

41. Because of the absence of simultaneous controls for income levels, family composition, and race, it is not possible to determine the portions of racial differences attributable to these other factors. Controls on the health status of the husband prior to his death also were not feasible because of reduced sample sizes.

References

Bixby, L. E. 1976. Retirement patterns in the United States: research and policy interaction. *Social Security Bulletin* 39 (August): 3–19.

Carpenter, J. O., McArthur, R. F., and Higgins, I. T. 1974. The aged: health, illness, disability, and use of medical services. In C. L. Erhardt and J. E. Berlin, eds., *Mortality and morbidity in the United States.* Cambridge, Mass.: Harvard University Press.

Cleveland, W. P., and Gianturco, D. T. 1976. Remarriage probability after widowhood: a retrospective method. *Journal of Gerontology* 31: 99–103.

Davis, J. M. 1972. Impact of health on earnings and labor market activity. *Monthly Labor Review* 95 (October): 46–48.

Duncan, O. D. 1961. A socioeconomic index for all occupations. In A. J. Reiss, Jr., O. D. Duncan, P. K. Hatt, and C. C. North, et al., eds., *Occupations and social status,* pp. 109–138. New York: Free Press of Glencoe.

Glasser, M. A., Loren, E. L., and Solenberger, W. E. 1970. *Survivor benefits of blue collar workers.* Lexington, Mass.: D. C. Heath and Company.

Glick, I. O., Weiss, R. S., and Parkes, C. M. 1974. *The first year of bereavement.* New York: John Wiley and Sons.

Heidbreder, E. M. 1972. Factors in retirement adjustment: white collar/blue collar experience. *Industrial Gerontology* 12 (Winter): 69–79.

Irelan, L. M. 1972. Retirement history study: introduction. *Social Security Bulletin* 35 (November): 3–8.

Kitagawa, E. M., and Hauser, P. M. 1966. Education and income differentials in mortality, United States, 1960. In M. Tachi and M. Muramatsu, eds., *Population problems in the Pacific: new dimensions in Pacific demography,* pp. 157–166. Tokyo: Eleventh Pacific Science Congress.

———. 1973. *Differential mortality in the United States.* Cambridge, Mass.: Harvard University Press.

Kobrin, F. E., and Hendershot, G. E. 1977. Do family ties reduce mortality? evidence from the United States, 1966–1968. *Journal of Marriage and the Family* 39 (November): 737–745.

Lando, M. E. 1975. The interaction between health and education. *Social Security Bulletin* 38 (December): 16–23.

Larson, D. L., and Spreitzer, E. A. 1971. The intrinsic and extrinsic meanings of work as related to disability inclination: another look at the sick role concept. *Sociological Focus* 4 (Summer): 88–98.

Lopata, H. Z. 1973. *Widowhood in an American city.* Cambridge, Mass.: Schenkman Publishing Company.

Mallan, L. B. 1975. Young widows and their children: a comparative report. *Social Security Bulletin* 38 (May): 3–21.

Moriyama, I. M., and Guralnick, L. 1956. Occupational and social class differences in mortality. In *Trends and differentials in mortality.* New York: Papers presented at the 1955 annual conference of the Milbank Memorial Fund.

Motley, D. K. 1972. Health in the years before retirement. *Social Security Bulletin* 35: 18–36.

———. 1975. Paying for health care in the years before retirement. *Social Security Bulletin* 38 (April): 3–22.

Nagi, S. Z. 1969. *Disability and rehabilitation: legal, clinical, and self-*

concepts and measurement. Columbus, Ohio.: The Ohio State University Press.

Ortmeyer, C. E. 1974. Variations in mortality, morbidity, and health care by marital status. In C. L. Erhardt and J. E. Berlin, eds., *Mortality and morbidity in the United States.* Cambridge, Mass.: Harvard University Press.

Parsons, D. O. 1977. Health, family structure, and labor supply. *American Economic Review* 67 (September): 703–712.

Scheffler, R. M., and Iden, G. 1974. The effect of disability on labor supply. *Industrial and Labor Relations Review* 28 (October): 122–132.

Schwab, K. 1974. Early labor force withdrawal of men: participants and nonparticipants aged 58-63. *Social Security Bulletin* 37 (August): 24–38.

Tuckman, J., Youngman, W. F., and Kreizman, G. B. 1965. Occupational level and mortality. *Social Forces* 43 (May): 575–577.

U.S. Bureau of the Census. 1978. Estimates of the population of the United States, by age, sex, and race: 1970 to 1977. *Current Population Reports,* Series P-25, no. 721. Washington, D.C.: U.S. Government Printing Office.

————. 1977. Marital status and living arrangements: March 1976. *Current Population Reports,* Series P-20, no. 306. Washington, D.C.: U.S. Government Printing Office.

U.S. Department of Health, Education and Welfare. 1978. *Vital statistics of the United States,* vol. 2, sect. 5, Life tables. Hyattsville, Maryland.

Chapter 8

Summary
and
Conclusions

Herbert S. Parnes

The preceding chapters have been diverse in subject matter and method of analysis. Indeed, only two elements are common to all. First, each has concentrated on an important problem or stage in the life cycle of men as they move from middle to old age. Second, each has analyzed the problem at issue by scrutinizing data collected in a series of interviews with the same sample of men between 1966 and 1976. At the end of this ten-year period the men under consideration constituted a representative sample of civilian males in the United States between the ages of 55 and 69.

A Review of the Studies

A Panoramic Overview (Chapter 1)

What were the principal changes over the preceding decade in the lives of men who in 1976 were between their mid fifties and their late sixties? A very simple way of answering this question is to tabulate the responses to the same set of questions asked at several points during the decade. The changes thus revealed in the characteristics and activities of the men reflect not only the consequences of their having aged ten years but also environmental changes over the decade, including manifestations of the civil rights movement, pronounced variations in economic conditions, and increasing liberality of private and public pension and disability programs.

A good example of the interaction of the two types of influence is provided by the record of labor market participation of the sample during the decade. In 1966 only 1 of every 25 men was out of the labor force; by 1976 this was true of more than 1 of 3. In large part, of course, this dramatic decrease in work activity reflected merely the effects of aging. That is, increasing proportions of the men reached the age at which pensions and Social Security benefits become available. Moreover, advancing age was accompanied by the increased availability of income from sources other than work and by greater inducements to seek such income arising from deteriorating health and decreasing burdens of dependency. At the beginning of the decade less than one-fourth of the men suffered a work-limiting health problem; ten years later this proportion had risen to about two-fifths. The proportion of men who had dependents other than their wives shrank from 60 percent in 1966 to about 25 percent in 1976.

But the aging of the cohort was only part of the story, since a decreasing trend is evident when one examines the labor force participation rates of men of the same age at several points over the decade. Among men 55 to 59 years of age, for example, the participation rate dropped by more than 10 percentage points between 1966 and 1976. Thus the increasing liberality of public and private pensions is also reflected in the data, perhaps along with cultural changes that have made retirement more acceptable to men at earlier ages. Plans for early retirement (before age 65) show a continuous increase over the decade 1966 to 1976. The proportion of men who had not yet reached age 65 by 1976 and who reported either that they had already retired or that they intended to do so before 65 doubled, from about one-fourth in 1966 to slightly over one-half in 1976. Thus, although some observers have questioned the likelihood of a continuation of the trend toward earlier retirement, there was certainly no evidence of either a reversal or an attenuation as late as 1976.

There are some recent contrary indications. A widely cited Harris poll released in February 1979 found that (1) 48 percent of workers 50 to 64 years of age said they expected to continue to work beyond age 65; (2) 46 percent of retired individuals would prefer to be working; and (3) 53 percent of those who had retired wished they had not done so.[1] High rates of inflation and the prospect of their continuation have been seen operating to reverse the trend toward early retirement. On the other hand, overt behavior has provided no evidence of a change in trend even by 1979. While the labor force participation rate of men 65 and older increased very slightly between 1977 and 1978—from 20.1 to 20.5 percent—the rate for 1979 was back down to 20.0, slightly below its 1977 level. The participation rate for men 55 to 64 declined continuously, from 74.0 percent in 1977 to 73.5 percent in 1978 and 73.0 percent in 1979.[2] Only time will provide a definitive answer to the question.

A majority of the men in the sample were employed more or less continuously over the decade, as evidenced by their status at the time of the surveys in 1966, 1971, and 1976. This group, some of whom were in postretirement jobs in 1976, appeared to enjoy relatively favorable labor market experience during the decade, at least on average. Median real hourly earnings for the entire age group, for example, were higher in 1976 than in 1966, even though many of those over 65 were in lower-paying postretirement jobs. For white men (but not for black), annual real earnings also rose over the decade on average, although for men 65 to 69 they dropped sharply, reflecting the prevalence of part-time work among those in postretirement jobs. The psychic rewards for work also remained high over the ten-year period. Three of every five men who were employed in 1976 reported that they were very satisfied with their jobs, about the same proportion that had prevailed in 1966. Almost half believed that they had progressed in their jobs over the preceding five years.

The financial impact of retirement is dramatically revealed by trends over the decade in total family income for men in the several five-year age categories. For the total cohort, median real family income rose between 1966 and 1971 and then declined by 1976 to a level about 12 percent below that of ten years earlier. But the difference between those who were not yet 60 years old in 1976 and those who were between 65 and 69 was pronounced. Real family income for the younger groups was higher in 1976 than in 1966; among the older group, on the other hand, there was a decline of nearly one-third in the case of white men (but not in the case of blacks). Because the decrease in dependency over the decade was greater than the decline in total income, real income per dependent increased substantially for the total age group, increasing over 1966 levels even for the oldest group of men. Real assets also increased, on average, for the total cohort, including those who by 1976 were in their upper sixties.

Trends in the Relative Labor Market Position of Black Men (Chapter 2)

Interpreting differences between blacks and whites in earnings or other measures of success in the labor market is a challenging intellectual exercise. That blacks do less well than whites by virtually every criterion is abundantly clear, but the reasons for the differences have been the subject of considerable debate. If racial differentials in rewards merely reflect differences in personal characteristics such as education, they are not evidence of racial inequality of opportunity in the labor market, although they may result from antecedent inequalities in educational opportunities.

Changes in the relative position of blacks over time are also susceptible to differing interpretations. Does an improvement in the black-white earnings ratio, for instance, signify greater equality of opportunity for blacks, or does it mean only that the educational background of blacks relative to whites has improved? The acknowledged improvement in black-white earnings ratios during the 1960s has been subject to these kinds of conflicting interpretations. In addition, some observers have argued that the data simply reflect improved economic conditions, during which blacks generally experience gains relative to whites. Which of these interpretations is correct obviously has a bearing on how one assesses the significance of the civil rights legislation of the 1960s. Not much credit can be given to that factor if black gains in the labor market simply reflect qualitative improvements in their productivity or better economic conditions.

The availability of data on earnings and unemployment for a number of points in time between 1966 and 1976 during which the economic climate varied considerably, together with information on many characteristics that affect an individual's productivity, has made possible a careful examination of this issue for men who had not retired by 1976. The analysis permits one to conclude that with characteristics related to productivity controlled, the ratio of black to white earnings increased over the decade from 0.84 to 0.92, and that employment security of blacks as measured by weeks of unemployment also improved relative to that of whites. Although there is evidence that the quality of black schools relative to white schools improved between the time that the oldest and youngest members of the age cohort were in elementary school, this factor does not account for these trends. In addition, the relative employment security of blacks was positively related to the level of economic conditions, implying that improvement along this dimension would have been even greater if economic conditions had not deteriorated during this period. Finally, there was close correspondence between changes in both aspects of black opportunities and changes in the amount of expenditures on antidiscrimination programs, suggesting that the civil rights movement did indeed have an effect.

The Fate of Displaced Workers (Chapter 3)

Job loss is particularly serious for middle-aged and older workers who have accumulated substantial equities in their jobs. Previous studies of displaced workers have generally focused on

257

the shutdown of a single plant and have typically been able to examine only the short-term experiences of the displaced individuals. Our longitudinal data, based on a national sample, permit generalization to the total population of this age group and allow an examination of both the antecedents and the reasonably long-term consequences of involuntary displacement.

Even when one excludes agriculture and construction, industries in which employment relationships tend to be tenuous, the involuntary loss of a job by long-service workers is by no means rare. Eight percent of wage and salary workers who had at least five years of tenure with their 1966 employers had experienced such a job loss by 1975. No amount of education reduces the risk of such a contingency, nor does membership in any broad occupational category. However, it is considerably less common in some sectors of the economy than in others—public service, for example, in contrast to manufacturing and trade.

Unemployment is the most obvious and immediate penalty of displacement from jobs, yet about two-fifths of the displaced workers moved directly into new jobs with no intervening idleness. At the other extreme, about one-fifth were unemployed for at least half a year. As might be expected, the general economic climate prevailing at time of displacement has an important bearing on the length of time that displaced workers are without work. Men who lost their jobs during the relatively tight labor market conditions of 1966 to 1969 were more likely than any others to experience no unemployment and had an average duration of less than 5 weeks; those displaced during the relatively depressed period 1971 to 1975 suffered an average unemployment duration of 22 weeks.

The long-term consequences of displacement can best be discerned by comparing the 1976 circumstances of the displaced workers with those of workers who suffered no involuntary job separation over the decade but were comparable in other respects. On the basis of this analysis it is clear that the displacement left its mark, since 10 percent of the displaced men were unemployed at the time they were interviewed in 1976, in contrast with only 2 percent of the control group. However, among the men who had been displaced as long as seven years earlier, that is, during the favorable labor market conditions of the late 1960s, the 1976 unemployment rate was no higher than among the control group.

The most serious long-term impact of displacement is not unemployment but a deterioration in earnings and occupational status. Average hourly earnings in 1976 were 20 percent lower for the displaced men than for the control group, and more than 40 percent of the displaced group had slid down the occupational prestige ladder between 1966 and 1976 in contrast with about 25 percent of the control group. There is no evidence that these adverse effects became less pronounced over time. They were just as discernible among men displaced in the early 1970s as among those who lost their jobs in the late 1960s.

Finally, there is evidence of psychological costs as well as the economic losses associated with displacement. The displaced workers were less satisfied with their 1976 jobs and less happy with life in general than members of the control group. They were also more likely to have developed a sense of alienation, with possible adverse effects on initiative.

The Impact of Poor Health (Chapter 4)

A considerable number of research studies have demonstrated that poor health has an adverse effect on an individual's labor market experience. One problem with many earlier studies, however, is the use of health measures that are to some degree tautological. For example, many studies, including some based on the National Longitudinal Surveys, have categorized respondents' health status on the basis of whether they report a condition that affects the amount or kind of work they can do. It is hardly surprising to find that health status measured in this way affects such labor market decisions as labor force participation and hours worked.

The 1976 interview instrument included a measure of health that does not suffer from this limitation, a series of questions about the extent to which respondents have physical or mental impairments such as difficulty in standing, sitting, reaching, walking, and dealing with people. On the basis of these responses, an index of impairment was calculated for each respondent, which provides the basis for several interesting types of analysis. For example, the factors associated with variations in level of impairment can be explored. Further, the relationship between this measure of health and labor market experience can be compared with the relationship yielded by the more conventional measure based on work-limiting conditions. Finally, because the same impairment questions were asked in the

1971 survey of the subset of the sample who reported work-limiting health conditions, the degree of change in level of impairment over the five-year period can be explored for this restricted universe.

When the impairment index is related to labor force participation or to hours worked, and when other factors are statistically controlled, a strong relationship is discerned. For instance, an average blue-collar worker with even a moderate degree of impairment is 9 percent less likely to be in the labor force than a comparable individual with no impairment. Even among men who are employed, impairment has an inhibiting effect on number of hours worked and a somewhat weaker effect on wage rates. The moderately impaired blue-collar worker, for instance, works 2 percent fewer hours per year and earns 1 percent less per hour than a comparable worker without impairment. The losses are larger for men with lesser amounts of education and, of course, also increase as level of impairment becomes more severe. Thus for the most severe impairment levels annual earnings losses are 26 percent and greater.

The analysis also supports the hypothesis that the effects of health on the amount of and compensation for work are sensitive to the measure used. The impairment index yields smaller estimates than the more conventional measure. Finally, the effects of impairments on labor market participation and hourly earnings do not vary across occupations, contrary to what might have been expected.

The Widening Disparity in Black-White Labor Force Participation (Chapter 5)

The secular decline in the labor force participation rates of middle-aged men has been considerably more pronounced among black men than among whites. Between 1948 and 1976 the participation rate of black men 55 to 64 years of age dropped by 23 percentage points, in contrast with a decrease of 14 points among whites. As a consequence, whereas white and black men in this age group had approximately equal probabilities of being in the labor force at the beginning of the 29-year period, by its end 75 percent of the white men but only 66 percent of the blacks were either working or seeking work.

No confident explanation of these divergent trends has hitherto been offered. A plausible hypothesis, however, is that they are attributable to the increasing availability and liberality of transfer payments—especially disability benefits—which have provided an alternative to continued work for those at the bottom of the economic ladder, among whom blacks appear in disproportionately large numbers.

There is some rather simple evidence that is consistent with this explanation. First, census data show that among both white and black men aged 45 to 64, nonparticipation in the labor force in 1970 was concentrated among those with limited education and therefore with low potential earnings. These same groups accounted for a disproportionately large share of the decrease in participation that occurred between 1960 and 1970. Second, the difference in labor force participation rates between white and black men all but disappears when educational attainment is controlled. Thus differences in educational attainment between the two races and the implied differences in physical and economic well-being appear to be sufficient to explain the differences in labor force participation.

Third, the difference in total family income between men who are working and those who are not is much smaller for men with very little schooling than for better-educated men. The difference is about $1,800 for men with less than four years of education and about $5,500 for men with high school diplomas. Thus the economic penalty for leaving the labor force is considerably less for workers with the lowest skill levels than for those at higher occupational levels. Finally, disability benefits account for a substantial portion of the family income of men out of the labor force, 29 percent in the case of whites and 48 percent for blacks. Of these, Social Security disability benefits account for over one-half among whites and as much as three-fifths among blacks.

All this suggests that the difference in the labor force participation rates of white and black men aged 55 to 64 may be due at least in part to differences between the two groups in health problems and in the relation between potential earnings, if employed, and potential social insurance or social assistance benefits (primarily disability), if out of the labor force. To test this hypothesis, statistical tests were performed to ascertain how much the gross difference of about four percentage points in the labor force participation rates of white and black men in 1966 would be reduced if the two groups were alike with respect to certain characteristics that are hypothesized to influence participation. Controlling first for age and health condition reduces the black-white differential by only one percentage point. When additional controls are introduced for the ratio of Social Security disability benefits and general welfare payments to potential wage, the racial differential in participation shrinks to only one percentage point. Finally, with additional controls for other characteristics such as schooling, marital status, and occupation, the black-white difference actually changes direction. In short, the lower participation rates of blacks are attributable not to behavioral differences between the two races but to differences in characteristics that condition labor force behavior.

To what extent do the factors that explain moment-of-time differences between the participation rates of white and black men also explain the divergent trends in these rates over time? Statistical measures of the 1966 relationships between the explanatory variables and labor force participation were applied to estimated values of the explanatory variables (such as wages, level of welfare benefits, level of disability benefits) in order to predict the labor force participation rates of men 55 to 59 years of age in 1976. These predictions were then compared with the actual participation rates for that group based on the 1976 interviews. The correspondence between predicted and actual trends is striking. For example, the predicted labor force participation rate for blacks falls from 84.7 percent in 1966 to 75.7 percent in 1976, while the actual rate falls from 85.0 percent to 77.5 percent. Thus one can conclude that the observed decrease in labor force participation among middle-aged and older men has been due primarily to increasingly attractive alternatives to work and that the larger decline among blacks stems from their less favorable opportunities in the labor market. The evidence also suggests that if wage rates for equally qualified whites and blacks are ultimately equalized, the difference in their labor force participation rates will disappear.

Routes to Retirement (Chapter 6)

The trend toward earlier withdrawal from the labor force and the growing proportions of older persons in the population have caused public attention to focus on the issue of retirement. Doubts have been expressed about the ability or willingness of society to accept the growing burden of adult dependency that these trends imply. At the same time, there is a widespread impression that many individuals are forced into retirement by mandatory retirement plans and that raising the mandatory retirement age under such plans or eliminating them entirely will keep many older workers in the labor force.

Much remains to be learned about the circumstances under which retirements take place. Most previous studies of this issue have asked respondents why they retired, but there is considerable ambiguity in the respondents. For example, a man who retires at a mandatory retirement age is likely to say that he retired because he had to. Yet he may have actually wished to retire at that age irrespective of the existence of the mandatory plan. As another illustration, "My health was bad," "I was tired of working," and "I had a good pension" are equally legitimate ways of describing the reason for retirement of an arthritic man in a dull job covered by a liberal pension.

An important advantage of longitudinal data in this context is that one can learn a great deal about the circumstances and attitudes of individuals before their retirement and thus resolve these ambiguities. For instance, if a man covered by a mandatory plan indicates before retirement that he would not choose to work longer even if he could, there is good reason to regard his retirement as something other than compulsory.

On the basis of the longitudinal records, it is possible to classify retirees with reasonable confidence into three categories: those who have unwillingly been forced out by mandatory plans; those who have retired because of poor health; and those whose retirement appears to have been in every respect voluntary. Of the approximately 1,600 members of the sample who had reported themselves retired by 1976, only 3 percent fell into the first category, 46 percent had retired because of poor health, and the remaining 51 percent had retired voluntarily. Even among men who were 65 to 69 years old as of 1976 (all of whom were potentially subject to mandatory retirement), only 5 percent had been forced out by mandatory plans. Thus the number of men driven to retire by poor health appears to be at least eight times as large as the number forced out by mandatory rules. This is not because mandatory plans are uncommon; it is because large majorities of men covered by them retire before the mandatory age or at the mandatory age with no desire to remain longer in their jobs.

Not only are relatively few retirees forced to retire, but a large majority of them demonstrate no desire to work. About one-fifth take postretirement jobs, a proportion that is remarkably invariant among the categories of retirees. However, very few of the large majority who are outside the labor force show any interest in working, regardless of the circumstances surrounding their retirement. Only 3 percent of such men said unconditionally that they would accept a job offer, and over four-fifths responded unconditionally in the negative. Moreover, only 1 percent attributed their absence from the labor force to the unavailability of work. Most of the retirees who hold postretirement jobs are working part-time and at lower wage rates than the jobs from which they had retired, so their annual wage and salary income is only about one-fifth (in real terms) of what it had been prior to retirement.

Family income, of course, shrinks after retirement. In dollars of constant purchasing power (1976) the average retiree's family income was about 40 percent lower in 1975 than in the year preceding retirement. This fraction varied between whites and blacks and among the several categories of retirees. The most prevalent source of family income among the retirees is Social Security retirement benefits, which are received by three-fifths of all retirees. The proportion would be higher than this among the total population of retirees; our sample ranged in age (in 1976) from 55 to 69. Pension and disability benefits are the next most frequent sources of income, but the relative frequency of their receipt differs between blacks and whites. About one-half of white retirees receive pensions and three-tenths receive disability benefits. Among black retirees, three-tenths receive each type. Social Security retirement benefits, private pensions, and disability payments make up about one-half of the average family income of white retirees and three-fifths of the much lower level of black family income.

Despite their reduced levels of income, large majorities of retirees appear reasonably satisfied, although this tends to be somewhat less true of blacks than of whites. Four-fifths of the retirees report that their preretirement expectations have been fulfilled or exceeded. At least three-fourths report that they would retire at the same or an earlier age if they had it to do over again. A majority report themselves to be very happy with their lives, although men who retired for health reasons are less content than the others. When this group is excluded, the remaining retirees express as great satisfaction with their lives as men with comparable educations who are still at work.

Family Adjustments to Poor Health and Mortality (Chapter 7)

About one-fifth of the more than 20 million males in the U.S. civilian population who were between 45 and 64 years of age in 1976 will not survive to age 65. The vast majority of these men will leave widows when they die.

These statistics are reflected in the National Longitudinal Surveys sample. Of the approximately 5,000 individuals in the original sample, 737 men had died by the time of the 1976 survey before reaching 65. The longitudinal records permit a comparison of the predeath work experience and income of this group with the experience of comparable men who remained alive in 1976. It is possible in this way to explore the extent to which deteriorating health or disability prior to death affect family income and the labor market activity of other family members. To assess the impact of the death of the breadwinner on survivors, an additional analysis has been made of data from the National Longitudinal Surveys cohort of mature women. The longitudinal records of a somewhat younger sample of women who were widowed between the ages of 30 and 53 are compared with those of a similar group of women whose marriages remained intact.

The racial difference in mortality rates is pronounced: the gross mortality rate of black men was one-third again as high as that of whites. That the differential persists when educational attainment is controlled but tends to disappear within occupational categories suggests that black men of this generation have been channeled into less desirable occupations than white men with ostensibly comparable educational backgrounds.

Within each racial group death rates are higher among non-married than among married men and, not surprisingly, among men who had previously reported health problems. White men who had reported health problems and had not been employed were more than three times as likely to die as were men without health problems. Among blacks the corresponding ratio was almost three to one.

As might be expected, the income and employment experience of decedents in the period prior to death depends on the extent to which the death had been presaged by poor health. A decedent who reported health problems in the survey before death worked an average of 812 hours in the preceding 12 months, in contrast with the average of 2,112 hours worked by a decedent who had not reported health problems. The resulting income deterioration in such cases in the period before death is not replaced to any appreciable extent by increased earnings of the wife. Thus the economic blow to the family is severe and is especially pronounced where the primary breadwinner had been in low-status occupations. In these cases the wife and other family members generally have below-average employment opportunities. In contrast, the prime-age man who dies without an extensive health problem usually continues to work until shortly before his death. Not only is family income not significantly impaired in such cases, but medical expenses are doubtless lower.

In contrast to their behavior prior to their husband's death, an appreciable number of white women enter the labor force once their husbands are gone. It seems plausible that the difference between the pre- and postdeath behavior is attributable to the husband's need for his wife's care during his terminal illness. The same pattern is not evident among the blacks, however, perhaps because the heavier burden of child care responsibilities and low potential earnings induce black women to seek other means of compensating for the lost income of their husbands.

Policy Implications

Research findings never provide unambiguous guidelines for public policy. Not until they are blended with value judgments can they point to courses of action. Nevertheless, the studies summarized here as well as the research reviewed in chapter 1 are relevant to a number of important policy issues.

Retirement

Contrary to popular impression, only a small minority of men are forced out of jobs by mandatory retirement plans. Eight times as many older men are compelled to leave jobs by poor health as by mandatory retirement. Among men 65 years of age or older who had retired by 1976 and who had been covered by mandatory retirement plans, 39 percent had retired prior to the mandatory age and 15 percent had retired at the mandatory age with no regrets. Only 15 percent of this group potentially liable to compulsory retirement, and only 5 percent of all recent retirees 65 to 69 years of age, left their jobs unwillingly because of a mandatory plan.

Thus if society is concerned with the high dependency ratio resulting from the increasing proportion of older workers and the trend toward earlier retirement, elimination of mandatory retirement is not likely to be an effective remedy. This is not to deny that mandatory retirement may be undesirable for other reasons. Insofar as it forces any productive workers out of the market, it deprives society of willing resources. Moreover, it represents a denial of the individual's freedom of choice. On these grounds alone its abolition may be justified.

What, then, are the policy instruments that are likely to cause men to remain in the labor force to older ages? In the long-run, whatever can be done to maintain good health into old age will remove a powerful stimulus to early withdrawal from the labor market. In the shorter-run, modifications in public and private pension plans would have the most immediate and direct effect, for there is abundant evidence from our studies and others that the availability and magnitude of expected retirement income is the most important factor affecting the retirement decision.

Programs of job sharing and flexible working hours might encourage some workers to remain in the labor force past the usual retirement age. A similar effect might be produced by programs that facilitate occupational change in mid life if such changes allowed workers to move into less demanding jobs or into those in which psychic rewards were higher, for job satisfaction has been found to bear an inverse relation to the likelihood of early retirement.

Most men who retire for reasons other than poor health are quite happy in retirement and would retire at the same age. However, a minority believe they made a mistake in opting for retirement. Among the voluntary retirees in our sample, for instance, 13 percent of the white men and 17 percent of the blacks said that they would choose to retire later. Preretirement counseling programs would help potential retirees make more informed assessments of the benefits and costs of retirement. Even with such programs, however, some who opt for retirement will regret it later. Policies should therefore be directed toward making the retirement decision as reversible as possible.

While it may be socially desirable to induce healthy workers to remain economically active longer than many are now choosing, our evidence indicates that many men retire at relatively early ages because of poor health. Among the retirees in our sample of men 55 to 69 years old who had retired for health reasons, almost nine in ten had retired before 65 and over one-half were still under 65 in 1976. Many of these suffer serious economic

adversity, particularly if they are not eligible for disability benefits. Thus a social judgment that retirement policy has been
more generous than it should be for individuals able to work is
not necessarily inconsistent with making retirement somewhat
easier for the medically impaired. One may ask which of these
two groups is more "deserving" of support and also consider
relative costs. The social cost of retiring a medically impaired
worker is, on average, less than for an able-bodied worker.
Foregone production is lower and benefit costs are lower because average earnings during the worker's productive lifetime
were lower.

Perhaps no issue illustrates better than this one the crucial
role of value judgment in policy prescription. More liberal disability and welfare benefits are an important factor in the secular
trend toward lower labor force participation rates among men
55—64 years of age. This trend may be retarded or even re-
versed by tightening eligibility requirements or by reducing benefit levels. On the other hand, it is also possible for society to
rejoice in having found humane alternatives to work for those
whose physical or mental conditions make work inappropriate.
In any case, our evidence clearly lends some support to the recommendation of past Social Security Advisory Councils that a
somewhat less restrictive definition of disability be adopted for
eligibility of workers 55 years of age or older.[3]

Health

In addition to forcing men into early retirement, health problems
have other serious consequences for the welfare of middle-aged
men and their families. By 1976 two-fifths of all white men in
the NLS sample and almost one-half of the black men reported
problems that affected the amount or kind of work they could
do. Among those 65 to 69 years of age these proportions were
one-half and two-thirds, respectively.

Health impairments have some adverse effects on wage
rates, and the effect on labor supply (hours worked per year) is
profound. The unhealthy worker's family suffers as well, especially in cases where a long illness is followed by death before
the worker reaches retirement age. Such workers tend to be
concentrated among those who also have lower earnings, and
their lost earnings are generally not replaced by increased work
of their wives. Because men who die before retirement age are

more likely to be in occupations with lower status and lower earnings, their wives have already suffered economic disadvantage relative to other married women before they are widowed. Moreover, they are less likely than other women to have the education and skills needed to compensate for their loss.

Thus improvement in the health of the labor force will significantly reduce labor market disadvantage and public dependency. Long-term policies to improve the health of the work force should be encouraged not only on humanitarian grounds but also because bad health deprives the economy of otherwise willing human resources. The principal causes of illness and death among older persons are related in major degree to the character of the individual's life-style. Increased research on effective methods of influencing the health-related behavior of individuals early in life would appear to have potentially high payoffs. No matter how successful such programs are, there will nevertheless continue to be deaths during prime working years. If widows of low-status workers are to live above the poverty line, either they must be helped to better jobs through training programs, or transfer payments must be increased by modifying eligibility requirements or by liberalizing benefits.

Discrimination

Even when education, training, work experience, initiative, and other factors associated with labor market success are controlled, black men have poorer jobs, more unemployment, and lower wages than whites. At the extreme these inequalities of opportunity in the labor market are reflected in higher death rates among blacks than among whites. At the same time there is evidence that the relative opportunities of black men improved significantly over the decade 1966 to 1976 and that this improvement was associated with government expenditures on antidiscrimination programs. Thus if society is committed to pursuing equality of opportunity in the labor market, the means of doing so are available.

Our studies have produced no evidence relating to the existence of age discrimination. We have shown, however, that as many as 1 in 12 men loses his job in mid life after building up substantial equity in it, and that he can by no means depend upon regaining an equally desirable position. Deterioration in earnings and occupational status is the most serious long-term consequence of job loss under these circumstances, but psychological costs are also observed. Compared with members of a control group, displaced workers were less satisfied with their jobs, less happy with life in general, and more likely to have developed a sense of alienation. These findings suggest the importance of strict enforcement of the Age Discrimination in Employment Act. Consideration might also be given to requiring early warning to workers of impending permanent layoffs and possibly the payment of some kind of reparation to workers to compensate them for whatever long-term earnings losses they incur as the result of job loss late in life.

The Pursuit of Full Employment

The studies in this volume provide additional evidence—if any further evidence is needed—that high levels of economic activity are an indispensable prerequisite to the achievement of social objectives relative to the labor market. Improving the earnings position or the economic security of blacks, for example, is much easier in tight than in loose labor markets. As another illustration, while it is clearly not possible to guarantee the jobs of middle-aged men, the impact of unemployment resulting from loss of jobs can be minimized by policies directed at maintaining high levels of employment opportunities. The principle can be stated in general terms and is well established: Workers who are disadvantaged, for whatever reasons, improve their relative positions when there is a high overall demand for labor.

Notes

1. National Committee on Careers for Older Americans (1979), p. 7.

2. U.S. Department of Labor (1978, 1979).

3. Advisory Council on Social Security, 1979.

References

National Committee on Careers for Older Americans. 1979. 'Older Americans: an untapped resource. Washington, D.C.: Academy for Educational Development.

Social Security Financing and Benefits: Reports of the 1979 Advisory Council on Social Security. Washington, D.C.: 1979, p. 1.

U.S. Department of Labor. 1978, 1979. *Employment and earnings.* Table A.4. February 1978–June 1979.

AGE
A continuous variable measuring the age of the respondent (in years) as of April 1 of the relevant survey year.

ANNUAL EARNINGS
The wage and salary income received by the respondent in the calendar year preceding the survey week. It is measured in actual dollar amounts.

ANNUAL INCOME
See *family income*.

ATTITUDE TOWARD JOB
The respondent's report of his feelings toward his job at the time of interview when confronted with the following four alternatives: like it very much, like it fairly well, dislike it somewhat, dislike it very much.

AVERAGE HOURLY EARNINGS
Usual gross rate of compensation per hour on the job held by a wage and salary worker during the survey week. If a time unit other than an hour was reported, hourly rates were computed by first converting the reported figure into a weekly rate and then dividing by the number of hours usually worked per week on the job.

BEST JOB 1966
A binary variable coded one if the respondent perceived, as of the 1966 survey, that his current job was the best in his career, and zero if the job was not the best.

BLACK
A binary variable coded one if the respondent's race is black and zero if it is white. Racial groups other than black (Negro) and white (Caucasian) are excluded from the sample.

BLUDUM
A binary variable coded one if the respondent's current or last occupation was manual (blue collar, farm, or farm laborer) and zero otherwise.

CENTRAL CITY
A binary variable coded one if the respondent resided in the central city of a Standard Metropolitan Statistical Area (SMSA) and zero otherwise.

CHILDREN
(See also *number of children*) A series of binary variables with a code of one indicating the presence of at least one child in the respective age range in the household at the survey date and zero otherwise. These variables include age 0–5, age 6–13, age 14–17. The reference group is women who have no children or children older than 17 years of age.

CLASS
A binary variable coded one if the respondent was working as a wage and salary worker at his current or last job measured as of the survey week 1976, and zero otherwise.

CLASS OF WORKER
Wage and salary worker: A person working for a rate of pay per unit of time, commission, tips, payment in kind, or piece rate for a private employer or government unit. *Self-employed worker*: A person working in his own unincorporated business, profession, or trade, or operating a farm for profit or fees. *Unpaid family worker*: A person working without

pay on a farm or in a business operated by a member of the household to whom he is related by blood or marriage.

COLLECTIVE BARGAINING
Indicates whether or not the respondent worked under a collective bargaining agreement at his 1966 job.

DELCJS
A binary variable coded one if the respondent's employer at his current or last job measured as of the 1976 survey week was the same as his employer for the current or last job measured as of the 1971 survey week, and zero otherwise.

DELDEP
A binary variable coded one if the respondent's number of dependents in 1976 was equal to his number of dependents in 1971, and zero otherwise.

DELHT
DELHT1: A binary variable coded one if the respondent reported that his health prevented him from working in 1971 and 1976, and zero otherwise. *DELHT3:* A binary variable coded one if the respondent reported that his health affected his work in 1971 but did not affect his work in 1976, and zero otherwise. *DELHT4:* A binary variable coded one if the respondent reported that his health did not affect his work in 1971 but that it did affect his work in 1976, and zero otherwise.

DELIND
A binary variable coded one if the respondent's current or last job measured as of the 1976 survey was in the same three-digit industry as his current or last job measured as of the 1971 survey, and zero otherwise.

DELMTL
A binary variable coded one if the respondent's marital status in 1971 and 1976 were the same, and zero otherwise.

DELOCC
A binary variable coded one if the respondent's current or last job measured as of the 1976 survey was in the same three-digit occupation as his current or last job measured as of the 1971 survey, and zero otherwise.

DELOFI
The difference (in 1976 dollars) between the respondent's family income less his earnings in 1975 and the corresponding measure in 1970. See also *OFINC*.

DELRES
A binary variable coded one if the respondent's county of residence in 1976 was the same as his county of residence in 1971, and zero otherwise.

DELRET
A binary variable coded one if the respondent reported himself retired from a regular job for the first time during the period 1973 to 1976, and zero otherwise.

DIMP2
A binary variable coded one if the respondent's health declined in the period between 1971 and 1976, and zero otherwise.

DIMP3
A binary variable coded one if the respondent's health improved in the period between 1971 and 1976, and zero otherwise.

DISPLACEMENT
A permanent, involuntary separation from a long-standing employer. It excludes those respondents whose separations occurred because of compulsory retirement.

DUNCAN INDEX OF SOCIOECONOMIC STATUS
Socioeconomic status is measured by the Duncan Socioeconomic Index of occupations. (See Otis Dudley Duncan, "A Socioeconomic Index for All Occupations," in Albert J. Reiss, Jr., O. D. Duncan, P. K. Hatt, and C. C. North, *Occupations and Social Status* [New York: Free Press of Glencoe, 1961], pp. 109–138.) The index assigns a two digit status score to each three-digit occupational category in the Census classification scheme. The Duncan scores range from 0 to 96 and reflect for each occupation (1) the proportion of male workers in 1950 with educational attainment of four years of high school or more and (2) the proportion of males with incomes of $3,500 or more in 1949.

DURATION OF HEALTH LIMITATION
Years of duration of health problem that limits the amount or kind of work the respondent can do.

EARNINGS
See *annual earnings*.

ED
See *educational attainment*. Specific values are assigned for specific attainments. For example, a person who received a bachelor's degree but no additional years of schooling is coded as having 16 years of education regardless of how long it took him to obtain his degree.

EDUCATIONAL ATTAINMENT
Highest grade of regular school completed by the respondent as of the 1966 survey. The range is from 0 to 18 years, and years of college completed are denoted 13, 14, 15, 16. Regular schools include graded public, private, and parochial elementary and high schools; colleges; universities; and professional schools.

EMPLOYMENT STATUS
A binary variable coded one if the respondent is employed and at work at the survey date, and zero otherwise.

EX
Civilian labor force experience. This variable is calculated as age minus education minus military experience minus 6 (AGE–ED–TEMP–MILCAR–6), except that a respondent could not be given credit for civilian labor force experience that occurred before age 12.

FADUN
The occupational status of the respondent's father (or head of household) when the respondent was 15 years of age measured by the Duncan Socioeconomic Index Score. See also *Duncan Socioeconomic Index*.

FAMILY INCOME
Income from all sources (including wages and salaries, net income from business or farm, pensions, dividends, interest, rent, royalties, social insurance, and public assistance) received by any family member living in

273

the household of the respondent in the calendar year preceding the survey week. Income of nonrelatives living in the household is not included.

FAMILY INCOME LESS WIFE'S EARNINGS
The arithmetic difference between family income and annual earnings of the wife (actual dollar amount). See also *family income* and *annual earnings.*

FARM15
A binary variable coded one if the respondent resided on a farm when he was age 15 and zero if he did not.

GVEXP
The combined appropriations for the year of interview, to the three federal government agencies whose primary purpose is to combat discrimination—the Equal Employment Opportuntiy Commission, the Office of Federal Contract Compliance Programs, and the Commission on Civil Rights.

HAPPINESS
A binary variable coded one if the respondent's answer to the question: "Taking things altogether, would you say you're very happy, somewhat happy, somewhat unhappy, or very unhappy these days?" was "very happy" and zero if the response was other than "very happy."

HEALTH STATUS
A binary variable coded one if the respondent's self-assessment indicates a health problem that limits the amount or type of work and zero if he reports no health problem.

FATHOCC
The occupational status, measured by the Duncan SEI score, of the respondent's father.

HL3YR
HL3YR1: A binary variable coded one if the respondent reports that his health has improved in the three-year period preceding the 1976 interview date, and zero otherwise. *HL3YR2:* A binary variable coded one if the respondent reports that his health declined in the three-year period preceding the 1976 interview date, and zero otherwise.

HLTH
See *health status.*

HOURLY RATE OF PAY
See *average hourly earnings.*

HOURS WORKED
Usual hours worked per week in the past year (see chapters 3 and 7). Annual hours worked in the past 12-month period preceding the interview date (see chapters 4 and 7).

HUSBAND'S HEALTH-MORTALITY STATUS
A series of binary variables interacting health status (1 = health problem, 0 = no health problem) with prospective mortality status of the husband by 1976 (1 = died, 0 = alive). A code of one on each variable indicates that the respondent fits the designated condition; a zero code means he does not fit the condition. The variables include no health problem, died; health problem, died; health problem, alive; data on health problem not ascertainable, died; data on health problem not ascertainable, alive; The

reference group for this series of variables is respondents who did not have a health problem and survived.

IMP
Impairment index. See the appendix to chapter 4 for a complete discussion of the derivation of this variable.

IMP*OCC
The product of the impairment index and occupation cluster. *IMP*OCC2:* The product of the impairment index and occupation cluster 2. Those respondents not in occupation cluster 2 are assigned a value of zero, *IMP*OCC3:* The product of the impairment index and occupation cluster 3. Those respondents not in occupation cluster 3 are assigned a value of zero. *IMP*OCC4:* The product of the impairment index and occupation cluster 4. Those respondents not in occupation cluster 4 are assigned a value of zero. See also *IMP* and *OCC.*

INDUSTRY
The ten one-digit (or more refined three-digit) classes of the Bureau of the Census classification of current or last employer on the basis of the nature of the final product.

JOB
A continuous period of service with a given employer. Thus a job change is a move from one employer to another. A change of occupation *within* a given firm is not included among job changes. *Current or last job:* For respondents who were employed during the survey week, the job held during the survey week. For respondents who were either unemployed or out of the labor force, their most recent job.

JOB ATTACHMENT
Degree of attachment to current employer. Respondents who said they would not leave their current employer no matter what rate of pay was offered were considered highly attached to their jobs. Those respondents giving any other response were classified as having low attachment.

JOB SATISFACTION
A binary variable coded one if the respondent reported some degree of satisfaction with his job and zero if he reported dissatisfaction.

JOBSAT
See *job satisfaction.*

LABOR FORCE AND EMPLOYMENT STATUS
In the labor force: All respondents who were either employed or unemployed during the survey week.

Employed: All respondents who during the survey week were either (1) "at work," those who did any work for pay or profit or worked without pay for 15 hours or more on a family farm or business; or (2) "with a job but not at work," those who did not work and were not looking for work, but had a job or business from which they were temporarily absent because of vacation, illness, industrial dispute, bad weather, or because they were taking time off for various other reasons.

Unemployed: All respondents who did not work at all during the survey week and (1) either were looking or had looked for a job in the four-week period prior to the survey; (2) were waiting to be recalled to a job from which they had been laid off; or (3) were waiting to report to a new job within 30 days.

Out of the labor force: All respondents who were neither employed nor unemployed during the survey week. This includes categories of individuals who were going to school, retired, unable to work, and other.

LABOR FORCE PARTICIPATION RATE
The percentage of the total civilian, noninstitutional population or of a subgroup of that population classified as "in the labor force." See *labor force and employment status*.

LIMIT
See *health status*.

LMS
Labor market status. A general term used to refer either to log hourly earnings or to weeks unemployed in the year preceding the survey.

LNWAGE
See *log hourly earnings*.

LOCUS OF CONTROL
The degree to which an individual perceives himself capable of influencing his environment. "Internal control refers to the perception of positive and/or negative events as being a consequence of one's own action and thereby under personal control; external control refers to the perception of positive and/or negative events as being unrelated to one's own behavior in certain situations and therefore beyond personal control" (H. M. Lefcourt, "Internal Versus External Control of Reinforcement: A Review," *Psychological Bulletin* 65 (1966): 206). This variable is based on responses to an 11-item abbreviated version of Rotter's 23-item Internal-External Control Scale. Each of the 11 responses was assigned a score from 1 to 4 in order of increasing external control. The scores were then summed and consequently ranged in value from 11 to 44 points.

LOG HOURLY EARNINGS
Natural logarithm of hourly earnings. See *average hourly earnings*.

LONGEST JOB 1966
A binary variable coded one if the respondent indicated that the job he held in 1966 was the longest job in his career, and zero if that job was not the longest.

MAR
MAR2: A binary variable coded one if the respondent was divorced, widowed or separated, and zero otherwise. *MAR3:* A binary variable coded one if the respondent had never married, and zero otherwise.

MARITAL STATUS
A binary variable coded one if the respondent is married and his spouse present at the survey date, zero otherwise.

MARRIED
See *marital status*.

MILCAR
Career military experience. This variable is the number of years of military experience beyond the first four years. The sum of TEMP and MILCAR equals the total number of years of military experience.

MILT
The number of years the respondents served in the armed forces.

MORTALITY
An index of mortality over the ten years subsequent to 1966. Specifically,

MORTALITY = MORTDUMMY 66–67 + 0.524 MORTDUMMY 67–68
+ 0.747 MORTDUMMY 68–69 + 0.593 MORTDUMMY 69–71
+ 0.560 MORTDUMMY 71–73 + 0.286 MORTDUMMY 73–75
+ 0.270 MORTDUMMY 75–76.

where MORTDUMMY $t-(t + 1)$ is a binary variable coded one if the death of the respondent occurred between the survey at t and the survey at $t + 1$.

NET ASSETS
The market value in the survey week of all family assets, real and financial, minus the value of debts outstanding.

NONSOUTH
A binary variable coded one if the respondent resided in a nonsouthern region of the United States and zero otherwise.

NUMBER OF CHILDREN
The number of children less than age 18 living in the respondent's household at the survey date.

NUMBER OF DEPENDENTS
The number of persons who receive at least one-half of their support from the respondent, including spouse, children, parents and other relatives regardless of whether they reside in the household.

OCC
OCC2: A binary variable coded one if the respondent is assigned to occupation cluster 2 on the basis of the activities he performed on his current or last job, and zero otherwise. *OCC3:* A binary variable coded one if the respondent is assigned to occupation cluster 3 on the basis of the activities he performed on his current or last job, and zero otherwise. *OCC4:* A binary variable coded one if the respondent is assigned to occupation cluster 4 on the basis of the activities he performed on his current or last job, and zero otherwise. See the appendix to chapter 4 for a complete discussion of the derivations of these variables.

OCCUPATION
Position on current or last job expressed as one of the ten one-digit (or more refined three-digit) group codes used by the Bureau of the Census in the 1960 census. In chapter 8 occupations are grouped as follows: White collar consists of professional, technical, managers, clerical and sales occupations. Blue-collar occupations include craftsmen, operatives, and service workers other than private household. Farm consists of farmers, farm managers, and farm laborers. Other includes other laborers, military personnel, and private household workers.

OCCUPATIONAL STATUS
See Duncan Index of Socioeconomic Status. In chapter 3 a change in occupational status is considered a difference of three or more points on the index.

OFINC
Total net income of the respondent's family less his earnings.

277

OTHER INCOME
A residual category of income composed of family income minus earnings of all family members, Social Security income, pension income, and welfare income (actual dollar amount). (See *annual earnings, family income, Social Security income, pension income, welfare income.*)

PARTIC
A binary variable coded one if the respondent was in the labor force during the survey week, and zero otherwise.

PENSION COVERAGE
Indicates whether the respondent was covered by a pension plan at his 1966 job.

PENSION INCOME
Actual dollar amount of income of all family members from private or government pensions (including Social Security Old Age and Survivors Benefits for the mature women's cohort only).

PER CAPITA NET ASSETS
Net assets divided by the number of family members living in the respondent's household. See also *net assets.*

PER CAPITA REAL NET ASSETS
Per capita family assets expressed in 1976 dollars using the average of the 12 monthly Consumer Price Indexes for the selected calendar years. See also *per capita net assets.*

PER CAPITA REAL NET FAMILY INCOME
Per capita net family income expressed in 1976 dollars using the average of the 12 monthly Consumer Price Indexes for the selected calendar years (12-month periods). See also *per capita net family income.*

PER CAPITA NET FAMILY INCOME
Family income divided by the number of family members living in the respondent's household. See also *family income.*

PERCEIVED AGE DISCRIMINATION 1976
A binary variable coded one if the respondent answered yes to the question, "During the past five years, do you feel that so far as work is concerned, you have been in any way discriminated against because of your age?" and zero if the response was no.

PERCENT BELOW POVERTY LINE
Number of persons whose value on the poverty ratio is less than 1.00 as a percentage of all persons having a value on the poverty ratio. See also *poverty ratio.*

PERCENTAGE OF PAST YEAR WORKED
Mean annual hours worked during the past year as a percentage of 2,080 hours (40 hours a week × 52 weeks). See also *hours worked.*

POPULATION AT RISK
Workers who, in 1966, worked for wage or salary, were outside agriculture and construction, and had been with their employer at least five years.

POVERTY RATIO
Ratio of family income in the past year to the government-designated line for that year. See also *family income.*

PREVENT
A binary variable coded one if the respondent's self-assessment indicates a health problem that prevents him from working, zero otherwise.

PROBLIM
See *health status*.

PROGRESSED 1971–1976
Response to the question, "All in all, so far as your work is concerned, would you say that you've progressed during the past five years, moved backward, or just about held your own?"

RACE
A binary variable coded one if the respondent's race is white and zero if it is black. Racial groups other than black (Negro) and white (Caucasian) are excluded from the sample.

REASON FOR LEAVING LAST EMPLOYER
Voluntary separation: Includes all reasons for quitting. *Involuntary separation:* Reasons include discharges, separations, layoffs, and (from 1973) compulsory retirement.

RECEIPT OF TRAINING IN THE PAST YEAR
A binary variable coded one if the respondent has taken any occupational training programs in the past year, and zero if no programs were taken.

RETIRE
A binary variable coded one if the respondent reported that he retired during the period from 1966 to 1976, and zero otherwise.

RETIRE71
A dummy variable coded one if the respondent reported himself retired for the first time during the period from 1971 to 1976, and zero otherwise.

ROTTER I-E SCALE
See *locus of control*.

SCH
See *educational attainment*.

SCHOOL
See *educational attainment*.

SCHW
Highest grade of regular schooling completed by the wife of the respondent as of the 1966 survey (0 to 18 years).

SIZE OF LOCAL LABOR MARKET
The number of individuals in the labor force in the area of the respondent's residence according to the 1960 census. In chapter 3 this variable is categorized as follows: SMALL equals a labor force of less than 100,000; MEDIUM is between 100,000 and 500,000; LARGE is a labor force over 500,000.

SIZELF
See *size of local labor market*.

SKLJ
The skill level (measured by the General Educational Development, GED) of the respondent's longest job prior to the initial (1966) survey. See chapter 2.

SMSA
A binary variable coded one if the respondent resided in a Standard Metropolitan Statistical Area (SMSA) and zero otherwise.

SOCIAL SECURITY INCOME
Income of all family members in the past year from Social Security payments other than disability (actual dollar amount).

SOUTH
A binary variable coded one if the respondent resided in a southern region of the United States and zero otherwise.

SQDA
An indicator of the relative quality of black schools to all schools in the year that the respondent was 12 years old. Specifically, it is the ratio of the average number of days attended per pupil in black Southern schools to the same measure for all schools in the United States (Source: U.S. Office of Education. Selected years. Biennial Survey of Education in the U.S. Statistics of State School Systems).

SQPT
An indicator of the relative quality of black schools to all schools in the year the respondent was 12 years old. Specifically, it is the ratio of the number of pupils enrolled per classroom teacher in black Southern schools to the same measure for all schools in the United States (Source: U.S. Office of Education. Selected years. Biennial Survey of Education in the U.S. Statistics of State School Systems).

SSB/W
The ratio of the respondent's potential Social Security benefits to the hourly wage rate in 1966. See the data appendix to chapter 5 for a more complete description.

SUBURB
A binary variable coded one if the respondent resided in the suburb of a SMSA and zero otherwise.

SURVEY WEEK
The calendar week preceding the date of interview; in the conventional parlance of the Bureau of the Census, the reference week.

TEMP
Temporary Military Service. This variable is continuous and measures the number of years of military experience up to and including the fourth year of experience. The sum of TEMP and MILCAR equals the total number of years of military experience.

TEN
See *tenure.*

TENURE
The number of years of service with the respondent's survey week employer.

TRN

TRN1: A binary variable coded one if the respondent completed any training courses or education programs in the period from 1971 to 1976, and zero otherwise. *TRN2:* A binary variable coded one if the respondent participated in, but did not complete, any training courses or educational programs in the period from 1971 to 1976, and zero otherwise.

UNEMP

The unemployment rate for males aged 20 and over for the year of interview.

UNEMPLOYMENT RATE

Rate of unemployment in the local area in which the respondent resides. The rate is based on the 12-month average for the specified year obtained from the Current Population Survey (CPS) for that area.

UNEMYR

See *unemployment rate.*

UNION

A binary variable coded one if the respondent is a member of a union, and zero otherwise.

WAGES

See *average hourly earnings.*

WAGE AND SALARY WORKERS

See *class of worker.*

WEEKS IN THE LABOR FORCE

The cumulative number of weeks in the 12-month period prior to interview (in the 1966 survey, the time reference is the calendar year 1965) that the respondent reported that he either worked, looked for work, or was on layoff from a job. This period is variable among respondents, since interviews generally occurred over a two- or three-month period and were not necessarily at the same time each year with each respondent.

WEEKS OUT OF THE LABOR FORCE

The arithmetic difference between 52 and the number of weeks in the labor force. (See *weeks in the labor force.*)

WEEKS UNEMPLOYED

A continuous variable measuring the number of weeks the respondent reported being out of work and seeking work in the 12-month period prior to the survey date. (For 1966, the reference period was the calendar year 1965, and for 1973 it covered the two-year period between interviews.)

WEEKS WORKED

The number of weeks worked in the year preceding the survey week, including vacation and paid sick leave.

WELFARE INCOME

Actual dollar amount of income of all family members from all public assistance programs including Aid to Families with Dependent Children and food stamps (in survey years where data were available).

WEL/W

The ratio of welfare payments in the respondent's state of residence to the respondent's hourly wage rate in 1966. See the data appendix to chapter 5 for a more complete description.

WHITE

See *race*.

WIFE WORKED

A series of variables based on weeks worked by respondent's wife during the past year. *1–26:* A binary variable coded one if weeks worked were between 1 and 26 and zero otherwise. *27–52:* A binary variable coded one if weeks worked were between 27 and 52 and zero otherwise. Reference group for this series of variables consists of women who did not work during the past year.

WORK COMMITMENT

A binary variable coded one if the respondent answered yes to the hypothetical question, "If by some chance, you were to get enough money to live comfortably without working, do you think that you would work anyway?" and zero if the response was no.

WUNLY

See *weeks unemployed*.

YEARS OF SCHOOL COMPLETED

See *educational attainment*.

YR$_t$

A binary variable representing the year of interview. A code of one indicates the observation occurred in year t and a code of zero indicates that the observation was not in that year. Thus YR69 indicates the observation was taken in 1969.

Appendix B

Sampling,
Interviewing,
and
Estimating
Procedures

The Survey of Work Experience of Mature Men is one of five longitudinal surveys sponsored by the Employment and Training Administration of the U.S. Department of Labor. Together these surveys constitute the National Longitudinal Surveys. Each of the four original NLS samples, of which the mature men's was the first, was designed by the U.S. Bureau of the Census to represent the civilian noninstitutional population of the United States at approximately the time of the initial survey in 1966. Because of attrition from the samples over the years of the surveys, they cannot be construed to be precisely representative of the civilian population in any year after the first.

The 1976 survey was the fifth personal interview conducted for the Survey of Work Experience of Mature Men. Interviews were also conducted in 1967, 1969, and 1971. A brief mailed questionnaire was used in 1968, and telephone surveys were conducted in 1973 and 1975. The respondents were between the ages of 45 and 59 at the time of the first interview in 1966; thus the age range in 1976 was 55 to 69.

Sample Design

The cohort is represented by a multistage probability sample located in 235 sample areas consisting of 485 counties and independent cities representing every state and the District of Columbia. The 235 sample areas were selected by grouping all of the nation's counties and independent cities into about 1,900 primary sampling units (PSUs) and further forming 235 strata of one or more PSUs that are relatively homogeneous according to socioeconomic characteristics. Within each of the strata a single PSU was selected to represent the stratum. Within each PSU a probability sample of housing units was selected to represent the civilian noninstitutional population.

Since one of the survey requirements was to provide separate reliable statistics for blacks, households in predominately black enumeration districts (EDs) were selected at a rate approximately three times that for households in predominately white EDs. The sample was designed to provide approximately 5,000 respondents, about 1,500 blacks and 3,500 whites.

An initial sample of about 42,000 housing units was selected and a screening interview took place in March and April 1966. About 7,500 of these units were found to be vacant, occupied by persons whose usual residence was elsewhere, changed from residential use, or demolished. On the other hand, about 900 additional units were found which had been created within existing living space or from what was previously nonresidential space. Thus 35,360 housing units were available for interview, of which usable information was collected for 34,662 households, a completion rate of 98.0 percent.

Following the initial interview and screening operation, 5,518 males aged 45 to 59 were designated to be interviewed. These were sampled differentially within four strata: whites in white EDs (containing predominately white households), blacks in white EDs, whites in black EDs, and blacks in black EDs.

The Fieldwork Over 300 interviewers were assigned to each of the surveys. Since many of the procedures and the labor force concepts used in the NLS were similar to those employed in the Current Population Survey (CPS), the Census Bureau used only interviewers with CPS experience.

In each of the surveys a two-stage training program was used to provide specific instruction to the interviewers. Two supervisors from each of the Census Bureau's 12 regional offices were trained in Washington. They in turn trained the interviewers and office clerks assigned to the survey in their regions. Each trainee was provided with a verbatim training guide prepared by the Census Bureau staff and reviewed by the Manpower Administration and the Center for Human Resource Research of The Ohio State University. The guide included lecture material and structured practice interviews to familiarize the interviewers with the questionnaire. In addition to the classroom training, each interviewer was required to complete at least one live interview before beginning an assignment. For the 1971 survey 28 training sessions were held in different regions of the country. For the 1976 survey, no training sessions were necessary. The interviewing in 1976 was conducted between July 26 and September 3.

In addition to training, a field edit was instituted to insure adequate quality. In the 1966 and 1967 surveys this consisted of a full edit of the first several schedules returned by each interviewer and a partial edit of the remaining questionnaires from each interviewer's assignment. The full edit consisted of reviewing the questionnaires from beginning to end, to determine whether the entries were complete and consistent and whether the skip instructions were being followed. The interviewer was contacted by phone concerning minor problems and, depending on the problem, was either told of the error or asked to contact the respondent for additional information or for clarification. For more serious problems the interviewer was retrained either totally or in part, and the questionnaire was returned for completion.

If problems arose, the complete edit was continued until the supervisor was satisfied that the interviewer was doing a complete and consistent job. The partial edits simply checked to determine that the interviewer had not inadvertently skipped any part of the questionnaire which should have been filled. Any questionnaire that failed the partial edit was returned to the interviewer for completion. In the 1969, 1971, and 1976 surveys a full edit was used on all the schedules.

Estimating Methods

The estimating procedure used in the NLS involved multistage ratio estimates.

Basic Weight

The first step was assigning to each sample case a basic weight consisting of the reciprocal of the final probability of selection. The probability reflects the differential sampling employed by color within each stratum.

Noninterview Adjustment

In the initial survey the weights for all those interviewed were adjusted to the extent needed to account for persons for whom no information was obtained because of absence, refusal, or unavailability for other reasons. This adjustment was made separately for each of eight groupings: census region of residence (Northeast, North Central, South, West) by place of residence (urban, rural).

Ratio Estimates

The distribution of the population selected for the sample may differ somewhat, by chance, from that of the nation as a whole with respect to residence, age, color, and sex. Since these population characteristics are closely correlated with the principal measurements made from the sample, the measurements can be substantially improved when weighted appropriately to conform to the known distribution of these population charac-

285

teristics. This was accomplished in the initial survey through two stages of ratio estimation.

The first stage takes into account differences at the time of the 1960 census between the distribution by color and residence of the population as estimated from the sample PSUs and that of the total population in each of the four major regions of the country. With the use of 1960 census data, estimated population totals by color and residence for each region were computed by appropriately weighting the census counts for PSUs in the sample. Ratios were then computed between these estimates (based on sample PSUs) and the actual population totals for the region as shown by the 1960 census.

In the second stage the sample proportions were adjusted to independent current estimates of the civilian noninstitutionalized population by age and color. These estimates were prepared by carrying forward the most recent census data (1960) to take account of subsequent aging of the population, mortality, and migration between the United States and other countries. The adjustment was made by color within three age groupings.

Sampling Weights   In each survey year after the initial interview, the sample was reduced for reasons of noninterview. To compensate for these losses the sampling weights of the individuals who were interviewed had to be revised. This revision was done in two stages. First, the out-of-scope noninterviews in each of the years were identified by the Bureau of the Census and eliminated from the sample of noninterviews. This group consisted of individuals who were institutionalized, had died, were members of the Armed Forces, or had moved outside the United States, that is, individuals who were no longer members of the noninstitutional U.S. civilian population.

The second stage in the adjustment acknowledged the non-random characteristics of the in-scope noninterviews. In each of the survey years the eligible noninterviews and those inter-viewed were distributed into strata (cells) according to their race, years of school completed, and years in 1966 place of res-idence. Within each of the cells the base year weights of those interviewed were increased by a factor that is the reciprocal of the reinterview rate (using base-year weights) in that year.

Coding and Editing   Most of the data on the interview schedules required no coding, since a majority of the answers were numerical entries or in the form of precoded categories. However, clerical coding was necessary for the occupational and industrial classification of the several jobs referred to in the interview. The Census Bureau's standard occupation and industry codes used for the CPS were employed for this purpose. Codes for other open-ended questions were assigned by the Center for Human Resource Research from tallies of subsamples of the returns.

The consistency edits for the interview schedules were completed on the computer by the Census Bureau. For the parts of the questionnaire that were similar to the CPS, a modified CPS edit was used. For all other sections separate consistency checks were performed. None of the edits included an allocation routine which was dependent on averages or random information from outside sources, since such allocated data could not be expected to be consistent with data from previous or subsequent surveys. However, where the answer to a question was obvious from others in the questionnaire, the missing answer was entered on the tape. To take an example from the initial (1966) survey, if item 39a ("Is there a compulsory retirement age where you work?") was blank, but legitimate entries appeared in 39b and 39c ("At what age?" and "Would you like to work longer?"), a yes was inserted in item 39a. In this case, only if 39a was marked yes could 39b and 39c be filled; therefore the assumption was made that either the card punch operator failed to punch the item or the interviewer failed to mark it.

Copies of the complete interview schedules are available from the National Longitudinal Surveys Public Use Office, The Center for Human Resource Research, The Ohio State University, Columbus, Ohio 43210.

Index